Wild Garlic, Gooseberries ... and Me

To the memory of my father,
Michael Cotter, a frequent
and often unexpected guiding
presence during the writing
of this book.

wild garlic, gooseberries ...and me

DENIS COTTER

Collins

The greatest service that can be rendered any country
is to add a useful plant to its culture.
THOMAS JEFFERSON

First published in 2007 by Collins, an imprint of
HarperCollins Publishers Ltd
77-85 Fulham Palace Road
London
W6 8JB

The Collins website address is: www.collins.co.uk

Collins is a registered trademark
of HarperCollins Publishers Ltd

12 11 10 09 08 07
10 9 8 7 6 5 4 3 2 1

A catalogue record for this book is available
from the British Library

ISBN 978-0-00-725197-1

Editorial Director Jenny Heller
Senior Editor Lizzy Gray
Cover illustrations Kathryn Milton and Stephen Raw
Cover design Emma Ewbank
Design Jon Hill Design
Photography Cristian Barnett
Props stylist Róisín Nield
Food stylist Linda Tubby

Colour reproduction by DOT Gradations Limited
Printed and bound in Italy by L.E.G.O.

Introduction

While I was writing this book, most people I know learned not to ask two particular questions: 'How is it coming along?' and 'What is it about?' Some kept asking anyway, which was actually much appreciated. The answer to the first question was almost always a moan, often very long, sometimes monosyllabic. To the second question I would answer simply, 'Vegetables,' and most of the time I really felt that it was enough of an explanation. Caught on a good day, I might have added that the book is also about my relationships with the vegetables I work with as a professional cook, and with the people who grow them. It is also about the place where this happens, and my place in that place.

Now that the book is done, I guess that's still the answer I would give. Food is life. We all know that intuitively but often forget it or lose touch with the importance of food in our lives beyond the basic need for sustenance. A healthy culture needs a healthy food culture, one that is built on trust and making the connections and relationships that shape a community.

I have been living with the structure of this book for so long that it seems completely natural to me, and I have to remind myself that it may not be quite so obvious to others. The vegetables I have chosen to write about are not listed in alphabetical order nor arranged in a pattern that reflects the seasons of a year. Instead, they are grouped according to shared characteristics, whether that be their colouring, as in the opening chapter 'It's a green thing', or their habitat as in both 'Wild pickings' and 'Growing in the dark'.

In 'A passionate pursuit' I suppose the grouping is less obvious, but these are the vegetables that are currently a major source of interest, even obsession, both to me and to Ultan Walsh, the grower who provides much of the local produce we use at Café Paradiso.

Very early, back in that innocent but hugely enjoyable stage of just sitting around talking about a potential book, I visited Ultan often, to pry further into something which I took for granted: the hows and whys of his work as a grower. I already knew that we shared a special affection for certain vegetables, such as the artichokes and asparagus that were thriving on his new farm. I knew too that we were both excited by the possibility of producing vegetables that might be thought of as non-native, or those that are difficult to grow in this part of the world. During those conversations, I came to understand better the deeply personal way in which a grower works with his produce and his specific piece of land. It was when he burst my linear notion of seasonality that I realised I needed to look at the produce from a new angle and to dig deeper into the characteristics of different vegetables and their potential.

The result, this book, is therefore a very personal take on the vegetables I have encountered in a year and a bit of concentrating on the possibilities of one small corner of the southwest of Ireland. It's a combination of things I know or believe to be true, things I have learned in the process, and some stuff that you might find amusing. Oh, and a pile of recipes that I hope you will find useful in the kitchen if the text gets your juices going.

It's a green thing

I t all comes down to the rain in the end. Of course it does. How could it be otherwise? Of the many clichés and myths surrounding Ireland, two of the most unavoidably true are that it's a green place, and it rains a lot. These are facts. It's a simple equation. The rain makes the place green. That, and the temperate climate, which means the land never gets scorched in summer or frozen in winter. The damned grass never stops growing.

Coming in to land at Cork Airport, you will still occasionally hear stifled gasps and hushed exclamations at just how green the fields are down below. Not just from first-time tourists – they expect it, they've read the brochure – but also from returning natives who've popped abroad for a spot of weekend shopping and martinis. We Irish may be a moneyed lot these days, but we still get excited at the sight of our little green home.

Those who know and care about these things say that green is the colour of hope. Hmm … I like that. Hope is a very strong force in life, nothing like the wishful thinking it is often taken for. It is a positive, purposeful energy, and in my green-tinged world, that connection makes sense.

Green has long been an obsession of mine. The colour, that is. My eye is drawn to flashes of green in every visual setting. Artwork, furniture, a row of books, crockery on a shelf or shoes in a shop window; clothes especially, whether on a body or hanging on a rack. I wear a lot of green, and feel comfortable with myself in green more than any other colour. I took to it quite young, glorying in its many shades – and there are so many, far more than the forty that the hoary old Irish ballad glorifies.

Some greens are fun in a shocking way, most just merge into the background – literally, in a rural context, of course. The ones in the dark green-black, olive-tinted sphere are almost soberly elegant. Almost. There are dozens that seem bearable when viewed in an indoor mirror, but in the light of day make you resemble a lost American tourist looking for Killarney. I actually love them all, in the way a good parent likes his children equally, or a cat lover pampers every one of her disdainful feline fold.

In the vegetable world, greens have long been lumped together. Mind you, now that I think of it, the political Greens are usually treated in the same way – tolerated, patronised, thought of as vaguely good for you, an off-centre sideshow to the real focus of the political table.

Green vegetables, if they are eaten at all, have very often been taken as if they were medicine, a source of some necessary but unidentified nutrients, and swallowed as such without any expectation of pleasure. 'Eat your greens', that familiar old war-cry, translates into: 'Enjoy your dinner but eat that dull but healthy stuff I put on your plate too; it's good for you.' It was inevitable

that this attitude led to greens being cooked as though they were medicine too, with little care given to how they might taste.

In the days before the arrival of modern calabrese broccoli to our shops, the range of greens eaten in most households where I grew up was narrow, and greens typically meant cabbage. Whatever was on the plate in the way of protein, the accompaniment was always cabbage, and the cabbage was 'good for you'. It was no great punishment to me, however. I liked cabbage, but that was just luck, it wasn't why it was fed to me.

It seems to me there are plenty of families now who don't even bother to inflict greens on themselves in this way. Sometimes it's a basic lack of health awareness, despite the burgeoning produce markets and the ubiquitous high-profile foodie campaigners on our TV screens. For those who do fuss over their nutritional requirements, the options for satisfying these has widened to include supplements, pills, fortified breakfast cereals and milk products, and other horrors. Believe in that lot if you will. Even if we were to accept that these fulfil all our nutritional needs, does it mean the end of usefulness of our traditional medicinal greens?

If anything, I think there is a certain freedom in it. A freedom to not bother, if you're that way inclined. But also, a freedom from thinking of greens as medicine. A freedom, if you like, to love them for the rich and complex flavours they bring to the table.

Eating greens for pleasure; now that's an interesting concept, and a real cause for hope. And yet, I only realised the extent of my own fascination with greens when teasing it out with another devotee. I have been fortunate in the last few years to be working with Ultan Walsh of Gortnanain Farm, a grower who, like me, has a passion for the food he produces. He grows vegetables that he loves, both as commercial crops and as food to use in his own kitchen. (In theory, he also grows what I want him to grow, even if it's not something he cares for. Somehow we don't get much of a supply of those crops. I must get to the bottom of that one day ...)

Ultan and I have often eaten some new variety of greens he has produced, and then launched into a post-mastication analysis of how it stands in the league of greenness, and how it compares to others like it. Does its texture compensate for a certain flatness of flavour? Does it have a wonderfully satisfying taste but look like a pile of sludge on the plate? This ongoing inquest has always existed between us to an extent, but it became a top-of-the-agenda subject when he trialled Chinese kale. The purpose was to check out this exotic vegetable, see how it behaved as a crop and test it in a few recipes. We were also interested at the time to find some new greens to fill those gaps in the seasons when the fields are almost bare. Ultan's first response was to declare it the best green he'd ever eaten! Well, I wasn't expecting that; it wasn't even on the agenda. The 'best'? How do you make such a declaration? What are the qualities of green? What is the vocabulary that speaks of greenness? The world of wine has a native language that allows those inside to speak fluently to each other about the endless intricacies of structure, flavour and all-round character of their subject. To outsiders, it can be an incomprehensible jargon, but there is no denying its fluency and the fact it has the practical usefulness of any proper language. Cheese and chocolate lovers sometimes aspire to creating a language of similar complex usefulness, though they still have a way to go.

So it is with the matter of greens. When Ultan and I eat some freshly cut Chinese kale or sprouting broccoli, cooked in olive oil with maybe a little chilli and garlic, we gush incoherently in praise of its very fine greenness indeed. 'By God, but that's a damn fine green, that's about as green as a green could get.' And so on, our enthusiasm compromised by a lack of vocabulary.

To me, there is a quality in the finest greens that can't be measured in terms of nutrients or flavour. Other vegetables provide pleasures of taste, but in the inherent pleasure of fresh greens there is what can only be called a 'life force'. It is like going straight to the source, accessing the most primal and vital food. It is engaging with life itself, in a pure and vibrant form that we can absorb but can't quantify. More prosaically, how to define the experience of eating greens must lie, of course, somewhere in the combination of texture, flavour and appearance.

The texture of greens can range from meltingly soft baby spinach to the crisp 'bite' of Savoy cabbage and the satisfyingly chewy kales. Soft is good and I will happily sing its praises later, but the most prized greens in our canon have a tougher textural character.

The flavour is hard to pin down. I call it 'green', but that's not really enough, is it? At the top of the scale, there is some element of a strong cabbagey character, earthy with a little bitterness. However, when cooked these greens reveal a sweet note underneath. This unique combination makes the best greens – such as sprouting broccoli and black or Chinese kale – a great partner for olive oil, various spices and the sweetness of tomatoes and peppers. Add some sheep's cheese and you have a sense of what my heaven tastes of. Of course heaven has a flavour! How could it not?

In this quixotic search for the ultimate green, colour is very important, and it may be the most telling element. Well, it would be, I suppose, given that we're talking about vegetables that share a name with a colour.

The vegetables that rate highest in our admittedly very subjective quest

DENIS AND ULTAN

have, in the raw state, a deep, dark shade of green, intense but self-contained. Toss them in a pan with some olive oil and they become vivid, glowing and translucent, a green unlike almost anything else in nature. Mind you, nature itself can get pretty vivid. One of the most electric greens I've ever seen lit up my journey one spring morning, while I was driving through the West Cork countryside. I was on my way to see my good friend Bill Hogan, to cook a dinner celebrating his wonderful artisan cheeses. I hadn't been out that way in a while, but felt familiar enough with the area not to pay too much attention to the scenery. Just enjoying the drive, listening to Grant McLennan sing his beautiful melancholy. The morning had that peculiar mixture of thin sunshine and comically heavy showers that is typical, yet never quite expected, of West Cork in May. (Why does the rain surprise us? Have you ever met an Irishman with proper rain gear? Do we not expect rain in our lives or do we just not take any notice of it? Never mind, we could get stuck on that tangent forever.) Suddenly, I came to the top of a long rise in the road just as the rain took a short break, allowing the timid but still blinding sun a moment of glory. Unfolding in front of me, as I sped along, was an idyllic rural scene. For some reason, probably the music, my attitude was different and I took notice of my surroundings. Small fields of grass and meadow of the most vivid green, dripping with moisture, lit by striped sunlight, and marked out by hedgerows in which the creamy hawthorn blossom was dominated by the shockingly bright yellow, bright orange of gorse flowers. There is something in the gorse that turns the fields of West Cork to eleven on the monitor. I kid you not. Go look for it if you get a chance.

The essential greens are those on your doorstep

So much for the notion of 'green', and the essence of what it is about green vegetables that turns me on so much. Perhaps it's time to take a look at the specific ones that do it for me. As with all the vegetables in this book, what follows here is a study of those that have been closest to my heart over the past year. Most are long-standing favourites, but even then they have become new again to me in the way that I work with them, which is constantly evolving, and, even more so, in the way that I procure them. Green vegetables, more than any others, have to be fresh to give their best, and the only sure way to get fresh greens is to grow them yourself or to source them from a local supplier who can deliver what you need when you want it. The shorter the journey from field to kitchen, the more we can access the almost magical qualities of foods that, being so recently picked, are simply bursting with life. It is in the forming and nurturing of the relationships essential to that transaction that we can change the way we value our greens. When it comes right down to it, the ultimate reason these vegetables are so important to me is because they are grown close to where I work by people I know and trust.

Here then, from cabbage to watercress, via asparagus and chard amongst others, is a personal take on the most truly vital ingredients of my kitchen.

The iconoclastic lover of heartless cabbage

Cabbages of all sorts have been playing a huge role in the diets of most parts of Europe for hundreds of years. So I'm told, anyway. They certainly played a big part in my youth, which concerns me a lot more. It may be subjective and provincial, but my youth, despite fading into the past, still affects my relationship with food more than European history does. If the opposite is true for you, I'd love to read your dissertation on cabbage and its role in the fall of the Austro-Hungarian Empire.

I know it's an old Irish cliché now, but I did in fact eat a lot of cabbage as a child. I can at least spare you the weary and hackneyed description of the smell of over-boiled cabbage permeating the house, simply because I have no memory of it. My mother never over-boiled cabbage. When she used it in classic bacon 'n' cabbage (yes, we did have it a couple of times a week), it was added to the pot lateish with the lid kept off, and cooked until soft but not disintegrating. How's that for enlightened?

I do, however, have a reference for the type of horrific food smells that can cause distressing memories. No, not from my friends' houses, because everyone in the town was similarly enlightened. (Thanks to the town council for sponsoring that comment.) In New Zealand, there is a similar modern trauma amongst the newly sophisticated regarding the smell of long-boiled mutton, often combined with cabbage as well. I knew about it from hearsay before I ever experienced it. Like the cabbage legend on this side of the world, their version is often used as a way to laugh at country cousins or the ignorance of an earlier generation.

When I finally came nose to nose with the olfactory reality, I was living in a small town in the middle of the North Island of New Zealand. One quiet day of many, I went out for a cycle to pass the time. I could have gone swimming or cricketing or rolling bowls around the green like everyone else, but I was feeling unsociable. Miles out of town, I was overtaken by one of those serious bike people, decked out in the kind of tight-fitting, outrageously gaudy outfit that would get cyclists thrown out of all but the most hedonistic of gay clubs. He pulled over and made small chat, always delighted to meet someone interested in bikes, and so on. He was not a young man, and thus was very proud of overtaking youngsters. He was also running a small cycling club in a part of the world that didn't care much for the sport, always on the lookout for new members. I wasn't exactly fit at the time, but I was young and had my own bike, so I guess I was fair prey. I was also foreign and way too polite. Against my better judgement, I followed him to his nearby house to sign up to a glittering cycling career.

It was one of those classic Kiwi country homes, a tiny shack of timber with a tin roof and a small front porch on which there is always an old couch with cushions held together by the dog or cat hairs of their usual occupants. While the club chairman went into the back room to get forms, I stood in the kitchen. There was a tall pot on the stove. I recognised it from the legend. In it goes a piece of a dead sheep with plenty of water, and maybe a couple of onions if you're really cooking. On goes the lid, heat turned down low, and off to work you go. When you get home, you call it dinner. Or maybe when you get home, you put the cabbage in – I never did pay enough attention. Anyway, the smell was vile, even sulphurous. I wasn't professional enough to do an analysis, but I would swear there was definitely cabbage in this one. The smell wasn't just coming from the pot – every part of the house reeked of it, from the endless daily ritual. By the time the chairman came back with the paperwork, I was a couple of miles down the road, moving a lot faster than when I'd met him. Saved by the reek of long-boiled dinner.

Because I have no childhood odour trauma about cabbage, I have never been uncomfortable with it, which must be why I still find it one of the most useful, affordable and flexible vegetables, both at home and in a restaurant kitchen.

The first book I usually turn to when trying to decide what flavours to pair with a vegetable is *Jane Grigson's Vegetable Book*. Although I've never knowingly cooked directly from it, the book works as a springboard to an almost endless range of possibilities because of Grigson's passionate but detailed research. True to form, she doesn't hide her disdain for what she considers the coarser greens. On spring cabbage and its inability, or disinclination, to form a heart, she quips that 'heartlessness is never a desirable quality'. It's a fun line she must have enjoyed writing. I would have liked an evening in her company to discuss it – wouldn't even have minded losing the argument, though an argument it would have been.

However, she clearly adored some cabbages, and rightfully placed the Savoy at the top of the pile. The Savoy is a highly cultivated vegetable, with a sweet flavour and wonderfully crunchy texture which makes it just as good eaten raw or cooked. Despite the recent trend against long cooking of cabbages, I think the best way to cook Savoy is to braise it for an hour or more in olive oil, wine and stock, with the possible addition of spices and the extra sweetness of tomato. After that you can add anything you fancy that goes with cabbage: I like chickpeas, lentils, seeds such as fennel, coriander, caraway and cumin, sweet peppers, fennel, even potatoes in a reverse of the classic method of adding cabbage to spuds. Not all at the same time, mind. Pick a well-matched two or three. In Paradiso we use it as a wrapping for dolmas and timbales, as well as a braised side dish. Savoy isn't the most obviously smooth wrapping material, but the flavour makes it worthwhile and it only takes a little effort to flatten the leaves if you need to.

Even after losing my imaginary argument with Ms Grigson, I still love spring cabbage, partly for its lovely soft, pliable leaves and its relatively mild flavour, but mostly because it arrives in early spring just when we are tiring of the stored winter foods. Putting away the winter things and moving on is one of the most exciting times in the vegetable year. It changes your focus from the past to the potential future. Spring cabbage has the flavour of new growth, of life and hope and the mad optimism of a new year.

The brassica that divides people most, however, is surely the Brussels sprout – an eccentric name for a gloriously eccentric-looking plant. Brussels sprouts are compact cabbages in mini form, with concentrated flavour. But what an astonishing-looking plant they come from. It grows about 60cm (2 feet) high with a few dozen sprouts clinging to the stalk, while out of the top it puts up what it clearly believes to be a decent attempt at a cabbage. And it's not far wrong. The leaves are indeed good cabbage, and have the advantage, culinarily speaking, of clinging to life when the sprouts and most other winter greens are gone. These should, however, be cooked like winter rather than spring greens. They are tough, having been hanging around all winter, and are best braised or thinly sliced and fried.

The sprouts themselves are as adaptable as the entire range of cabbages put together. They are best known as a simply boiled vegetable – hard or soft, as you like it. But they also fry well, with spices and tomato. They are good in creamy gratins with strong cheeses. The sprouts can also be shredded leaf by leaf and added to salads, soups or stews. Brussels sprouts with chestnuts is a classic combination, one that gets a frequent run-out at Christmas, but they also go well with other nuts, including walnuts, hazelnuts and macadamias. I believe they work with blue cheese too, but not everyone agrees with me. You have to admire that about Brussels sprouts – as much as they are pigeonholed by local tradition, they are also just as happy dressed up in exotic gear.

The thing about sprouts is that very few people can agree on how to

ABYSSINIAN CABBAGE

cook them. Leaving out those who simply can't abide the vegetable at all, the rest of us who profess to love them – there is apparently no middle ground with sprouts – are very subjective about how they should be cooked, so it is very difficult to say anything other than this is how I like mine. For everyone who likes them lightly steamed, there is another who likes them almost mushy, and really loves them that way, so you can't say it's wrong or ill-advised. Every winter at Paradiso I try a new twist on sprouts. The recipe to follow later with a blue cheese cream and spiced potato gnocchi is this year's model. I love it, but I accept that it's a personal thing.

There is also a relatively new cabbage that we used for the first time last winter. In fact, it's relatively new to everyone except the Ethiopians. It was only in the late 1950s that it was first brought to Europe and America. It is called Abyssinian cabbage, but you may have come across it as 'Texsel greens', a very unglamorous name given to it by people trialling it as a crop in, er, Texas, would you believe? Ultan first grew it to fill that gap in mid-to-late winter. It can survive outdoors in our summer, but the fields and tunnels are full of greens then. So instead, he grows it in a tunnel in the dull days of November to February, to give us some badly needed variety at that time, something softer and lighter than most winter greens.

We harvest it in two ways for Paradiso: firstly as a cut-and-come crop where small-to-medium leaves are picked from closely sown plants; and secondly as a plant grown to full maturity when the leaves are almost the size of spring cabbage. The younger, cut-and-come leaves are close to spinach in texture, and can be used in almost the same way, bearing in mind that they do have a slightly tangy cabbage flavour. This works well with the sweetness of tomato and garlic, and it is comfortable too with the zing of ginger and some of the sweeter spices like nutmeg, paprika, fennel and cinnamon.

Even at full size, the leaves are relatively soft, somewhere between a coarse spinach and spring cabbage. This is a refreshing food to have in the depths of winter, when you want the flavour of fresh greens but are not in the mood for the full-on hit of kale. You can even eat the sprouted shoots, which cook like sprouting broccoli. The large leaves make a good wrapping for dolmas, timbales and terrines, but they are best cooked simply in any way that works for spring cabbage, especially stir-fried and seasoned with sesame and soy sauce.

Flowering brassica – the true cabbage royalty

When I think of great brassica, however, it isn't the headed cabbages I dream about at all, but the flowering heads of broccoli and the loose leaves of kale. It is astonishing that purple sprouting broccoli has been grown for hundreds of years, yet it has remained relatively obscure in recent times. Meanwhile, the vegetable generally known as broccoli or, properly, calabrese, has taken over the Western world in a mere thirty years.

On the other hand, sprouting broccoli has the drawback of being a vegetable that doesn't accord with the average supermarket buyer's criteria. It has a long growing season, is time-consuming to harvest on a large scale, and it needs to be eaten when very freshly picked. But for the consumer, the flavour of sprouting broccoli has an intensity, richness and complexity that shows up the big-headed green version as the one-dimensional thing it is.

It doesn't take much imagination to see how those attributes can be seen as positive attractions to those whose main priority in food is not mere convenience. This is a vegetable that sits in the ground over winter, then produces the most beautiful and intensely flavoured shoots in late winter, and continues producing more for eight to ten weeks. Its arrival at this lean time of year gives it a very special place in the hierarchy of all vegetables. There are varieties that crop even earlier, depending on the mildness of the winter, and others that go on producing into late spring. This is an area where the breeding of varieties to extend the season can only be seen as a good thing. The autumn in which I wrote this piece was so mild that many broccoli plants due to sprout early, as in shortly before Christmas, were already putting out a crop in early November. What is a grower, or a cook, to do? Scold the plant for unseasonal behaviour and ignore the crop? Or be grateful for such an early treat? I value the principle of seasonality as much as anyone, and I love those vegetables which remain resolutely and stubbornly seasonal. But there is a big difference between growers using their skill and knowledge to extend the season of a plant and a supermarket flying the stuff in from the opposite hemisphere because we can't go a week without it. It is mainly because of this intelligent and useful extending of sprouting broccoli's season that we are finally beginning to see it more frequently in markets and even in some supermarkets.

The last time I wrote about purple sprouting broccoli, in *Paradiso Seasons*, I suggested that the only hope for wider recognition of its virtues was if both the public and the growers viewed it as a vegetable on a par with asparagus in terms of perceived value and price. I didn't know then that in Italy, where it has been loved for centuries, it has long been treated as such when sold at markets. It was even referred to as 'Italian asparagus' in eighteenth-century England.

Purple sprouting broccoli has a big rich flavour; a little bitter, yes, but with that essential innate sweetness too. It is great in stir-fries with hot spices like chilli and ginger, but is just as comfortable in pasta dishes with the sweetness of tomato or peppers, and herbs like thyme, basil and oregano. It works with most cheeses, but especially soft sheep's milk cheeses like Knockalara, or mild blues. One of the nicest and simplest ways to prepare it is to simmer it in a small amount of water in a covered pan until just tender, and then dress it with olive oil, salt and pepper. This simple dish is equally good whether served at room temperature or piping hot.

Cime di rapa, or broccoli raab, is a somewhat similar vegetable, but it is grown more for its leaves than for the flowering stalks. The leaves are wonderfully bitter, yet cook as quickly and as softly as spinach. When cooked in olive oil, the leaves shrink quickly but become the most darkly vibrant shade of green. The edible stalk is sweeter than the leaves, which makes the combination such a deliciously balanced flavour. The skin of the stalks can be slightly stringy, so it's best to either peel them or chop them finely. As I write, we have only eaten a trial crop, but it is a vegetable I am very excited about for the coming years. It is wonderful in pasta, as a perky side dish for a comforting risotto and cooked with the tomatoes and chillies that complement dark greens so well.

There is a great love of flowering brassica in Chinese cooking, and most of the favourites are from a range of greens going under the general name of choi sum. One that we have taken to using in the restaurant is Chinese broccoli, sometimes known as Chinese kale. (Well, it isn't technically one of the choi sum family at all, but it is grown and used in the same way.) For some reason, faced with the choice of names, Ultan and I decided to go with 'kale' at first. I think he had kale on his mind that week, trying to find ways to make sure we always had a couple of kale varieties on the menu.

To confuse the matter even more, if you are lucky enough to come across this gem in a Chinese restaurant, as I did in a wonderful place in London doing a modern take on dim sum, then it will probably be called 'gai lan'. Probably. Don't bet your house on it. It might be 'kai lan', or any of a number of variations on the two. Outside of horticultural books, these terms can be more casual tools for communication. We choose one and go with it. That way, I know what the grower means, my cooks and floor staff understand what I mean and, hopefully, so do the people eating in the dining room. Nonetheless, when it came to serving the vegetable, I reverted to 'Chinese broccoli'. Next year, I'll go for broke and use 'gai lan'. It must be a brassica thing, this confusion over names. I'm sure the rest of the vegetable world is much more conformist.

While not exactly a fast grower, Chinese broccoli gives results much faster than its Western cousins, putting out flowering stems with soft leaves attached. As with sprouting broccoli, these stems are the prized part of this amazing vegetable. It has that classic combination of sweetness and slight bitterness, and the young leaves are delicious too. The texture of the stem, picked at the right time, is tender and juicy, with a little bite. In the pantheon of greens, it has it all. It is often picked as a young whole plant, when every part can be eaten, and can be presented on the plate as one piece, which looks very striking.

Chinese broccoli has strong enough flavours to carry quite a lot of spices, and works especially well when flavoured with chillies, ginger, soy sauce or sesame oil. But if you think of it as having a character close to sprouting broccoli, then you can see how it can be used with European seasonings, with garlic, tomatoes and herbs, even with cheeses, as well as in the usual contrasting role with risotto and other comfort foods. It is great with eggs too, especially served straddling a soft omelette.

The timely revival of lowly kale

Not fifteen years ago, the only kale to be found was the curly green one. Even then, most people believed it to be fit only for cattle; a tiny minority enjoyed it from their own gardens, but it never showed up on shop shelves. Kale may have suffered from its association with poverty and hunger, something it shares with the wonderful but often derided swede turnip.

There is something tragi-heroic in kale's history, in the way it fell from a dull but important survival food to something looked on with disdain. Kale is a tough character, it survives well in cold weather and in poor soil, and it is a low-maintenance, cut-and-come source of food. Most importantly, it over-winters well and can go on through the lean months of March and April, the notorious 'hungry gap' months. So much for the heroic. Foods that nourish through times of deprivation are quickly left behind when the good times roll in. Throwing off the badge of poverty, the survival food is discarded, denied even, and replaced by the exotic, by what can be afforded.

Years ago, I was discussing roots with a German grower working in West Cork, who supplied me with local and imported vegetables, a man who went by the descriptive name of Organic Joe. I was moaning about the high price of imported roots like celeriac and salsify, and the humble turnips too, though I never bought those from him. He said that for a new generation of growers and foodies in Germany, Holland and other parts of Europe, roots were something of an exotic. They had largely disappeared once the post-war economic boom kicked in and people could finally put away the foods that helped them survive when rationing was necessary. As one generation shied away from roots and the associations they brought to the table, the next generation went back to them as something with the dual appeal of being both exotic and traditional. So it may have been for poor old kale in these parts. I don't think this is a conscious thing or an overt snobbery; it just happens that people unthinkingly move away from the things that have associations with the parts of their history they would rather forget.

In the early 1990s, as Ireland became more self-confident due to its increasing wealth, there seemed to be the beginnings of a new lease of life for kale, echoing Organic Joe's theory on roots. Kale, having been rejected by a generation or three, was at once new to us and obviously part of our food history. At first, there was a renaissance for the traditional curly kale. Not long after, other more exotic varieties began to show up. By the late 1990s, we were seeing kale as a newly fashionable ingredient. Put away that dull old cabbage, dear, we're having kale for dinner tonight.

The first of the immigrant kales that I fell in love with was cavolo nero, the Italian variety, and still my favourite. Again, the issue of naming comes up here. We've always called it by the loose translation 'black kale', not for any reason other than that it became the term in common usage between grower and kitchen. I know this can seem annoyingly careless to those who are fastidious about the proper names of vegetables. I'm generally as fussy as the next person about attention to detail but, in naming things, common usage often dictates the rules.

Black kale is a strikingly handsome plant, growing up to 1 metre (3 feet) high, with long leaves fanning out from the stem. The leaves are the most fantastic colour. Definitely a green, but purple too at the same time, a very intense purple that is almost black. Take a look at the water in the pot next time you boil some. It will be a beautiful, bright, shade of green. No purple there at all. Meanwhile the kale itself will have become more intensely dark. What's going on here? Most greens become brighter and more translucent when cooked. This one leaks its green colour, intent on becoming a black vegetable. Cooked in olive oil and stock, its deep colour glistens, and the strong flavour has the perfect balance of bitter and sweet elements.

A new favourite is Red Russian, though the colour is really more of a magical blend of a silvery translucent green with pink shading. It has a softer, more open leaf than the black kale, and it cooks faster to give a more tender vegetable. We still persist with the curly green variety too, but I admit it is only as a back-up to the current two favourites. Others we have tried and liked, and will definitely come back to, are Pentland Brig, Red Bor and Raggedy Jack.

All kales can be cooked in the same ways, making allowances for their toughness. If you are using leaves with a thin stalk, simply chop them coarsely. This is especially good when you are adding kale to stews, as the stalks cook down to a softly chewable texture. If the stalks are thicker or seem tough, pull the leaves from the stalks, discarding the stalks, and then take one of two options. The first is to boil the kale in a large pot for anything from four to ten minutes. If the cooked kale is to be part of a dish, such as in pancakes, frittata, tarts or gratins, cool it by dropping it into cold water. Squeeze out the water and chop the kale. How thorough you need to be in squeezing out the water depends on the dish. If you intend to add the kale to a soup or risotto, it's not such a serious issue, but if you are making gnocchi or putting it in a frittata, try to get it as dry as possible. Alternatively, for a simple side dish, wilt the kale by frying it in olive oil over medium heat, splashing regularly with stock or water until the kale is tender. This simple method makes kale a perfect foil for rich food, such as egg or cheese dishes. Most kales are strong enough to take quite a lot of spicing, especially chillies, cumin and coriander seeds, and ginger.

Kale is traditionally a winter crop, and, as such, it is a vital part of our repertoire during those lean months. However, we also use it in summer, sometimes even from plants grown in a tunnel. Kale in a tunnel? In summer? That may seem to go against the accepted thinking on the subject of kale, and indeed on the whole notion of serving vegetables according to their season. Over the years, Ultan has developed growing patterns to ensure that we always have a variety of different greens to work with. In fact, because of kale's affinity with different ingredients and flavourings (it loves tomatoes and herbs, but also chestnuts and potatoes), I like to have one or two varieties around most of the year.

In the early summer, when the spring greens are disappearing, kale from the tunnel is very welcome, and is followed by outdoor kale which crops through the summer. The kale of deepest winter is the hardiest, with the toughest leaf and the strongest flavour. Kale grown in a tunnel is a different beast. It grows quickly, producing softer leaves. These cook faster too, giving a softer texture and a sweeter, milder flavour. The Red Russian is particularly successful this way, finishing up closer in texture to coarse spinach than to winter kale. It's a lovely summer green, simple as that, and very welcome on my plate and in my menus.

Another misleading theory about kale is that it is bitter in early winter before the first frost. Bitterness in greens is a good thing, but the theory suggests that at this time of year it is not balanced by any sweetness when the vegetable is cooked. The frost theory is applied to other brassica too, especially Brussels sprouts. Some go as far as to say these greens need a few weeks of frost. (Weeks of frost? Brr … no, thanks.) I would agree that the first outer leaves of kale in early winter are not as sweet as the inner ones later on, but they are far from unusable or completely lacking in balance. To rigidly await the arrival of frost only makes sense in a location where the weather patterns are predictable and there are plenty of alternative greens. Many vegetables with a long season go through changes in flavour and texture during their picking time. This is something to be celebrated and savoured, even if some adapting of recipes is called for. The best analogy I can make is with the Sungold tomatoes that Ultan grows all summer long. Through the season, their flavour moves across the spectrum from acidic to sugary sweet, and few people agree on when they are at their best. They are, however, always good. In any case, while the climate in West Cork may not be a sub-tropical nirvana, the winters here are not very cold. If we were to wait for a decent number of consecutive frosty nights before we picked the crop, then some winters we'd never get to eat kale at all.

Whether growing kale or doing any other kind of gardening, you can only ever take a manual or instruction book as a guide, not a bible. The rest depends on your own circumstances, as well as your needs and tastes. This is true of cookery books too, including this one. Ultan puts it succinctly when he says that every locality, every field or side of a hill, every tunnel or glasshouse is a micro-climate. In her classic book *Grow Your Own Vegetables*, Joy Larkcom says that all gardeners need to be experimenters who have to co-operate with the conditions and requirements of their particular garden, as well as with the local weather patterns. By the same token, all cooks in their own kitchens have to be experimenters too.

Asparagus, perennial king of a gardening renaissance

I received an e-mail from a man I know, let's call him 'Harry', who contacts me occasionally with proposals for business opportunities. Mostly they involve me working very hard and him adding to his stash. Still, I like looking at projects, fantasising about dream kitchens with more chefs than I need or can afford, turning out food I haven't yet imagined. I can even get as far as thinking about what I'll do with my share of the millions. Alas, the projects never happen, yet each time I mull over the possibilities with the same enthusiasm.

However, this most recent e-mail opened with news of his asparagus bed. Doing well, apparently, and giving the best asparagus in the world of course, though the slugs are causing sleepless nights. Now, Harry is young and wealthy. He knows the ways of the business world and has the tough streak needed to function in it. He also takes a good chunk out of life and is equally partial to a New York nightclub or a weekend's ice-climbing. So, this e-mail was a new twist. (By the way, one of the many methods used by organic growers to deal with slugs is to crawl around at dusk, snipping them in half with decently sharp scissors. Now, that takes character. Good preparation for the cut-throat world of business, I would think.)

I tell this story to illustrate the fact that gardening, especially the growing of vegetables, is becoming fashionable, infecting people's imaginations like some sort of virulent contagion. I have been told by people who give talks about vegetable cultivation that the audience is growing and the age profile is dropping alarmingly. Encouragingly, I should probably say. It is surely a bit ironic that while we cram our modern cities with hideous shoebox apartment blocks, those who have access to land, even a tiny piece of earth to dig, are turning to the ancient activity of growing food. There is a different focus this time round, however. Sure, people are growing a few spuds and onions, but there is greater emphasis on speciality and 'heirloom' vegetables, on the varieties that you can't get in shops, as well as on those vegetables that need to be eaten very fresh and which are therefore usually in poor condition by the time they appear in a shop. Even where potatoes are being grown, the focus is on early varieties that are immeasurably better to eat when freshly dug. This new gardening is more about a love of food than saving on the household budget.

In a sense there is a new model being created for the kitchen garden, where the old staples are being replaced by vegetables further up the hierarchy; higher up the social ladder, one might say. Opinion on the aristocracy of vegetables may vary, but in almost everyone's list you will find asparagus. In a rapidly growing minority, you will also find seakale. Both asparagus and seakale require a commitment of time and energy that gives a return that can't be measured in volume, only in depth of pleasure. This makes them more than a mere luxury, because they can only be had through work and careful attention. And I say this as someone who doesn't garden but who envies those who engage in this primal pastime.

It is ironic that, for such a classy vegetable, an asparagus bed is not much to look at during its productive season. The beautiful shoots poke their heads up, quickly grow to a size worth picking and eating, and then they're gone, cut down and off to the kitchen to make someone's day. Your typical asparagus bed, therefore, is a brown patch of earth with a mixture of a few short juvenile spears and some long grassy stalks, the ones that were never fat enough to pick, waving in the breeze.

The first time I saw an asparagus bed, however, it was a thing of beauty indeed. The bed was in its first year and Ultan had sensibly picked none of the shoots for eating, instead allowing them all to grow as they wished. The spears had grown to be long, delicate fronds, almost 2 metres (6.5 feet) high, and they were a pretty sight. Letting the asparagus grow would strengthen the plant below ground and set it up for good cropping in later years. The following year, he did it again, though I suspect he cheated a little this time, sneaking the occasional tea-time treat. We finally got some for Paradiso in the third year, although he picked for a fortnight only. It was worth the wait. Fresh asparagus has an intensity of flavour that might shock a palate used to pale supermarket imitations.

Freshly cut asparagus, from a variety grown for flavour as well as for yield, is indeed the king among aristocrats. It sets a benchmark for the flavour of other vegetables. How often do you hear or read that a certain vegetable has a hint of asparagus? Usually it is said in hope or bluff more than truth. And yes, good asparagus does have an element of primal green in its complex and intense flavour. It also has a definite earthy sweetness that leaks easily after picking, which is one of the best reasons to buy locally grown asparagus when it is available.

Asparagus has a proud history. It has been cultivated for close to forever, at least as far back as Roman times, and was produced on a large scale around Venice in the sixteenth century. All that time, and continuing today, it has been the jewel in the vegetable market of every culture lucky enough to be able to grow it, and smart enough to embrace it. It is shocking, then, to think of how, in Ireland, it went from being the most exclusive exotic to the mundane in what seemed like the vegetable equivalent of the speed of light. As well as shocking, it is perhaps a wry reflection on the values of a newly rich society.

Asparagus certainly played no part in the Ireland in which I grew up. Years later, it was rumoured to be occasionally available in the finest restaurants. Or, you might come across it on your holidays in France. (If, that is, you were the sort to take holidays anywhere other than the nearest beach.) There may have followed a short time when Spanish asparagus appeared in good greengrocers (remember them?) for a short season and at a high price.

If there were such a time, it was brief and quickly shoved aside by the scenario of mediocre asparagus on the shelves all year round. Usually European in origin for the traditional six- or eight-week season of May to June, for the rest of the year it is imported from Peru. So, before we even had a chance to divide ourselves into those who could afford or appreciate

ASPARAGUS IS THE KING OF ARISTOCRATS

asparagus and those who couldn't or wouldn't, the beautiful vegetable has been reduced to a bog-standard ubiquitous imitator. Think about this: has anyone ever gushed excitedly to you on a cold winter's morning about the amazing asparagus they had for dinner the night before, and which they bought cheaply at Tesco? Not likely.

One of the finest qualities of asparagus as a crop is the way it resolutely sticks to its seasonal pattern. By the same token, one of the worst qualities of the people purchasing for supermarkets is their myopic belief that you, the punter, will only be interested in a vegetable if it is in the same place on the same shelf every day of the year. And going cheap. When almost all vegetables have been manipulated, teased and tricked into lengthening their productive seasons, the few that have remained unbendable hold a special place in the hearts of those who enjoy the pleasure of taking part in a feast that passes by briefly, and only once a year. And I think that, deep down or otherwise, that's most of us.

If it is true that there is a rebirth in the art of growing food, there may yet be another heyday for asparagus, and a better one. The smartest gardeners will take the trouble to make an asparagus bed a part of their future. When this happens, it should go a long way to helping us to see asparagus as the outrageously bountiful vegetable it is when in season. Whether you grow your own or have access to a decent crop in late spring, do try to feast on it at least a couple of times while it is around. I mean really feast on it – cook a couple of kilos and call it dinner, served with some melted butter and a few new spuds if you need the carbs.

In recipes for asparagus, you will often find references to thin and fat spears, and many food writers seem to favour thin ones. I don't really get this, unless you are after a very delicate flavour. I rarely am. A good spear of asparagus should have the thickness of your little finger, at least, and is often better if it is the size of the next one along. At this size, the flesh inside has a juicy, nutty sweetness that is balanced by the texture of the skin and its green, almost grassy, flavour. Thin asparagus spears, however, can be fantastic in salads or strewn over softly cooked eggs, especially if the asparagus is raw or merely introduced to boiling water for a few seconds. A simple way of approaching this is to think about the proportion of skin to flesh. The thin skin of asparagus coats the sweetly succulent flesh with a mildly astringent, truly green flavour. At a certain point, there is a perfect balance, and it's not at the skinny end of the scale.

There is, too, disagreement about peeling the stalks. Here again, I go for the simple life, and rarely peel at all. Simply snap the spear just above the point where it changes colour. However, if the spears are very fat or it is obvious that the skin is tough, then peeling is the only solution. And it is worth it, because the flesh inside is usually still tender and juicy. Never say never.

There are two basic ways to prepare asparagus, three if you count eating it raw. And, definitely, very fresh asparagus is fantastic raw, either as an indulgent snack coming back up the garden path, as finger food with a dip, or thinly sliced in salads. Once indoors, asparagus can be boiled, steamed, fried, roasted or grilled. Boiling or steaming leaves the flavour pure and fine, and this is best if the asparagus is to be used in cooked dishes like tarts, gratins, pasta, risottos or pancakes. I like asparagus lightly cooked and still crunchy, so I would cook it for no more than three minutes. That's a subjective matter, though, and you have to find your own way. Always serve it immediately, or plunge it into cold water to cool it down if you are adding it to a dish later.

If you are serving the asparagus on its own or with a dip, perhaps as a starter, then you can get a more intense flavour by grilling or roasting it. Lay the spears on a flat oven tray, sprinkle them very lightly with olive oil and salt flakes, and roast in a hot oven for four or five minutes. Cooking them under a grill, on a griddle pan, or on a barbecue, works too, but I think the oven gives a juicier result. Done either way, the asparagus will be crunchy, slightly browned and somehow more intense and sweeter than when boiled. You can't leave it hanging around at this stage, nor can you cool it in water, so be sure that everything, and everybody, is ready before you put asparagus in the oven or under a grill.

When asparagus takes a partner, it really marries well. Classically, asparagus has an affinity with new potatoes, butter, lemon, chives, tarragon and with eggs of all kinds cooked any way. Asparagus is comfortable with a surprisingly wide range of cheeses, but has a special affinity with hard mature cheeses with some sweetness or the mellow sharpness of fresh goat's or sheep's cheeses.

Asparagus also loves a hint of rosemary or lemon thyme in an olive oil-based aïoli for dunking. In a twist on this, we sometimes replace the herbs in the aïoli with blood orange juice. It makes a striking starter that will make you appear to be very clever and modern. Be careful whom you try to impress, however, as quite a lot of people already know that this is not a new trick at all, but a classic combination from Malta. We found the inspiration for this version in *Jane Grigson's Fruit Book* while looking for interesting things to do with blood oranges. The combination of orange and asparagus also works beautifully in a salad.

SEAKALE

Seakale, a prince from the shoreline

Asparagus will remain at the top of the aristocratic pile for a while yet, but if there is a vegetable with the potential to match it for unique flavour and appearance, it is surely seakale.

Seakale has a dual personality of extreme characteristics. It is at once ancient and modern, both highly cultivated and utterly wild. It was eaten as a prized wild seashore plant around the coasts of much of Europe long before it was cultivated, and it has persisted as a favourite wild food still, for those lucky enough to know where to find it and who still appreciate its rugged qualities. And yet, it has for centuries also been grown as an exquisite garden vegetable. This transformation from rugged and wild to delicate and cultivated is achieved by the gardening practice known as blanching, whereby the young shoots of a plant are covered to keep the sunlight away. The stalks grow long and thin, with little foliage, and, most importantly, with a subtly delicious flavour and tender texture.

Perhaps in the renaissance of domestic vegetable growing, seakale will become once again, along with asparagus, one of the prized jewels of those who love to eat as much as they love to grow. However, I would urge anyone growing seakale to leave some of the plants uncovered, to be enjoyed as one of the most intense and succulent winter greens. This dual role is why seakale is the only individual variety of vegetable to feature twice in this book, both here and in the chapter 'Growing in the dark', where I look at the blanched version in more detail. If I had found any in the wild, it would have been featured in the 'Wild pickings' chapter too, but it has become very scarce in Ireland.

Although I did some research for this book (those who know more than me will have noticed, and I look forward to some witty letters), I tried not to do so much that it would discolour my approach to the vegetables I love. To be honest, after a while I had only a small handful of trustworthy books close by when I felt in need of facts. I'm a lazy reader, but still I began to see patterns of repetition in reference books, patterns that made me nervous.

The myth about seakale, repeated in so many books that it has practically become fact, is that it is 'bitter and inedible' as a green vegetable. This may be because it is so sublimely unique when blanched – an understandable extension of thought, if you like, but the myth is actually untrue. It is a myth that must have been promulgated by those who have never eaten unblanched seakale. Surely if you are going to say that something that grows easily in your climate is bitter and inedible, you should take a bite of it first?

Of course, it is necessary to accept the validity of expert sources when writing history or science, and there is a lot of both in gardening and food reference books. So there is bound to be repetition. But as little as I know about gardening, I came to realise very quickly the importance of trying to get to original sources of information. In that context, Joy Larkcom's books, especially *Grow Your Own Vegetables* and *Oriental Vegetables*, are so idiosyncratic you just know that there is nothing in there that she hasn't tested in her own field. Literally. Joy never wrote of seakale, but knowing her love of greens, you can be sure she would not have been able to resist testing it in the end.

I might well have gone on to propagate this notion too if I hadn't had a call from Ultan, way too early one damp Monday morning in March. He had been diligently leaving the first year's crop of seakale to grow out, unblanched. All the books tell you to do this simply to strengthen the crowns below ground, and so he did ... sort of. Being a fiend for good greens, he kept looking at them, thinking they must be edible. In my interpretation of the scene, I imagine him drooling a little, maybe even a lot. Anyway, the night before (a wet, boring Sunday) he ate the damn things. No, not all of them, but enough to know the truth. Again, I imagine there was drooling, maybe even slobbering. I would have known about it immediately, except that I was out at a 'fine' restaurant eating crap food. Ah, the glorious joys of urban life.

The next day I collected some green seakale and cooked it for the first time. I admit I was a little nervous, especially of feeding it to my fifteen-year-old son. He's a willing guinea pig, though I wouldn't go so far as to say he trusts me completely. I even warned him that the literature describes this stuff as inedible in its green state.

In fact, there was no more than a trace of the bitterness that is written of in those dozens of books. All good greens have some bitterness, so if anything, the taste was a little milder than many of my favourite greens, such as sprouting broccoli or black kale. Seakale has the essential vibrant colour, and a softly melting but chewy texture. Sprouting broccoli is a good reference point for seakale. Pick it young, when the stems, the soft leaves and the budding flower heads are all edible. Discard the tough leaves and cook the rest in an open pan with a little water, just enough to keep it moist. When it is tender, dress it with olive oil, salt and pepper. Don't leave any juices behind in the pan when you serve. Until you become bored with that, nothing more is called for. And yes, the fifteen-year-old liked it.

Next year we will have both green and blanched seakale. How cool is that?

Watering the cats and putting manners on the plants: the rainbow chard diaries

I spent ten days in late spring minding the house of friends who had gone off to France in a camper van that I didn't expect to make it off the ferry. Oh well, to each their own sense of adventure. Mine was to live alone for ten days in their lovely old farmhouse with an acre or so of garden near the coast in West Cork. 'Garden' might be a bit of an understatement. It is more an exquisite arrangement of plants, the edible and the purely aesthetic, blended together in deliberate patterns but not fussily pristine. Parts of it are handsomely geometric, but look as though it might have happened by happy chaos, that it is simply the inherent beauty of nature that has caused it to fall together so perfectly. I know how much work goes into achieving that look. I say that as someone who fusses over plates and the appearance of food, and who likes the result to look as if it fell on to the plate in a pleasing but slightly off-centre sort of way.

Up at the very top of the garden, in the pink and purple area (yes, indeed) was a chard plant almost 1.8 metres (6 feet) tall, flanked by two purple-tinted kales, slightly shorter. All three were the previous season's crop, which were allowed to carry on growing for their statuesque beauty and fabulous colours. In fact, the stem and leaf stalks of the chard were close to a screaming shade of red, with just enough hint of pink to qualify for the theme of the area. (This is one of chard's great qualities as a garden vegetable. It is very beautiful, especially if you grow varieties with different-coloured stalks.) Elsewhere in the garden there was a patch of the more sedate but classic white-stemmed chard, and in another corner still a scattering of what is known as a 'rainbow mix', with yellow, orange, white and pink chards mingling vividly. And all this beauty provides such good, and easy, food.

I was in the house for the peaceful environment and to find the time that I had been wilfully wasting in the city, for writing and reading. But this was to be a mutually beneficial arrangement, so I had chores as well. Two duties mainly: the cats and the garden. The cats were easy. I moved them out of the house, lecturing them on the potential joys of getting in touch with their inner tiger. The catflap, their portal between wild nature and indoor pampering, was temporarily sealed. Not wanting to be totally heartless, I gave them access to a tiny hallway where there would be mats to sleep on, and food to eat, albeit smaller rations than they were used to. Well, I reckoned, quickly getting up to speed on cat evolution, a fat lazy cat has no chance of finding that tiger. She needs some hunger motivation. Some great wise (and probably very rich) old man is bound to have said that.

The garden was another matter. I don't garden. I admire and love those who do, and I know a lot of the theory, but I've never really got my hands dirty in one. Not the best person to leave in charge, then. I can do chores, if they are clearly laid out. So I did what I do in the restaurant kitchen – made a checklist for every day, with space to tick off jobs as they were completed: watering, ventilating the greenhouse, moving plants here and there for light and shade, covering and uncovering new plantings depending on weather, recording temperature and rainfall levels. (Golden rule: never go to bed with an unfinished checklist.) Yes, that's right: I was Met Man for West Cork briefly.

The first night, it lashed down, heavy rain falling in bucketfuls. The wind whipped around the house and every door latch twitched noisily all night. In my few fitful snatches of sleep, I imagined it was the cats coming for me, all tigered up. In my more frequent wide-awake state, I felt a tiny bit sorry for them. Next morning, there was more water in the rain collection jar than had fallen in the entire previous month. The cats were alive and dry, if a little sorry for themselves. I took a ramble round the garden, trying to be masterly but not really knowing what I was looking for. I mean, in the city I would have been looking for roof tiles and broken downpipes, maybe glass everywhere. So, to my untrained eye, it all looked fine, a bit windswept maybe, but fine, until I came to the chard. One entire plant had fallen over. It wasn't broken, more like it had stood up to the wind and rain for a long time, then gradually tilted sideways until it lay flat on the ground, dejectedly unable to fight any more, yet relieved that the battle was over. It reminded me of seeing Spencer Tracy in *The Old Man and the Sea*, putting a gloomy downer on one Christmas holiday afternoon in my youth. Watching the film, you cheer him on for an hour or so, but then, seeing that he is dying a slow death, you just want it over and done with. I did the only thing a self-respecting cook could do – snipped off a handful of leaves for lunch (just a simple dish of wilted chard flavoured with lemon and pine nuts). Two days later when the plant had made no recovery, I took the best of the rest and made a very tasty gratin.

Chard grows willingly and can be harvested by taking a few leaves at a time. It will kindly go on producing more. It has never made much of an impact as a commercial crop, except in farmers' markets to a small extent. This is not necessarily a bad thing. It really does need to be used very fresh. This is true of the softer greens in general, but especially of chard because the stalks start to become tough and stringy in a day or so after picking, and the leaves lose their sweetness. It's worth mentioning too that while the coloured chards will add to the beauty of your garden, their stalks

CHARD

are thinner and tougher than the white variety. I rarely cook the coloured stalks at all.

Spinach is a good starting reference point for what to do with chard, though the leaves are coarser and hold their texture and substance better than spinach. This makes chard leaves really good in tarts, frittata, stews, soups and pancakes, and as a wrapping for 'parcels' like dolmas and timbales. The flavour also has a stronger, earthier element than spinach.

Chard stalks are a vegetable in their own right, and it is worth thinking of them as such once the stalk is about 3cm ($1^1/4$in) wide below the leaf. If the stalks seem stringy, it is possible to peel away the thin layer of stringy film. At that size and beyond, I like to trim the leaves off and braise the stalks by slicing them across 2cm ($3/4$in) thick, then putting them in a heavy pan with olive oil, white wine and stock to barely cover, and cooking over a low heat with the lid on until the stalks are soft and succulent. In soups or stews, the stalks don't need to be cooked separately, of course, but just added earlier than the leaves.

Chard, whether using leaves, stalks or both, is wonderful with eggs, tomatoes, earthy Puy lentils, olive oil and spices, and with almost all cheeses from strong blues to feta, and from hard, aged cheeses to soft fresh ones. It is also great in any variation of hearty Italian soups and stews, rich as they are with olive oil and herbs, and often laced with lemon juice.

Back at the farmhouse, there was one other chore, which I never managed to tick off. (So much for the golden rule of the checklist.) I was to kill snails and slugs at dusk, the scissors method being optional. I tried it the first evening, bolstered by a few glasses of wine. But I managed to fool myself that I couldn't find more than a half dozen of the enemy, that the problem was exaggerated, and I admit to simply chucking those few over the fence. I went on fooling myself on that one for the rest of the tour of duty. At least I was honest enough not to tick the checklist.

Popeye's fighting fuel – spinach or whiskey?

While we were diligently eating our cabbage here in Ireland, children in other parts of the world, particularly America, were shovelling back the spinach. Nutritionally, its strongest card is iron, which it has in spades, if you'll excuse the pun, and is surely what that crazy fiend Popeye was supposedly benefiting from when he glugged down those cans. Was that guy invented by a committee of lunatic nutritionists? I know it must have seemed like a good idea to have a cartoon character that encouraged kids to gobble up their greens, but couldn't they have come up with a role model with rather more admirable characteristics? Popeye was a rough sailor, not the brightest fish in the sea either, with a shockingly poor grasp of grammar and vocabulary. OK, he loved his girlfriend, and that's a sweet message, but I can't help thinking she might have been better off with someone else. Whenever there was a problem, and sometimes when he merely imagined there was one, he lashed back a couple of cans of spinach and came out, fists blazing, walloping people clear out of the scene with ferocious violence. Whiskey would have had the same effect. (In fact, he surely must have been drinking off screen, in one of those seedy waterfront dives populated by cartoon lowlife.)

As it turned out, the information that fuelled not only Popeye but also the enormous canned spinach industry was erroneous. Big time. When the US research of the 1890s was retested by German scientists in the 1930s, it was found that the original results had put a decimal point in the wrong place, multiplying the potential benefits of spinach tenfold. Just in time to start a huge industry. Oh, dear. You wouldn't want to be cynical, would you? If only Popeye's foes were aware that he was fuelling himself on a fallacy.

Spinach is still a highly nutritious vegetable, even so, and it does have a decent amount of iron. But even if it wasn't so healthy, we would still eat it for its flavour and all-round usefulness. Spinach is, in many ways, the ultimate green. Granted, in the company of some of the other greens here, it may not seem a big hitter, having neither the complex flavour nor the strong texture of the likes of sprouting broccoli and black or Chinese kale. But that is not what spinach is about. It has a mild flavour and a soft texture, which makes it easily the most useful, multi-functional green. Available all year round now, spinach is almost always on the menu in Paradiso, often in more than one dish. There is always spinach, the other greens come and go.

Spinach is also the benchmark of leaf greens, the one that the others are judged by. Is this or that kale softer or tougher than spinach? Sweeter or more bitter? Longer to cook? Easier to grow? Can it step into classic recipes that call for spinach or is it too strong, bitter or tough?

Recipes for spinach? There are thousands. For hundreds, and in some cases thousands, of years, it has been served in tarts both sweet and savoury, curries, soups, inside ravioli, as a component of pasta dishes and even as a colouring for the pasta itself; in gnocchi and other dumplings, omelettes and endless egg dishes, pancakes, salads, and much more besides. Not forgetting that it is also wonderful served on its own, whether in the English style with butter, or with olive oil, as the Italians prefer.

There are many varieties of spinach, but it's best to think of them as two types. The soft 'true' spinach, as it is sometimes called, can be used raw in salads, especially with the likes of soft cheeses or hard sweet ones, fennel,

NEW ZEALAND SPINACH

oranges and oily nuts such as walnuts or pine nuts. It can certainly also be cooked, and has a meltingly soft texture and beautifully dark, glossy colour. However, you have to be very careful, as it cooks very quickly and reduces to less than a tenth of its volume. The other type is generally known as 'perpetual' spinach. It has much larger, thicker leaves of a lighter shade. For general cooking, I prefer to use this one. The flavour is less exquisite, but it carries, and stands up to, other flavours very well. It also loses much less volume when cooked. Oh, it shrinks all right, but not so much that it breaks your heart and sends you scurrying to the shops for more.

There is one variety that needs to be looked at in its own right, however. It goes by the name of 'New Zealand spinach' or 'tetragonia'. Although I have spent a bit of time in New Zealand, I have no memory of this vegetable there. However, it is documented that the great (or terrible, according to your perspective) Captain Cook brought it back from his first voyage down under. Or perhaps I should say it came back on his ship. I don't know if Cook was that interested in plants, but he was lucky enough to have someone on board who was – a certain Joseph Banks, a botanist with an appetite for exploration.

Back on this side of the world, however, despite its flavour and suitability to the climate, New Zealand spinach is still very rare, and little used as a vegetable. Unlike other spinach varieties, this one can tolerate dry, and even hot, conditions. This has sometimes been mistakenly believed to be because it doesn't go to seed as easily as the others do when stressed. The truth is that the plant is forever going to seed, hence those beautifully sweet buds that add greatly to its flavour and texture. New Zealand spinach grows well in a tunnel or glasshouse in spring and autumn, and has proven to be perfectly happy outdoors during our warm but often damp summers. In fact, the only conditions it really doesn't like is a combination of very hot and very wet. Should be safe as houses in Ireland, then. We can do wet with gusto, but hot is rare enough to be a tale for the grandkids. Both together would mean the whole island had slid down to the equator.

There are, I think, a couple of reasons for the lack of success of this spinach variety. New Zealand spinach grows as a creeping plant and covers the ground in a fiercely territorial way. The tips of the shoots, with the top few leaves and the tiny bud attached, are the best parts to pick and cook, though the lower leaves are excellent too. Because of the way it grows and the way it is harvested, it is never going to be well enough behaved to be of any use to supermarkets. And so it remains a defiantly domestic vegetable or, at a stretch, one grown by dedicated professionals for specific customers. I always admire that in a vegetable – one that is clearly great homegrown but can't be tamed for the convenience market. When people ask in the restaurant where they can find this gem of a green, it is great to be able to say that the best thing is to grow your own.

The second drawback is that there comes a time when the sweet little buds become too coarse and tough. The leaves are still good at this point, but the work involved in preparing the vegetable, picking off the buds, is almost doubled. I've tried asking Ultan to do it, but only by leaving a phone message as I didn't really want to hear his reply. It is no problem doing this at home for a small number, but in a restaurant kitchen, preparing for multiple meals, the cooks quickly grow to despise the chore. When it comes to that, it's time to give up on the troublesome vegetable. A grumpy kitchen is no fun, and not much good at the sensitive job of cooking dinner either.

So why persevere with New Zealand spinach, then? Although it is very close in character to standard spinach, and it can be used in any recipe that calls for the latter, it has two important advantages. Texture and flavour. Yes, those two! The matter of flavour is subjective, of course, and I may well be taken to task for saying it, but New Zealand spinach is somehow richer and greener than other spinach varieties, yet still sweet and without any of the bitterness of the coarser greens. It really stands alone in terms of texture. The shoot tips, with a tiny bud and some leaves attached to a thin stalk, hold their shape beautifully when cooked, as indeed do the other individual leaves. This is a wonderful asset to a restaurant kitchen, where the aesthetics of food is always high on the agenda. A good-looking vegetable that doesn't sacrifice flavour is a restaurateur's dream.

Taking to the watercress: the holy herb

Watercress has been gathered from the wild for thousands of years, providing a source of essential vitamins and iron long before these qualities were isolated and recognised. Watercress is one of those foods that are so overtly good for you that it really doesn't take a scientist to explain it. You can see it in the vibrant green colour and taste it in the punchy flavour: this is a loaded vegetable.

It has traditionally been picked from flowing streams and ditches and can be found all year round, except that it doesn't really like extremes of temperature and often disappears temporarily during the coldest part of winter and the hottest summer months.

Because the plant will absorb any water-borne pollutants, especially agricultural slurry washing off nearby fields, I am not advocating the consumption of wild watercress. Liver fluke is a particular worry as it seems to thrive in watercress, and can pass to humans. While the idyllic image of

WATERCRESS – THE HOLY HERB

collecting wild cress is attractive, it is essential that you really know the source and are certain that the water in which the cress grows is free from any pollution. For most of us, that means it is simply not a good idea to eat watercress from the wild. Similarly, if you are buying watercress from a market stall, do make sure you can trust the source.

Most watercress is now commercially grown in carefully controlled flowing water beds, an industry that already goes back over two hundred years. The watercress we use in Paradiso comes from a source that is somewhere between the wild and controlled. It is grown in a deep pond in the bend of a stream on a small vegetable farm in West Cork. The pond was created in the late 1970s by a number of very enlightened blow-ins who began their lives here as self-sufficiency advocates, moved on to trading and bartering amongst themselves, and eventually took the bold step of selling excess produce to the public. Fatefully, they formed a co-op. From there it was the usual slide towards outbreaks of feuding, accusations of capitalism, fascism and plain old fraud. The good ones are still round and about, still growing and sometimes selling great food. Luckily the stream and the cress survived not only the fall-out, but numerous changes of ownership of the property that the stream flows through. Each time the farm changes hands, I fear for the future of our watercress supply.

Somehow it's not surprising that research is well advanced on the attributes of watercress that are believed to be cancer inhibitors. This is a very modern take on a plant that has been seen as a miracle for as long as humans have been eating it. Way back as far as Greek and Roman times, and continuously through the centuries since, watercress has been revered for qualities beyond its simple nutritional content. At various times it has been credited with the powers of everything from curing freckles and hangovers to reversing baldness and restoring lost beauty; and it has been extolled as, among many other things, an aphrodisiac and an intellectual stimulant.

Whatever the validity of some of the more outrageous of these claims, there is definitely something to be said for the plant's ability to stimulate the mind. In Ireland, it has a special place in the mixture of folklore, myth and history that makes up what we know of the lives of saints, sages and holy men. Monks were known to spend long periods living on watercress alone, or sometimes supplemented with a little bread. This wasn't a case of self-flagellation but an attempt to stimulate their thinking powers. The combination of the plant's cleansing and healing properties with its reputed effect on the brain would have been a powerful stimulant to those who set themselves apart in isolation to confront the great issues of mind and soul. Even if the effect were not purely scientific, the very deliberate act of putting yourself in that situation of 'taking to the watercress' would surely sharpen and focus the mind. Whatever gets the work done, I say. And they certainly got some work done. The religious communities in Ireland have been credited with carrying the torch of civilisation during the Dark Ages. They took on the task of writing down as much as possible of European literature, even as the barbarians were destroying it, and later disseminating it back across the continent. Many of these communities were fiercely isolationist, putting themselves in seemingly uninhabitable places, like the Skellig rocks off the south-west coast, in order to have the physical freedom and safety as well as the sense of remove that were needed to carry out their visionary work.

Perhaps it's just foodie wishful thinking, but I'd like to think that, although taking to the watercress was a form of fasting, it was done with such positive and specific purpose that these holy men would have enjoyed the stuff. Watercress is one of the most flavourful and easily digestible greens, so it certainly must have been better than if they had attached mind-enhancing properties to nettles or the like.

The taste of watercress is a pungent mix of mustard-like heat, an aromatic freshness and a slight bitterness. Some varieties of land cress are available, similar in appearance to their watery cousin but grown in soil, and the flavour is usually a much more direct hit of unadulterated heat with none of the subtleties of watercress. It is only in direct comparison that you really appreciate the exquisite and complex flavour of the original.

Watercress makes a great salad green, bringing a peppery vibrancy to any mix. It's delicious with orange, fennel, the oily nuts like walnut and pecan, as well as pears and green apples. Blue cheese is fabulous with cress, as are soft mild cheeses, especially those made from goat's or sheep's milk. Despite all that, I actually cook it as often as I serve it raw, although cooking is probably not quite the right word. If you heat it for much more than a minute or so, you risk losing both the vivid colour and the full impact of the flavour. In risotto, pasta, sauces and even soups, I add the cress at the last second so it just warms through. Eaten as part of dishes such as these, you may not get enough to turn you into a seer, but it certainly adds a kick to your dinner.

The future might be greener than you think

There is no doubt that we've come a long way from regarding greens as a purely medicinal form of food. Or maybe it's not so much that we've moved on but that we have eased into a more comfortable relationship with green vegetables. We live in an age where we could easily give them up for a few supplemental pills, and yet vegetables are actually becoming more embedded in our food culture than ever. This is partly due, in an era of extreme health-consciousness, to the wonderful research conducted on the healing and disease-inhibiting characteristics of so many greens, especially watercress and almost all of the brassicas. But it is also true that, released from the slavery of feeling we have to chuck the stuff back to keep us off our deathbeds, we have actually come to love green vegetables for their flavour, texture and almost indefinable life-force quality. When greens were medicine, they were cooked as such and swallowed reluctantly. I especially pity the poor kids of America who had to swallow whole cans of slimy spinach in an effort to grow protruding muscles and strong jaws. Now that we are free to enjoy our greens, we are constantly playing with new ways to flavour the familiar, as well as looking for new varieties to add to the repertoire.

Almost half of the vegetables discussed here are new to me, in the sense that up to two years ago I didn't have sufficient quantities of them to cook with. You only have to walk through the markets of small towns in Italy or China, or to browse through the vegetable-growing books of pioneers like Joy Larkcom, to see that the potential for further growing and cooking experimentation has barely been touched. Next time you eat some wonderfully exotic, if bitter, greens in Italy, don't come home only extolling the joys of Italian food culture. Wonder, too, why it is we don't grow them here. Yet.

Sprouting Broccoli and Oyster Mushrooms in Ginger Broth with Pumpkin and Macadamia Dumplings

First make the broth by bringing the water to the boil in a large saucepan and adding all the ingredients except the soy sauce. Turn down the heat and simmer for 20 minutes. Remove from the heat, add the soy sauce and leave for 20 minutes more. Strain through a sieve into a bowl saving the broth and discarding the vegetables.

Steam the pumpkin until tender and mash it. Stir in the nuts, lemon zest and juice and coriander, and leave to cool.

Place the wonton wrappers on a work surface, with a corner facing you. Put a teaspoon of the pumpkin filling across the centre, shaping it into a rectangle. Moisten the uncovered wonton pastry and fold up first the nearest corner, then the sides and finally the top corner, to make a neat rectangular parcel. Repeat with the rest of the filling to make eight dumplings.

Reheat the ginger broth gently in a large saucepan and keep warm over a low heat. Heat a little vegetable oil in a wok or large frying pan, and fry the broccoli and mushrooms over a medium heat for 5–6 minutes, occasionally ladling in a little of the broth to keep the vegetables moist. Add the spring onion and continue cooking for 2 minutes more.

When the vegetables are almost tender, bring the broth to the boil, drop the dumplings in, lower the heat and simmer for 2 minutes, then remove them and place two each (or four if serving as a main dish) in warm shallow bowls. Divide the cooked vegetables between the bowls and ladle in the broth.

Serves 4 as a starter, 2 as a main dish

vegetable oil

4 small handfuls (about 350g/12oz) purple sprouting broccoli

100g (3½oz) oyster mushrooms, sliced or torn if large

4 spring onions, diagonally sliced

FOR THE BROTH

1.5 litres (2¾ pints) water

1 medium onion, roughly chopped

2 celery sticks, chopped

1 carrot, chopped

4 garlic cloves

85g (3oz) fresh root ginger, sliced

1 fresh chilli, sliced

1 handful fresh coriander leaves

1 handful fresh parsley leaves

100ml (3½fl oz) soy sauce

FOR THE DUMPLINGS (MAKES 8)

100g (3½oz) pumpkin flesh, diced

1 tbsp shelled macadamia nuts, finely chopped

finely grated zest of ½ lemon

½ tsp lemon juice

2 tsp chopped fresh coriander

8 wonton wrappers

Spring Cabbage Dolma of Pumpkin and Chickpeas with Sesame Yoghurt Sauce

Serve these lightly spiced dolma with couscous, either simply steamed or flavoured with lemon and herbs. Any squash with reasonably dense flesh will work in this recipe, including the widely available hokaido and butternut squash.

Preheat the oven to 200°C/400°F/Gas Mark 6. Chop the pumpkin into 1cm (½in) dice. Toss these in a little olive oil in an oven dish that is large enough to spread them out in a single layer, then roast them in the oven for 20–30 minutes, until lightly coloured and tender. Lower the oven temperature to 180°C/350°F/ Gas Mark 4.

Cut the leek in quarters lengthways, wash it and slice it thinly. Heat 2 tablespoons of olive oil in a pan, and fry the leek over a medium heat for 5 minutes.

While the leeks are cooking, toast the cumin and coriander seeds in a heavy pan over a low heat, then crush them lightly in a pestle and mortar, just enough to crack them open. Add the seeds to the leek pan with the garlic and chilli, and fry for 2 minutes more.

Mash the chickpeas coarsely with a fork, then add them to the pan and continue frying for 5 minutes more. Gently stir in the roast pumpkin, season with salt, take off the heat and leave the mixture to cool.

Bring a large saucepan of water to the boil. Remove the stems from the cabbage leaves, either by cutting them out to give two pieces of leaf, or in the smaller leaves by trimming them to the thickness of the leaf. You will need twelve pieces of cabbage leaf (about 4cmx10cm [1½inx4in] in size) to make the dolma. Boil the leaves in the water for 4–5 minutes until tender, then drain and immediately cool in a bowl of cold water.

Gently pat the leaves dry with some kitchen paper. Place a leaf on a worktop and put a tablespoon of the filling at one end. Roll the cabbage leaf up one turn and fold in the sides, then continue rolling to the end, to make a cylindrical parcel about 6cm (2½in) long and 3cm (1¼in) thick. Make twelve parcels and place them close together in an oven dish brushed with olive oil. Brush the parcels generously with olive oil too, sprinkle them with enough water or stock to barely cover the bottom of the dish, and cover it with foil. Make a few steam holes in the foil, then cook in

Serves 4

FOR THE DOLMA

1.2kg (2¾lb) peeled and seeded Crown pumpkin or similar
olive oil
1 medium leek
1 tbsp cumin seeds
1 tbsp coriander seeds
4 garlic cloves, finely chopped
2 fresh mild green chillies, halved, seeded and sliced
250g (9oz) cooked chickpeas, or one 240g can, drained
salt
1 head spring cabbage
about 200ml (7fl oz) water or stock

FOR THE SESAME YOGHURT SAUCE

175g (6oz) tahini
2 garlic cloves, crushed
1 tsp ground cumin
1 pinch cayenne pepper
juice of ½ lemon
175g (6oz) plain yoghurt

the oven for 20 minutes, until the parcels are lightly coloured. Check once or twice that the dish isn't too dry. You might also want to remove the foil cover for the last 5 minutes of cooking.

For the sauce, whisk approximately 150–200ml (5–7fl oz) water into the tahini to get a pouring consistency, then add the garlic, cumin, cayenne and lemon juice. Stir in the yoghurt and season with salt.

Serve three dolma per portion with some of the sauce drizzled over the top (or serve it separately on the side).

Fresh Pasta with Abyssinian Cabbage, Dried Tomato, Chilli, Pine Nuts and Sheep's Cheese

This recipe is for two only, because I think it is a very tricky business mixing anything more than a simple sauce into long, fresh pasta, often resulting in the pasta becoming overcooked in the process. If you are cooking for more than two, dress the cooked pasta in olive oil and a little finely grated cheese, and put it in warm bowls before spooning the vegetables on top, encouraging people to mix their own.

Heat the olive oil in a wide pan and cook the onion, garlic and chilli over a medium heat for 1 minute. Add the cabbage leaves, tomatoes and pine nuts, and cook for 2–3 minutes more until the cabbage has softened. Season with a little salt and pepper.

At the same time, bring a large saucepan of water to the boil and cook the pasta for 2–3 minutes until just tender. Drain well and add to the vegetables with a sprinkling of the cheese. Toss to mix the vegetables through the pasta, then serve in warm bowls, with the rest of the cheese sprinkled over the top.

Serves 2

3 tbsp olive oil

1 red onion, halved and thinly sliced

2 garlic cloves, sliced

1 mild red chilli, halved, seeded and thinly sliced

2 handfuls Abyssinian cabbage leaves (about 160g/5³/₄oz), roughly torn

2 tbsp sun-dried tomatoes, thinly sliced

1 tbsp pine nuts, lightly toasted

salt and pepper

250g (9oz) fresh tagliolini or other thin pasta

60g (2¹/₄oz) Cratloe Hills or other hard sheep's cheese such as Pecorino, finely grated

Fresh Tagliolini with Shredded Brussels Sprouts, Sage and Pine Nuts

Quarter the sprouts, cut out the core and separate the leaves. In a wide pan, heat the olive oil and cook the sprouts, shallots, sage and garlic over a medium heat for 2 minutes. Add the tomatoes, orange zest and pine nuts, and season with salt and pepper. Simmer for 2 minutes more.

At the same time, bring a large saucepan of water to the boil, add the tagliolini and cook for 2–3 minutes until just tender. Drain well.

Add the butter, cheese and cooked pasta to the sprouts and mix well. Serve immediately.

Serves 4

250g (9oz) Brussels sprouts

2 tbsp olive oil

150g (5½oz) shallots, thinly sliced

12 fresh sage leaves, sliced

4 garlic cloves, sliced

4 canned tomatoes, finely chopped

finely grated zest of 1 orange

1 tbsp pine nuts, lightly toasted

salt and pepper

450g (1lb) fresh tagliolini, or other thin pasta

50g (2oz) butter

50g (2oz) Desmond, Parmesan or other hard cheese, finely grated

Brussels Sprouts with Roast Shallots and Spiced Potato Gnocchi in a Blue Cheese Cream

These quantities will give you very generous portions for a rich winter meal. The shallots and gnocchi can be prepared in advance. The uncooked gnocchi will keep for a few hours in a fridge or for a week in a freezer.

For the gnocchi, peel the potatoes, chop them into even-sized pieces and steam until tender. Gently mash them and leave them to cool. Stir in the cheese, egg yolks and cayenne, then quickly work in most of the flour. Season well with salt and pepper. If the dough seems firm enough, cut off a small piece, roll it into a ball and drop it into boiling water. If, after a few minutes, the ball floats without breaking up, the dough has enough flour. Bear in mind that the flour helps the gnocchi to hold together but too much flour can make the dough tough.

Cut the dough into three pieces and roll each piece with your hands into a 2cm (³/₄in)-thick tube. Cut each tube into pieces 1cm (½in) long and shape each piece into an elongated ball. Put the gnocchi to one side on a lightly floured plate as you go.

Preheat the oven to 180°C/350°F/Gas Mark 4. To roast the shallots, toss them in a little olive oil in an oven dish, cover loosely with baking parchment and roast in the oven, checking and stirring occasionally, until the shallots are soft and golden.

Halve or quarter the Brussels sprouts, depending on size. In a wide pan, heat the butter and cook the sprouts, garlic and caraway over a medium heat for 3 minutes. Add the stock or water, bring it to the boil, lower the heat, cover and simmer for 5 minutes, until the sprouts are almost tender. Add the cream and turn up the heat to boil for 30 seconds. Crumble in the blue cheese then turn off the heat and stir to melt the cheese.

While the sprouts are cooking, bring a saucepan of water to the boil and drop in some of the gnocchi, being careful not to overcrowd the pan or the gnocchi will stick together. As the gnocchi float to the top, remove them with a slotted spoon. Keep them warm in a buttered frying pan over a low heat while you cook the rest.

To serve, place some gnocchi in four warm plates or shallow bowls. Spoon the sprouts in their sauce around each portion, pouring some of the sauce over the gnocchi. Arrange some roasted shallots over each portion and finish with nutmeg.

Serves 4

400g (14oz) Brussels sprouts
15g (½oz) butter
4 garlic cloves, finely chopped
½ tsp caraway seeds
150ml (5fl oz) vegetable stock or water
300ml (10fl oz) double cream
85g (3oz) mild blue cheese, such as Cashel Blue
freshly grated nutmeg, to serve

FOR THE ROAST SHALLOTS

200g (7oz) small shallots, peeled (roots left intact)
olive oil

FOR THE SPICED POTATO GNOCCHI

400g (14oz) floury potatoes
60g (2¼oz) Desmond, Parmesan or other hard cheese, finely grated
2 egg yolks
½ tsp cayenne pepper
85g (3oz) plain flour
salt and pepper
butter

Braised Savoy Cabbage with Apricots, Pecans and Caraway

Soak the apricots for 1 hour in just enough water to cover them, then slice them thinly.

Heat the olive oil in a large pan and put in the cabbage, onion and garlic. Cook for 5 minutes over a medium heat until the cabbage has softened a little. Add the apricots, caraway, brandy and a pinch of salt. Bring back to the boil, turn the heat down to low, then cover loosely with baking parchment and simmer for 20 minutes, or until the cabbage is soft and sweet, stirring occasionally to ensure the cabbage doesn't stick. Stir in the pecans and serve.

Serves 4 as a side dish

30g (1¼oz) dried apricots

2 tbsp olive oil

400g (14oz) Savoy cabbage, shredded

1 medium white onion, halved and thinly sliced

4 garlic cloves, finely chopped

1 tbsp caraway seeds

50ml (2fl oz) brandy

salt

30g (1¼oz) shelled pecans, halved

Watercress Hummus

Serve this variation on the classic chickpea and sesame dip with warm pitta bread, crispbread or corn chips. It also makes a nicely peppery sandwich filling or topping for crostini.

Put the watercress in a food processor with a tablespoon of the olive oil, and blend to a smooth purée. Transfer to a bowl, then put the remaining ingredients, including the oil, into the processor and blend again. Add this purée to the watercress and stir. Season with salt. When serving, drizzle a little more olive oil over the hummus.

Serves 8–10 as a snack

100g (3½oz) watercress

100ml (3½fl oz) olive oil, plus a little extra to serve

200g (7oz) cooked chickpeas, from dried or canned

2 garlic cloves, crushed

1 tsp ground cumin

1 pinch cayenne pepper

1 tbsp tahini

juice of 1 lemon

salt

Chinese Broccoli with Cashews and Fresh Chillies

I like most Chinese broccoli dishes with the stems whole, about 12–15cm (4½–6in) long. This side dish has enough flavour to be served as a simple main course for two or three, with some rice or noodles.

Cut the chillies in half lengthways and remove the seeds. Slice the flesh in thin diagonal strips.

In a wide shallow pan, heat the olive or vegetable oil, add the chilli slices and cook for 1 minute over a medium heat. Add the Chinese broccoli, garlic, soy sauce and stock or water. Cover the pan and simmer for 5 minutes or until the broccoli stems are just tender.

Stir in the cashews and serve.

Serves 4 as a side dish

1–2 fresh red chillies

1 tbsp olive or vegetable oil

400g (14oz) Chinese broccoli

2 garlic cloves, sliced

1 tbsp soy sauce

100ml (3½fl oz) vegetable stock or water

40g (1½oz) shelled cashews, lightly toasted

Roasted Asparagus with Blood Orange Aïoli

Preheat the oven to 150°C/300°F/Gas Mark 2. Snip the ends off the garlic cloves. Put them on a small oven tray, drizzle them lightly with olive oil and roast them in the oven for 10–15 minutes until they are soft. Once they are done, squeeze the flesh from the skins.

Put the blood orange juice in a small pan and heat gently until reduced by half. Leave to cool for a few minutes.

For the aïoli, put the roasted garlic, egg yolks, egg and dill in a food processor and blend for 1 minute. With the motor still running, pour in the olive oil very slowly until the aïoli is very thick. Gradually add in the blood orange juice until you are satisfied with the colour and flavour and you have a dipping consistency. Season with a little salt and pepper. Taste the aïoli and add a little lemon juice if you wish.

Turn the oven up to 200°C/400°F/Gas Mark 6. Snap the tough ends off the asparagus and discard. Lay the asparagus on an oven tray, drizzle with a little olive oil and season with salt. Roast in the oven until just tender and lightly browned, but still crisp, about 4–5 minutes. Serve immediately with the blood orange aïoli as a dip.

Serves 4 as a starter or side dish

500g (18oz) fat asparagus spears

olive oil

FOR THE BLOOD ORANGE AÏOLI

2 garlic cloves, unpeeled

200–300ml (7–10fl oz) olive oil

juice of 2 blood oranges

2 egg yolks

1 egg

1 tbsp chopped fresh dill

salt and pepper

juice of ½ lemon (optional)

Sprouting Broccoli with Leek and Shallot Farrotto

'Farro' is the common name in Italy for a very old wheat variety. It is sometimes translated as 'spelt', though some references suggest it is not the same grain but a similar and equally ancient variety. It is often sold in a semi-pearled state, which means that most of the husk has been polished off. This makes it very useful for making a rustic but strongly flavoured risotto-style dish, hence the name 'farrotto'. It needs long, slow cooking, longer than the 20 minutes the pack might say, to get a rich, creamy finish. I like to make it with a lot of onion, both for flavour and texture.

The intense flavour of sprouting greens makes a great match for farrotto, as indeed do mushrooms. The recipe calls for a hard sheep's cheese, and I generally use Cratloe Hills, from County Clare, whenever I need that tangy sweetness. Italian Pecorino or Spanish Manchego would be good too.

Serves 4

3 tbsp olive oil
500g (18oz) purple sprouting broccoli
1 medium red onion, halved and thinly sliced
1 fresh hot red chilli, halved and sliced, seeds included
4 tomatoes, halved and sliced
salt and pepper

FOR THE FARROTTO

1.5 litres (2¾ pints) vegetable stock
3 tbsp olive oil
250g (9oz) leeks, washed and thinly sliced
250g (9oz) shallots, thinly sliced
4 garlic cloves, finely chopped
leaves from 1 sprig fresh thyme
1 tbsp chopped fresh sage leaves
200g (7oz) farro
100ml (3½fl oz) white wine
100g (3½ oz) butter
85g (3oz) hard sheep's cheese, freshly grated

Bring the stock to the boil in a large saucepan then turn down the heat and keep at a low simmer.

In a large saucepan, heat the olive oil and cook the leeks, shallots and garlic for 5 minutes over a medium heat. Add the herb leaves and the farro, and cook again for 5 minutes, stirring occasionally, to toast the grains. Add the wine, lower the heat and simmer for approximately 5 minutes until it has been absorbed. Pour in a ladle or two of hot stock and simmer, stirring occasionally, until it has been absorbed. Carry on adding stock in this way until the grains are soft and chewy. This may take 40–50 minutes.

As the farrotto nears the end of its cooking time, heat two tablespoons of the olive oil in a pan and cook the sprouting broccoli, red onion and chilli for 2 minutes over a medium heat. Add the tomatoes and the remaining olive oil, and cook for 2 minutes more. Then add a few tablespoons of stock and some salt and pepper, and cook for 1 minute.

When you are happy with the texture of the farrotto and all the stock has been absorbed, stir in the butter, cheese and some salt and pepper. Serve the sprouting broccoli with the farrotto, pouring the juices from the pan over each portion.

Sesame and Ginger Chinese Broccoli on an Oyster Mushroom Omelette

Preheat the oven to 140°C/275°F/Gas Mark 1.

Fry the mushrooms and garlic in a little oil for a minute or two, then stir in the coriander and a pinch of salt. Set this aside.

Heat a little oil in a wide shallow pan, and put in the Chinese broccoli, ginger, soy sauce, stock or water and the sesame oil. Bring to the boil, then lower the heat, cover and simmer for 5 minutes.

At the same time, heat an omelette pan over a high heat, and brush it with oil. Lightly beat the eggs with the water and season with salt and pepper. Pour half into the pan, leave it for a few seconds until the edges begin to solidify, then lift the cooking edges and tilt the pan to allow the uncooked egg to flow underneath. Scatter half of the cooked mushrooms over one half of the omelette, fold the uncovered side over and slide the omelette on to a plate. Keep this warm in a low oven while you repeat the process with the remaining eggs and mushrooms.

Cut each omelette in half to make four portions. Use tongs to place some Chinese broccoli on each, then spoon the juices over the top.

Serves 4

150g (5½oz) oyster mushrooms, shredded

2 garlic cloves, sliced

olive or vegetable oil

1 tbsp chopped fresh coriander

salt and pepper

400g (14oz) Chinese broccoli

1 tbsp grated fresh root ginger

1 tbsp soy sauce

100ml (3½fl oz) vegetable stock or water

1 tsp toasted sesame oil

FOR THE OMELETTES

olive oil

8 eggs

4 dsp water

Black Kale with Sweet Peppers, Olives and Smoked Cheese Polenta

I use smoked Gubbeen, a semi-hard cheese, to flavour the polenta because it is so delicately smoked. If using a stronger cheese, you may want to reduce the quantity.

For the polenta, bring the stock to the boil in a large saucepan, then whisk in the maize and a large pinch of salt. Reduce the heat and simmer over a very low heat, stirring often, for 20 minutes until the polenta has a thick consistency, like that of mashed potato. Stir in the cheese, butter and sage. Season with black pepper and some more salt if needed. Serve immediately or keep the polenta warm by placing the saucepan over a slightly larger pan of simmering water.

Remove the stalks from the kale and discard them, then slice the leaves into strips. Quarter the peppers, remove the seeds and pith and slice the flesh about 5mm (¼in) thick.

Heat 4 tablespoons of the olive oil in a large pan, add the kale and cook over a medium heat until it has shrunk: 2–3 minutes. Add the peppers, chilli, garlic and olives, and cook for 2–3 minutes more. Add the stock or water and a large pinch of salt, cover loosely with baking parchment and simmer for 15 minutes until the vegetables are soft. Check occasionally to make sure the dish is moist, adding more water if necessary. Just before serving, add a generous splash of stock and a tablespoon of olive oil.

Spoon the polenta on to serving plates or shallow bowls. Serve the kale and its pan juices over the polenta.

Serves 4

500g (18oz) black kale (cavolo nero)

2 sweet red peppers

5 tbsp olive oil

1 mild red chilli, halved, seeded and chopped

2 garlic cloves, sliced

2 tbsp black olives, halved and stoned

200ml (7fl oz) vegetable stock or water, plus an extra splash to serve

FOR THE SMOKED CHEESE POLENTA

1 litre (1¾ pints) vegetable stock

200g (7oz) coarse maize

salt and pepper

60g (2¼oz) smoked Gubbeen or other lightly smoked cheese, grated

40g (1½oz) butter

1 tbsp chopped fresh sage leaves

Cime di Rapa with Sweet Pepper and Fried Hazelnut Gougères

This recipe works with any strongly flavoured greens. Gougères are usually baked choux pastries, but in this instance the dough is deep-fried.

For the gougères, put the flour and hazelnuts in a food processor. Put the water and butter in a pan and bring to a boil. Start the food processor and pour in the hot water and butter, beating it in for 30 seconds. Add one egg and beat until fully incorporated, then add the second egg and repeat. Finally, beat in the cheese and some salt and pepper. Transfer the batter to a bowl.

Heat some vegetable oil in a deep-fryer or heavy-based saucepan to 170°c (325°F). If using a pan, test the oil by dropping in a little of the batter. If it floats and begins to colour in a minute or so, turn the heat down to hold the temperature.

Meanwhile, in a large wide pan, heat the 2 tablespoons of olive oil over a medium heat. Add the cime di rapa, red pepper, garlic and ginger, and fry for 2–3 minutes, stirring often. Add the sherry and the 2 tablespoons of water and simmer for 5–7 minutes more, until the greens are tender. Add a little more olive oil and water at the end to ensure that the dish is moist. Season with a little salt and pepper.

While the vegetables are cooking, take a heaped teaspoon of the gougère batter and, using a second spoon, slide it into the hot oil. Repeat with some more batter, to cook as many gougères as possible without overcrowding the oil. Fry them for 4–5 minutes, turning once if necessary, until the gougères are browned. Keep the cooked ones warm while you fry more batches.

Serve the cime di rapa in its juices, surrounded by some of the fried gougères.

Serves 4

2 tbsps olive oil, plus an extra splash

600g (1¼lb) cime di rapa

1 red pepper, quartered, seeded and thinly sliced

2 garlic cloves, sliced

1 tbsp fresh root ginger, thinly sliced

2 tbsp sweet sherry

2 tbsp water, plus an extra splash

FOR THE GOUGÈRES

110g (4oz) strong white flour

25g (1oz) hazelnuts, roasted and finely chopped

170ml (6fl oz) water

60g (2¼oz) butter

2 medium eggs

80g (3½) Gabriel, cheddar or other hard cheese, grated

salt and pepper

vegetable oil for deep-frying

Red Russian Kale with Orange and Nutmeg

Remove the thicker stalks from the kale and discard them. Chop the kale coarsely.

Heat the olive oil in a wide pan, toss in the kale and cook over a medium heat for about 2 minutes until it has shrunk and become glossy. Add the vegetable stock or water, the orange zest and juice and the nutmeg. Cover with baking parchment, lower the heat and simmer for 3–5 minutes until the kale is soft. Season with salt and pepper and serve.

Serves 4 as a side dish

500g (18oz) kale

2 tbsp olive oil

2 tbsp vegetable stock or water

finely grated zest of 1 orange

juice of ½ orange

¼ tsp freshly grated nutmeg

salt and pepper

Asparagus with Pine Nuts, Red Onion and Capers

This highly flavoured side dish is also excellent with a light dusting of finely grated hard cheese. In fact, adding some cheese and salad leaves makes it a great warm salad for a first course.

Snap the tough ends off the asparagus spears and cut the spears in half widthways. Steam the asparagus for 3–4 minutes until just tender.

While the asparagus spears are cooking, heat the olive oil in a pan and fry the red onion for 1 minute over a medium heat. Add the pine nuts and capers and cook for 1 minute more. Season with a little salt and pepper.

Put the cooked asparagus in a serving dish and scatter over the onion mixture.

Serves 4 as a side dish

500g (18oz) medium asparagus spears
2 tbsp olive oil
1 medium red onion,
halved and thinly sliced
1 tbsp pine nuts, lightly toasted
1 tbsp small capers, drained
salt and pepper

Warm Couscous Salad with Watercress, Avocado and Citrus-marinated Feta

This salad can be served as a simple lunch, as part of a buffet, barbecue or picnic, and it even makes a nice starter, in which case the recipe will make 6–8 portions.

For the feta, whisk together the olive oil, lemon, orange and lime juices and all the zest. Pour over the feta in a small dish, turn to coat the cheese, cover and leave to marinate for at least 2 hours.

Put the couscous in a bowl with a large pinch of salt and stir in 280ml (9½fl oz) warm water. Leave for 10 minutes, then fluff up the couscous with a fork.

Heat the olive oil in a large flat pan or wok and cook the spring onions, garlic, spices and chilli for a minute, then add the couscous and stir for a minute or two to warm it through. Remove from the heat and stir in the herbs, cherry tomatoes, watercress and avocado.

Serve the salad with some of the feta and its marinade scattered over and around each portion. Finish with a squeeze of lime juice.

Serves 4 as a main dish, 6–8 as a starter

300g (10½oz) couscous
salt
1 tbsp olive oil
4 spring onions, thinly sliced
2 garlic cloves, sliced
1 tsp cumin seeds
1 tsp fennel seeds
1 fresh mild red chilli, halved,
seeded and thinly sliced
2 tbsp chopped fresh mint leaves
2 tbsp chopped fresh coriander leaves
100g (3½oz) cherry tomatoes, halved
115g (4oz) watercress, chopped
1 large avocado, peeled and diced

FOR THE CITRUS-MARINATED FETA
100ml (3½fl oz) olive oil
finely grated zest and juice of 1 lemon
1 tbsp orange juice
finely grated zest of 1 orange
finely grated zest and juice of 1 lime
200g (7oz) feta cheese,
cut into 2cm (¾in) dice

Black Kale and Aubergine Spring Rolls with Ginger and Tamarind Dipping Sauce

Preheat the oven to 180°C/350°F/Gas Mark 4. Remove the stalks from the kale and discard them. Bring a large saucepan of water to the boil and drop in the kale. When the water comes back to the boil, remove the kale, drain and cool it in a bowl of cold water, then squeeze out all the water. Dry the kale fully with kitchen paper or a tea-towel so that the spring rolls do not become soggy, then chop into thin slivers about 3cm (1¼in) long.

Toss the aubergine in olive oil and arrange in a single layer in an oven dish. Cover loosely with baking parchment and roast in the oven for 15 minutes, checking and tossing occasionally to ensure the pieces are fully cooked and lightly coloured. Mix the tomato purée, soy sauce and sugar together and stir them quickly into the cooked aubergine.

While the aubergine is cooking, make the tamarind sauce. Put the tamarind and water in a small saucepan, bring to the boil, then lower the heat and simmer for 10 minutes. Press the liquid through a sieve and return it to the pan with the rest of the ingredients. Simmer again for a further 10 minutes until the sauce is slightly thickened. Sieve again to remove the ginger and chilli, and leave the sauce to cool.

In a mixing bowl, combine the kale, aubergine, spring onions, chilli and spices to make the spring roll filling. Lay a sheet of spring roll pastry on a worktop with one corner facing you. A quarter of the way up, put one and a half tablespoons of filling in a line (not to the edge) and brush the edges of the pastry with water. Fold the bottom corner over the filling and roll the spring roll to just beyond the halfway point, keeping it as tight and even as possible. Fold in the sides and continue rolling. Repeat with the rest of the pastry sheets and filling.

In a wide frying pan, heat 1cm (½in) vegetable oil to a medium temperature, about 160°C/325°F. Carefully slide in some of the spring rolls, making sure you don't crowd the pan. Cook for a few minutes on each side until the spring rolls are crisp and coloured. You can also cook them in a deep-fryer but make sure the temperature is not too high or they may burst. Remove the spring rolls and place them on kitchen paper to drain off any excess oil.

Serve the spring rolls with the tamarind sauce as a dip.

Serves 4

FOR THE SPRING ROLLS

200g (7oz) black kale (cavolo nero)

400g (14oz) aubergine, finely diced

olive oil

1 tsp tomato purée

2 tsp soy sauce

1 pinch caster sugar

4 spring onions, thinly sliced

1 fresh red chilli, halved, seeded and thinly sliced

1 tbsp coriander seeds, ground

4 cloves, ground

1 pinch freshly grated nutmeg

8 spring roll pastry sheets

vegetable oil, for frying

FOR THE TAMARIND SAUCE

3 tbsp tamarind pulp

300ml (10fl oz) water

3 tbsp caster sugar

1 tbsp rice wine vinegar

3cm (1¼in) piece fresh root ginger, chopped

1 whole dried bird's eye chilli

Asparagus, Spinach and Durrus Cheese Egg Rolls with Balsamic Beetroot Sauce

I love this earthy, sweet and sharp beetroot sauce (or syrup as it might properly be called) with the flavours in the egg rolls. You can make the sauce well in advance and it keeps for days.

It isn't always easy to tell if it has reduced enough in the pan, so if it isn't nicely syrupy when cooled, you can simply put it back in a pan and reduce it some more. The sauce can be very pretty on the plate or it can make a terrible mess, as beetroot always can, so it is best to put it on in a nice pattern from one of those squeezy bottles with a thin nozzle.

The rolls are also lovely with a tomato salsa, possibly with capers and/or avocado too.

Serves 4

FOR THE BALSAMIC BEETROOT SAUCE

500g (18oz) beetroot, cooked and peeled
500ml (18fl oz) water
500ml (18fl oz) balsamic vinegar

FOR THE EGG ROLLS

500g (18oz) medium asparagus spears
500g (18oz) spinach
2 tbsp tomato pesto, see recipe on page 227
salt and pepper
6 large eggs
3 tbsp milk
1 tsp chopped fresh chives
olive oil
200g (7oz) Durrus or other semi-soft cow's milk cheese, thinly sliced

Preheat the oven to 180°C/350°F/Gas Mark 4. For the sauce, chop the beetroot into small dice and put in a large saucepan with the water. Bring this to the boil and simmer for 5 minutes. Blend the beetroot and water to a fine purée, pass this through a fine sieve, and return to the pan. Add the balsamic vinegar, bring it to the boil and simmer until the sauce has thickened slightly. This may take 20–30 minutes. Leave the sauce to cool, when it will thicken some more.

Snap the tough ends off the asparagus spears. Slice any fat spears in half lengthways. Blanch the spears by dropping them in boiling water for 2–3 minutes until tender but still crisp, then cool them in a bowl of cold water.

Drop the spinach into boiling water for 2 minutes or until soft, then drain and cool it in a colander under cold running water. Squeeze the spinach dry and chop it very finely. Stir in the tomato pesto and season with salt and pepper.

Beat the eggs and milk lightly together in a bowl, season with salt and stir in the chives. Heat a heavy or non-stick 15cm (6in) frying pan over a low heat and brush it lightly with olive oil. Pour in enough of the egg mixture to make a very thin omelette, and cook it until set but only lightly coloured on the bottom. Flip the omelette over and cook the other side for 1 minute, then remove from the pan. Oil the pan again and repeat. The mixture should make eight omelettes or egg rolls.

Lay an omelette on a work surface and place a layer of cheese across the middle. Place some asparagus pieces on top to cover the cheese evenly. Then press some of the spinach mixture on to the asparagus. Fold over the omelette from the near end first, then the top, to make a tight roll. Repeat with the rest and place the egg rolls, seam-side down, on an oven tray lined with baking parchment. Brush the tops lightly with olive oil. Place the egg rolls in the oven for 3–4 minutes until the cheese is just beginning to melt. Drizzle some of the beetroot sauce on each of the serving plates and place the egg rolls on top. Serve the rest of the sauce in a jug at the table.

New Zealand Spinach, Puy Lentils, Fennel and Sheep's Cheese on Tomato Crostini

Because New Zealand spinach holds its shape so well, this looks good enough to be served as a starter, but it also makes a nice light lunch or late night snack.

Preheat the oven to 180°C/350°F/Gas Mark 4. Cook the lentils in boiling water for 12–15 minutes until tender but firm. Rinse briefly under cold running water to stop the cooking, but leaving the lentils warm.

    To make the crostini, brush the bread lightly with olive oil on both sides, place it on an oven tray lined with baking parchment and bake in the oven for about 10–12 minutes until crisp on both sides but still a little soft in the middle. You may need to turn the bread slices once during cooking to get an even finish on both sides. Leave for a few minutes to cool to room temperature, then spread a little tomato pesto on each one.

    Bring a large saucepan of water to the boil, drop in the spinach and cook for 1 minute. Drain well.

    At the same time, heat two tablespoons of olive oil in a large pan and cook the onion, fennel, garlic and lentils for 5 minutes. Add the spinach and stir to combine. Season with salt and pepper.

    Place one of the crostini on each plate and put the spinach mixture loosely on top. Squeeze some lemon juice over each portion. Coarsely grate or thinly shave the sheep's cheese and sprinkle it over.

Serves 4

60g (2¼oz) Puy lentils
800g (1¾lb) New Zealand spinach
olive oil
1 medium red onion, halved and thinly sliced
1 fennel bulb, quartered and thinly sliced
2 garlic cloves, finely chopped
salt and pepper
1 lemon, to squeeze over the finished dish
60g (2¼oz) Cratloe Hills, Pecorino or other hard sheep's cheese

FOR THE TOMATO CROSTINI

4 slices day-old sourdough bread
olive oil
2 tbsp tomato pesto, see recipe on page 227

Artichoke, Asparagus and Quail Egg Salad with Citrus Dressing

Snap the tough ends off the asparagus and discard them. Cut each spear in three, then bring a large saucepan of water to the boil and drop the asparagus into boiling water to cook for 1 minute. Cool under cold running water briefly, then drain well.

Pull off the outer leaves of the artichokes until only the paler, less green flesh is visible. Cut the leaves across below the tops. Trim the stalk with a knife and discard the tough outer skin to reveal the tender edible part at the centre. Cut the artichokes into quarters and scoop out any hairy choke. Drop the artichoke quarters into water with a little of the lemon juice. Bring a large saucepan of water to the boil, add the artichoke pieces and cook for 5–7 minutes until just tender. Cool briefly under cold running water and drain well.

Cook the quail eggs by dropping them into boiling water for just 1 minute, then cool them in a bowl of cold water. Peel the eggs carefully – the yolks should still be soft.

Make a dressing by whisking or shaking together the orange and remaining lemon juice, the orange zest and the olive oil.

Toss the asparagus and artichokes together with the chives and enough dressing to coat the vegetables. Season with salt and pepper. Place some rocket on four plates and share out half of the vegetables on top. Scatter on some more rocket and top with the rest of the vegetables. Cut the tops off the eggs, and tuck them into the salads. Drizzle some more of the dressing over and around the salad.

Serves 4

16 medium-sized asparagus spears
4 small artichokes
juice of 1 lemon
12–16 quail eggs
juice of 1/2 orange
finely grated zest of 1 orange
200ml (7fl oz) olive oil
1 tbsp chopped fresh chives
salt and pepper
200g (7oz) rocket

Spinach, Aubergine and Chickpea Curry

I like to make this curry with a strong chilli hit
and then serve it with another, milder curry,
either yoghurt or coconut based, and of course
some rice or bread.

Cook the spinach in boiling water for 2 minutes, then
cool it under cold running water and squeeze gently
to remove most of the liquid. In a food processor, chop
the spinach to a coarse purée.

    Heat half the olive oil in a large pan and cook the
onion, chickpeas, garlic, chilli and spices for 5 minutes
over a medium heat. Add the remaining olive oil and
the aubergine. Cook for 10 minutes, stirring often,
until the aubergine is coloured. Add the tomatoes and
a pinch of salt, then cover the pan, lower the heat and simmer for 15 minutes until
the aubergine is soft. Stir in the spinach purée and serve.

Serves 4

- 1kg (2¼lb) spinach
- 4 tbsp olive oil
- 2 medium red onions, diced
- 200g (7oz) cooked chickpeas, from dried or canned
- 2 garlic cloves, finely chopped
- 2 fresh hot green chillies, halved and thinly sliced, seeds included
- 1 tbsp coriander seeds, ground
- 1 tbsp cumin seeds
- 1 large aubergine, approx. 400g (14oz), cut into 2cm (¾in) dice
- 1 x 400g (14oz) can tomatoes, chopped
- salt

Green Seakale with Orange, Tomato and Fresh Sheep's Cheese

In a wide pan, heat the olive oil, and cook the onion
and garlic over a medium heat for 1 minute only.
Put in the tomatoes, then the seakale and the stock
or water. Turn down the heat, cover and simmer for
7–10 minutes, or until the seakale is tender.

    Stir in the orange zest and juice and the nutmeg.
Season with salt and pepper and transfer to a serving
dish. Crumble the cheese over and serve.

Serves 4 as a starter or side dish

- 4 tbsp olive oil
- 1 small red onion, thinly sliced
- 2 garlic cloves, sliced
- 1 x 400g (14oz) can tomatoes, drained and chopped
- 400g (14oz) seakale shoots, about 10cm (4in) long, leaves attached
- 200ml (7fl oz) vegetable stock or water
- finely grated zest of 1 orange
- juice of ½ orange
- 1 pinch freshly grated nutmeg
- salt and pepper
- 125g (4½oz) Knockalara or other fresh sheep's cheese

Chard with Couscous, Raisins, Pine Nuts and Lemon Oil

This can be a side dish or a simple meal. Or make it the centre of a mezze or tapas-style meal with some marinated feta, olives, fresh tomato salad, roasted sweet peppers and the like. (See photograph on following pages.) A chilli kick from Moroccan harissa sauce, served on the side, would be fun too.

Soak the raisins in just enough water to cover them for 10 minutes. Place the couscous in a large bowl, pour over the warm vegetable stock and stir once. Leave for 15 minutes before fluffing up the couscous with a fork.

Separate the chard leaves and stalks. Slice the stalks across about 5mm (¹/₄in) thick. Cook the leaves in boiling water for 5 minutes, until soft, then drain, cool under cold running water, drain again and chop coarsely.

Heat some olive oil in a large pan and cook the chard stalks, onion and garlic for 5 minutes over a medium heat. Add the spices and cook for a few minutes more, then stir in the chard leaves, pine nuts and the raisins with their soaking liquid. Add a little extra stock or water to keep the dish quite moist, then stir in the couscous, and turn off the heat. Season with salt and pepper.

Whisk or blend the lemon zest and juice and the olive oil together. Mix two tablespoons into the couscous, then serve immediately. Divide the couscous between four warmed serving plates, sprinkle some more lemon oil over the top and put the rest of the oil on the table in a jug or bottle for people to help themselves.

Serves 4

85g (3oz) golden raisins

300g (10¹/₂oz) couscous

280ml (9¹/₂fl oz) warm vegetable stock

1kg (2¹/₄lb) chard, including stalks

olive oil

1 medium red onion, halved and thinly sliced

2 garlic cloves, finely chopped

2 tsp cumin seeds

1 tsp fennel seeds

1 tsp turmeric

2 tbsp pine nuts, lightly toasted

salt and pepper

FOR THE LEMON OIL

finely grated zest and juice of 1 lemon

200ml (7fl oz) olive oil

Chard, New Potato and Chickpea Soup with Lemon and Roast Garlic

Although this recipe calls for new season potatoes, it works best if you can get a variety that is a little floury so that the potato thickens the soup slightly. Queens and Home Guard, the varieties favoured by growers of the renowned Ballycotton new potatoes, are perfect, but others will do nicely too, such as Nicola and Charlotte, both of which hold their shape but are not quite at the waxy end of the scale.

Serves 4
10 garlic cloves, unpeeled
olive oil
finely grated zest and juice of 1 lemon
600g (1lb 5oz) chard, including stalks
1 medium red onion, diced
100g (3½oz) cooked chickpeas, from dried or canned
400g (14oz) new potatoes, washed and diced
1 litre (1¾ pints) vegetable stock
1 tbsp chopped fresh basil leaves
1 tbsp chopped fresh mint leaves
salt and pepper

Preheat the oven to 150°C/300°F/Gas Mark 2. Put the garlic in a small oven dish, drizzle with olive oil and roast in the oven for about 10-15 minutes until soft and sweet. Squeeze out the flesh and discard the skin. In a food processor, purée the garlic with the lemon zest and juice, and 100ml (3½fl oz) olive oil.

Separate the chard stalks and leaves. Cook the leaves in boiling water for 2 minutes, then drain and coarsely chop them. Keep to one side. Slice the chard stalks across, 5mm (¼in) thick.

Heat a little olive oil in a large saucepan and cook the onion, chard stalks and chickpeas for 5 minutes over a medium heat. Add the potatoes and stock and bring to the boil. Add the herbs and chard leaves, and simmer until the potatoes are beginning to break down, about 10–12 minutes.

Stir in the roasted garlic paste, season with salt and pepper and serve.

Chard, Lentil and Roast Plum Tomato Gratin

Serve this gratin with some crusty bread or some mashed or roast potatoes.

Preheat the oven to 180°C/350°F/Gas Mark 4. Slice the plum tomatoes thickly, discarding the top and bottom, and place the slices in a single layer on an oven tray lined with baking parchment. Drizzle with olive oil, season with salt and roast in the oven until the tomatoes are beginning to colour but are still moist, about 15 minutes.

Cook the Puy lentils in plenty of boiling water for 15–20 minutes until tender but with a little bite. Cool under cold running water, then drain.

Separate the chard stalks and leaves. Cook the leaves in boiling water for about 5 minutes until soft, then cool them under cold running water, drain and chop finely. Season well with salt and pepper and mix with the lentils.

Slice the chard stalks across, 1cm (½in) thick. Heat two tablespoons of olive oil in a medium pan, add the stalks, garlic and thyme leaves, and cook over a medium heat for 5 minutes. Pour in the wine, cover with some baking parchment pressed down onto the vegetables, and simmer gently for 20 minutes until the chard stalks are soft. Add a little stock or water if it gets too dry. Season with salt and pepper.

Brush an oven dish, about 24 x 20cm (9½ x 8in), with olive oil and put in the roast tomato slices. Cover these with the chard and lentil mixture, then pour over the chard stalks and their juices and press gently to level the dish. Combine the breadcrumbs and cheese and scatter over the top. Place the dish in the oven or under a grill to brown the top.

Serves 4
400g (14oz) fresh plum tomatoes
olive oil
salt and pepper
100g (3½oz) Puy lentils
1kg (2¼lb) chard, including stalks
2 garlic cloves, finely chopped
leaves from 1 sprig fresh thyme
100ml (3½fl oz) white wine
50g (2oz) fresh breadcrumbs
50g (2oz) Desmond, Parmesan, Pecorino or other hard cheese, finely grated

Watercress Soup with
Walnut and Sweet Pepper Salsa

Melt the butter in a large saucepan and cook the onion and garlic for 8–10 minutes over a medium heat, then add the potatoes, wine and thyme leaves and cook for 1 minute more. Add the stock, bring it to a boil, cover, then lower the heat and simmer for 15–20 minutes until the potatoes are soft.

Meanwhile, bring a large saucepan of water to the boil and plunge the watercress into it for a few seconds before removing and cooling immediately under cold running water. Put the watercress in a food processor and blend it with a little water to get a green paste. Liquidise the soup, reheat it if necessary, and stir in the cream and the watercress purée. Season with salt and pepper.

While the soup is cooking, combine all of the salsa ingredients. Ladle the soup into bowls and spoon some salsa on to each portion.

Serves 4

FOR THE SOUP

15g (1/2oz) butter

2 medium onions, chopped

2 garlic cloves, finely chopped

250g (9oz) floury potatoes, peeled and chopped

50ml (2fl oz) white wine

leaves from 1 sprig fresh thyme

600ml (1 pint) vegetable stock

200g (7oz) watercress

75ml (2 1/2fl oz) double cream

salt and pepper

FOR THE SALSA

1 red pepper, seeded and finely diced

1 mild red chilli, halved, seeded and finely diced

1 shallot, finely diced

12 walnut halves, chopped

juice of 1 lemon

1 tbsp olive oil

Wild pickings

Before we go wandering out into the countryside – the beautiful, sometimes mystical, sometimes elusive and often stunning countryside – I have a confession to make. I'm not a fan of confessions in food books, but this is relevant. I am a townie. Where I grew up, the lines of distinction were always clear between those who trod the muddy fields in rubber boots and those of us who were privileged enough to have concrete pavement under our platform shoes. Even in a town of less than 3,000 people, in our own grand delusions we were as sophisticated as the denizens of London or New York, at least when compared to the savages from the farming country that enclosed us.

I'm sure that people from small towns are the most determinedly urban, the ones who are most insistent on that definition of themselves. We cling to concrete as our badge of civilisation. City folk are so removed from the country that they can take long weekends using its aesthetic beauty as a tranquil backdrop to their badly needed 'chilling' time. A townie living right on the edge of it, surrounded by it, is more likely to experience a reaction to it that combines a little deep-buried love with more overt and explicit hatred. I think it scared us a little. Not so much physically, though it did that too, but its sheer proximity was a constant reminder of how close we were to what we snobbishly saw as the poverty, savagery and endless toil that our ancestors had only recently escaped. The country was the past; and in our fantastic future we wanted to work indoors in nice shirts and soft shoes.

And yet, while the townie desperately wants to be sophisticated and recognisably urban, the countryside calls, and it knows how to make him listen. We are closer to it than we might like, genetically as well as geographically. In our hearts, the countryside is our natural playground, and we are drawn to it. While, as teenagers, we sauntered around the market square with an air of studied leisure, or leaned against lamp posts in poses of elegant boredom, our genes tugged at us, urging us to go out there: to run through the fields, jump in the streams, race bikes up and down the grassy lanes and explore tiny but imposing sets of trees we thought to be forests.

I can say now, with hindsight, that we went out into the countryside for the simple, pure pleasure of being in it. And we went often. But, in our confused relationship with it, we rarely went without a purpose. An excuse, you might even call it, lest the natives think we had reverted. No, we're here for a purpose, Mr Farmer; making it perfectly obvious with our buckets and baskets, plastic bowls and cloth sacks. Food was frequently the purpose, especially in late summer and into the autumn, and it was far more than an excuse. We set out to collect mountains of blackberries and crab apples, field mushrooms, wild berries, damsons and sloes. Always, of course, it was two

blackberries for the bowl, one for me ... then later, after the picking was done, just a few more to shorten the road home. Or we might have sucked the sweet nectar of honeysuckle from the flowers in the hedgerows. People traded, bartered and shared. A good day's mushroom picking yielded far more than a family could eat at one go. They wouldn't keep for long and, sure, there would be another sackful poking through the next morning.

Even so, we were relative amateurs. Others knew about watercress, dandelions, nettles, elderflowers and elderberries, hazelnuts, and the wilder mushrooms of the forests and hills that we were too scared to pick and too ignorant to identify safely. There is so much to know, so much food to be found.

For all that we saw ourselves as urban, we were, and are, deeply connected to the land. Everyone is. There are connections of memory, both personal and collective, connections that sometimes manifest themselves simply as longings to get out to the countryside. Some people need to feed these more regularly than others. I am still resolutely townie by nature, and can happily tread the pavement for many a month uninterrupted by the feel of soil under my shoe. But, a few times a year – twice, maybe, but rising – I get what can only be described as a yearning to stand in a field. Not to walk on a beach or climb a mountain, but to put my feet on farmland. I don't count my grower Ultan's vegetable farm because it's familiar, cultivated, a place of gentle nurturing, and going there is part of my work. It's slightly odd because I'm not even comfortable standing in a field, not alone anyway. I need a volunteer to come with me, if only to shield me from my own paranoia. I understand the pull, know that it is partly related to my childhood games, but even more so to the fact that my father and most of my relatives grew up on farms. I recognise the call and answer it when it becomes irresistible, but there's no real romance in the feeling. My father felt the same pull, but much more often, every week at least. Walking narrow roads with their Mohican tufts of grass running down the middle, crossing fields to slyly look over the herds, surveying the subtle changes in landscape and farm practice, he stayed in touch with the land but kept his good shoes on. It never changed the fact that he had been happy to leave the farm, hit the pavement and stay on it.

The strongest, most fundamental connection between us and the earth, the countryside, is food. No matter how sophisticated and technological our world becomes, the source of almost all of our food remains the ground we walk on. This might not always be obvious from some of the produce on our shop shelves, but even the most appalling processed rubbish is made from ingredients produced by the soil of this planet. Hard to believe sometimes, but true. Neither is it always obvious from the farming practices used to squeeze more and more out of the same ground, stripping it of its intrinsic goodness and leaving it as nothing more than blank holding material.

West Cork is not unique in the world, nor even in Ireland, in the way it tries to maintain a balance between what the earth is capable of giving up and what we increasingly demand of it. But it mostly manages to keep a good balance, in its landscape and its way of life. Agriculture moves forward as it must, but respectfully, aware of its place in the scheme of things. There has been some opening up of fields, but the hedgerows that support so much life are more intact than destroyed. Stands of trees and small forests shrink but survive enough to support the systems that produce so much life and the food that nourishes it. Some of that food is to our taste also. Besides the bounty that is produced for us by those who care for the land, there is a wealth of food to be picked, foraged, searched out. Free. Well, not completely free; you have to go and find it, and it will cost you an hour, an afternoon, maybe a weekend if you are lucky.

It is not so long ago that foods from the wild were an important part of some people's diet, either for reasons of nutrition or necessity. For us, as children, searching for it was part tradition and part adventure. The cupboards at home were well stocked. Now, more than ever, it could be said that we no longer 'need' to forage for food. We can buy anything we desire – or so the mantra of our age goes. Foods that were previously rare, expensive and exclusive are now widely available and affordable.

Yet this absolute availability has actually distanced us from any feeling of connection with it or its source. Food is simply stuff on shelves, and shopping for it is a weekly chore – an alienating and depressing chore, at that. The emotional black hole that this creates is causing us, often subconsciously, to try to re-connect. It causes us to forego the supermarket and take the trouble to source food from farmers' markets, cheese shops, vegetable stalls, grocers, bakers, and our own gardens if we're fortunate enough to have one. And it is one of the reasons that we like to go out and find food for ourselves.

In common with the act of growing food, foraging for it demands knowledge from the consumer, information about where and when as well as an understanding about what to pick and how to prepare it back at home. This knowledge is hugely empowering, giving us a strong link with, and a sense of control of, our food supply that ironically is lost to us in the mystifying plenty of the supermarket shelves.

When we set aside a day or half a day to go in search of wild food, we are making, re-making or reinforcing connections. The pleasure of food picked in the wild, in the context of a day out, is different from food bought, or even from food grown. It has the quality of treasure found, even when you had a good feeling that the treasure was there to be found. The primal thrill is intact, still available to new generations: it's in the scaling of a broken wall to gain access to the small stretch of brambles where the blackberries are biggest and most plentiful, or crossing a meadow littered with cowpats but with no visible beasts, to get to the holy grail of an inner field where, someone had whispered, there were fresh mushrooms just two days before.

Searching for food, like growing your own, edits out all middlemen and the process of trade, putting you in direct contact with the produce, with the land that is the source of your food, and with the locality itself. If it is a place that is new to you, it will remain in your memory, forever connected with the food you brought home, as the food when you encounter it again will conjure images of the place where you originally found it. Sometimes there is even an element of pilgrimage to the day out. Going back to the blackberry lanes or mushroom fields of our past, consciously connecting with that past, perhaps with our own childhood or the lives of parents or ancestors, we are acting out rituals that nourish our souls as well as our bodies.

But hang on a minute, I can hear the rural associations all over the country cry, you can't have the place swamped with city folk getting in touch with their inner savage while looking for good blackberry hedges. Of course not, I agree. There are fundamental rules and codes of behaviour that have to be followed. Most could be filed under decency, common sense and respect.

● Don't forage on private land without permission.
● A great many plants in the wild are protected and shouldn't be picked at all. If you're not sure, leave them alone.
● When picking, be careful not to damage or destroy the plant, or take so much that it has no chance to regenerate.
● Take the fruit, the leaves or flowers, as the case may be, but don't uproot a plant unnecessarily.
● And, for heaven's sake, as you've been told a thousand times before, don't eat any mushrooms you're not absolutely 100 percent certain you've identified correctly as safe.

There are many books on wild food, one of the best of which is Wild Food by Roger Phillips. It's a fascinating tome that covers just about everything that you could eat from the wild in this part of the world, including some stuff even the author isn't too keen on. The book is fairly comprehensive, but only a small percentage of it will be of more than a passing interest for most of us. If the number of people who will go out to forage is a minority, the ones who will do so to supplement their diet in any substantial way by shoving down acrid wild greens is a dot on the graph.

In the course of what I might call 'research' for this book, and what others might call 'walking across a few fields', I tasted many things that count as wild foods. Some might make interesting additions to salads, others would only ever find their way into your kitchen if you were starving, impoverished and impervious to the sneering looks of your peers as they noted your sinking social status. It is true that the early leaves of hawthorn and oak are edible, as are clover, chickweed, hop leaves, comfrey and other foliage. The value may largely be in the novelty, however. If you are inclined towards serious foraging and living off a largely wild and free diet, get Roger Phillips' book. What am I saying? Of course, you already have it.

Wild treasures of the hungry gap

It is one of the beautiful symmetries of the seasons that the proverbial 'hungry gap' in cultivated foods – the months when little fresh food is available (usually March and April) – coincides with a time of year when the hedges, forsaken corners of fields and the edges of hidden streams offer up vital nourishment. That fallow time in late spring, before the arrival of summer crops, is when people traditionally turned to the wild, especially for those essential nutrient-loaded greens. As much as the wild greens were appreciated in times of need, however, they inevitably took on the badge of poverty.

When we became well off enough to buy our way out of the hungry gap, we stopped walking along the edges of fields with our heads down looking for sustenance. In a society struggling to better itself, to haul itself into modern times and prosperity, as Ireland did right through the last century, collecting from the wild gradually became a taboo. Instead, we have taken to shopping as though it were a salvation-promising religion. We are now heroic shoppers, European champions of the high-street frenzy.

The foods that survived the taboo to any extent were the ones that simply have no comparable replacement in cultivated produce. Blackberries, damsons, elderflowers and wild mushrooms are some that were still valued during the time when we were putting away the past and trying desperately to catch up with the twentieth century. Seen as luxuries, glamorous additions to the routine diet or seasonal treats, these held their status and, maybe more importantly, encouraged the current resurgence in picking wild foods.

I hope it is safe to say that we are far enough removed from poverty for the stigma of foraging to now be gone. Indeed, there may even be a new glamour attached to it, as we search for new ways to stimulate our jaded palates. For those who can buy anything, all that is left is the stuff you simply have to go find for yourself.

Sorrel

Wood sorrel straddles the border between the peripheral wild greens, the ones with more curiosity value than flavour, and those that still have the potential to actually excite our taste buds and widen our repertoire of ingredients. It has a very pretty shamrock-like leaf with a flavour that makes it an intriguing element in mixed salads. It has the same lemony taste as cultivated sorrel, though they are not related. Wood sorrel seems to release its flavour later. Pop a leaf in your mouth, chew awhile and, just when you're about to conclude that there's not much to the stuff, the acidic citrus-like taste takes you by surprise. It's a fun way to add a little oral stimulation to a walk in the forest, and one that goes back hundreds of years. In the sixteenth and seventeenth centuries, accounts were written on the state of the Irish nation, its customs and lifestyles, mostly designed to justify its colonisation by the British. These ridiculed some of the barbaric practices of the natives that needed to be improved, such as their awful cooking and music, the guttural language, ugly clothing and peculiar marital arrangements. Oh, and their disgusting habit of strolling through the woods chewing this shamrock-type plant. Time to send in the troops! Clearly, ignorance can be subjective, and one man's idea of barbarism is another's idea of culture.

There are, of course, wild sorrels which are related to the cultivated variety so beloved of French cuisine. If you find them, they are likely to have decent-sized and plentiful leaves. Some are coarse-leaved and bitter, while others have a sweet lemony zing and are soft enough to melt in the pan. Use them chopped into mixed salads and in potato-based soups, or to give a lively twist to fritters, tarts and pancake fillings.

I came across some sorrel one afternoon on the side of a narrow road that goes nowhere much, but conveniently past a few houses on the way. I wouldn't be given much penance in church for saying that it is the windiest place on earth. The people there could be divided into two groups: those who walk face up and smiling into the wind as though it were a pleasant face massage; and those who huddle away from it, developing stoops and permanent grimaces. Every living thing in that place is either curved by the wind or cutely skulking in the shadows.

The sorrel was hiding, tucked in and low down. According to the keen-eyed expert who was with me and who spotted it (I was keeping my eyes on the mangy and low-slung dog trying to sneak around behind us for a guerrilla attack), sorrel is happy to grow in shade, not caring too much whether it gets sunlight or not. This was a dull autumn day in October but the leaves had the vivid sheen of early spring growth. Although associated with spring, sorrel is one of those plants that is daylight-hour dependent, meaning that it goes for it and puts a spurt on when the number of daylight hours is in a certain proportion to those of darkness. Sorrel doesn't much like winter or summer but loves spring. And so it actually likes a mild autumn too. Or maybe it can't tell the difference. Plants, however much we like to deify their relationship with nature, are not always so smart. They take a gamble sometimes on which season it actually is, and can be easily fooled. If they weren't so gullible, it would have been very difficult to get them to adapt to our liking as we have done over the centuries.

Dandelions

Dandelions are many things to many people. They may represent a curse on your perfect lawn, a stubborn weed with a flower that holds no beauty for those who like a decent stretch of perfect putting green. Our childhood word for them was 'pissabeds', the joke flower of the plant world, guaranteed to cause bedwetting if hidden under a sibling's mattress. Strangely, although this was commonly said, I don't know of anyone who tried it or was the victim of it. Maybe we all believed it more than we realised. I doubt if many children are even acquainted with the legend any more.

To others still, the dandelion is a wonderful food with edible roots as well as leaves. Some say the flowers are also edible, but that's a taste too far for one brought up on the pissabed legend. They do make a decent wine, however, if you're that way inclined.

Of course, dandelion leaves are now grown as a commercial crop, often blanched or whitened to lessen their bitterness. Wild dandelion leaves have a wonderful pungency that can really add a kick to salads. In fact, they make a great salad in themselves, if you enjoy bitter greens. Add a sweet element for balance, such as peppers, orange, ginger, and walnut or hazelnut oil. Poached or hard-boiled eggs work really well with the astringency of dandelion. As with most wild leaves, it is best to pick the leaves young in spring, before the plant flowers.

Dandelion also cooks well, especially when wilted in olive oil and stock, which softens their cough a little. Even the older leaves can be good when cooked, especially if you add sweet elements to the dish, as with salads.

Nettles

The garden behind the house I grew up in had a pretty serious slope to it. Put a football anywhere on it and it took off for the bottom, where the ground levelled out for a couple of feet in an almost mockingly useless way. The pretty, planted shrubs there took a battering but at least they prevented the ball ending up in what was accurately known as 'the dump', the place where we kept stuff we might possibly use in another life after the dreaded bomb was dropped. There were blackberries in there but you just couldn't get to them. (You wouldn't dare try because there were almost certainly monsters there too.) The only way to win a football match in the garden was to play downhill in the first half and drag the second out until tea was on the table.

At the other end of the garden there was what could only properly be called a stand of nettles. Proud as a forest of pines, they were always there, occupying what we didn't know was the only part of the garden that was level, an area about 3 metres (10 feet) deep. The word, probably put about by our father, who had had enough of digging in his life, was that the damn things had incredibly deep and complex roots and were not easily shifted. They would have been all over the garden but for the furious football and show-jumping activity. (No, we didn't have ponies; don't ask.) One year, a man came and removed the nettles, like some gardening messiah. I never saw him, don't know his name or anything about him. For a long time I believed it was some nomadic saviour of domestic gardens who had the awesome power to defeat the unstoppable nettle. My mother put a garden bench and a deck chair on the new flat space, to sit in on sunny afternoons, and we built a shed which became the headquarters of a secret society. Never in our wildest dreams, not even in the event of the bomb being dropped, did we contemplate eating the nasty, stinging, space-grabbing plants. How things change.

Nettles have long been a mainstay of the hungry gap. The young shoots of spring are the best to eat, both for flavour and nutrition. In larger nettles, the tops of the plants are edible. They are a wonderful source of iron and have always had a reputation for great blood-purifying properties, which is probably responsible for their continued use as a food long after our absolute need for them has passed. Many people still eat nettles either as a soup or a vegetable every day for a week or two in May. The soup is more commonly consumed, and I hope it's not sacrilegious to say that nettle soup is usually potato soup with nettles in it. Nettles also make a good coarse unblended soup with barley and mushrooms. Really, nettles can be used in any way that suits simple greens such as spinach. Once boiled, cooled and chopped, they are good in egg dishes, risotto, pasta, as a cream sauce or as a

NETTLES HAVE LONG BEEN A MAINSTAY OF THE HUNGRY GAP

flavouring for gnocchi. I've read of them being used in salad, but I haven't had the nerve to try it, and I certainly wouldn't encourage anyone to eat raw stinging nettles. It is true that if you grasp a nettle quickly and firmly, as in the old saying, you may be rewarded for your courage and decisiveness by avoiding a painful sting. Then again, you may not always be so lucky. So if you go out to pick nettles, do take a decent pair of gardening gloves along.

Wild garlic

Wild garlic was the first wild food that excited me, as an adult and as a cook. It appeared in the garden one spring, its pretty flowers like bluebells but white, elegantly nodding on the end of slender grass-like stalks, and giving off a scent that was clearly more culinary than floral. I'm not a fan of perfumed floral flavours in food, though I accept that others value it. Discovering a flower growing wild within arm's reach that tasted of mild garlicky onion was a new food experience. I picked a bunch and went to the kitchen to play. The flowers were its best part. The stalks, too, were perfectly edible, if slightly grassy in texture.

Later, a know-all in the food business told me this was not actually garlic at all but 'three-cornered leek or onion', and I should really get hold of some 'true' wild garlic. Of which he had a supply. At a price. Ho hum, the food business. I persevered with my garden source, but noted that the one he advocated had a broad leaf with a softer texture. When he sacked one of his best employees, I asked the ex-worker to pick wild garlic for me. Ho hum, the food business.

Commonly known as ramsons, this broad-leafed garlic is undoubtedly a more useful plant, partly due to its sheer size but also because of its soft leaf and mild flavour. The leaves make great pesto and are mild enough to be added generously to salads, pasta, stews and risotto dishes. It grows in damp woodland as a floor covering, which looks extravagantly beautiful in flower. The 'three-cornered' garlic is mostly a hedge dweller. It will take over your garden if you let it but will happily shrink back to the edges if mowed. In late spring it flowers profusely in the densely populated hedges lining the narrow roads of West Cork. The heady scent and its elegantly fragile beauty make a defining image of the place in its time, in the same way that the fuchsia and montbretia do later in the year.

For the record, neither is actually garlic in the true sense. There are dozens, if not hundreds, of plants that are called wild garlic across Europe, North America, South Africa and Asia. Of these hundreds, I still use the only two I have access to, and I'm happy with both. It's a question of using what is available, and that is surely the essence of cooking with wild foods.

Elderflowers

There are a few contradictions associated with the elder tree. Both the flowers and berries look beautiful in their season: the flowers delicate like crocheted lace, followed by shiny black berries that hang from the slender branches in alarmingly heavy bunches. Yet, although both flowers and berries are harvested to be eaten, you couldn't guess it from how they taste when raw. The flowers, even at their prime in May and June, have an unpleasant smell and taste, acting as a useful warning since they contain small amounts of a poisonous alkaloid, though luckily this is destroyed in cooking. The berries that show up in autumn are as bitter as they are handsome, so there is little danger of anyone eating large quantities of them. And in the folklore surrounding elder, for every way that it is said to invoke evil there is another that suggests an association with good magic. Witches were thought to take the form of an elder tree as a disguise, but the trees were also grown to ward off witches! Elder has been used as a folk cure for pains, yet it was considered to bring with it a curse if brought indoors to be used as firewood.

So, it's really no surprise that it can be both horrible and delightful to eat. Cooked elderflowers have a delicately floral flavour, especially when made into a syrup or cordial. Over the last couple of years we've made a lot of this, using it to flavour gooseberry fool as a dessert, Prosecco as an aperitif and sparkling water as a refreshing drink.

The flowers make delicious and very attractive fritters. The first time I made these, I didn't really get it, finding the result too floral for savoury use. I nearly always think in terms of savoury flavours and had to be pointed in the other direction, as usual. Served in the manner of Spanish churros, sprinkled generously with sugar as a sweet fried snack, they are compulsive eating.

A stroll along the shore (with an eye on the waves...)

Given that we live on a small island off the north-west edge of Europe, it is surprising how little the Irish have traditionally looked to the sea for food. Any of you hoping that I am going to set all of that straight here and now with a comprehensive account of what is edible out there in the ocean and the amazing things you can do with it will be disappointed to hear that I am typical of my generation. I grew up thirty miles from the sea, but culturally it was in another part of the world, far removed from our lives. We went to paddle at the edges of it on a few sunny Sunday afternoons a year and spent a couple of weeks in a beach cottage every summer. The time there was

passed more in the sand dunes than in the water. Whether as children playing innocent games of mystery and intrigue, or as teenagers playing with the idea of falling in love, the dunes were more use to us than the cold sea. To this day I remain a man more inclined to roll his trousers up for a stroll along the edge than to plunge into the waves. No metaphor intended.

However, in recent years and with something like an open mind, I have been led to the terrain along the edge of the ocean, and to see it as an unlikely but inspiring source of ingredients. The vegetables that thrive in the halfway house between land and sea bring something of both to the kitchen in a unique way.

Carrageen

By and large, with the exception of pockets of communities who developed a taste for dillisk, aka dulse, if we've had any use for seaweeds, it has been to spread it over fields as fertiliser. More recently there has been a new growth in the industry, as it branches off into cosmetics, skincare and hair products. We're still not eating a lot of the stuff, though.

Of course I have eaten seaweeds, and even enjoyed them. I like sushi, with its nori wrapping, but I can't say I like nori on its own. Similarly, I have enjoyed arame and wakame in soups and salads, but not enough to motivate me to really get into them and develop some recipes of my own. I have eaten dillisk in a wonderful cheese made in Dingle in Kerry, and it certainly adds a complex new flavour to the cheese, but when I buy, I prefer the version without seaweed.

Then there is carrageen, probably the most widely used Irish seaweed. It is traditionally used as a gelling agent to make a simple pudding, the point of which I have always assumed is to get the combined goodness of milk and highly nutritious carrageen in one easy-to-digest package. A couple of years ago we started to use it in the restaurant to make a panacotta of sorts with sheep's milk yoghurt and honey. I liked the idea of using a native gelling agent. The yoghurt gave the pudding a richer texture and a sharp flavour which doubled as a mask for the carrageen, because the truth is that carrageen has what I can only describe as an unpleasant, spit-it-out flavour. The trick with using it, it seems to me, is to find the balance, the point where you use just enough to gently set the pudding, but not so much as to flavour it. In this sense, too, of course, it is not really a wild food, but rather a dried product from a health-food store. Use half of what it says on the pack. If you get it right, the pannacotta makes a wonderful foil for simple fruit compotes, especially ones made with the autumn fruits such as blackberries or figs.

Shortly after I started work on this book, I was given some seaweed products to sample. It seemed like a good coincidence and a stimulus to get me thinking positively about the bounty of the sea. I decided to go for broke and try the strong-smelling pickle first. Using all my powers of self-hypnotism to shut out my natural fear, I put some in my mouth and chewed for a few seconds. Then the floodgates of my self-control caved in and my mind became aware of what it was that I had in my mouth, and how utterly unlike food it tasted. I gagged, and by gagged I mean a form of rejection very close to emptying my stomach. I know this is psychological more than anything. The idea of fear of food is a hobbyhorse of mine. I'm not talking about the pain of a habañero chilli or the rank smell of Norwegian cave-matured blue cheese. Most of us have a fear of some foods which are considered quite unusual by a sizeable percentage of the population. Some children will go hungry for a week rather than eat a Brussels sprout. Grown men who are almost physically fearless will refuse to put a harmless foodstuff in their mouths – something as simple as parsnip or beetroot, a slightly unusual mushroom, maybe a strong cheese. So it annoys me that there are foods that I find disgusting without actually having tasted them, and I would like to overcome this prejudice, but the taste of that seaweed dish was more than I could tolerate. There and then, I gave myself permission to go on with the book without having to do seaweeds.

Two weeks later, I was out sea kayaking on a staff outing. The leader, Jim, has a gently convincing way about him. He takes you on the water for the Zen-like experience and just pushing off from the quay allows you to very quickly leave the earth – or at least the solid part of it –and its troubles. You become a floating element of a beautiful part of the planet – the wet part – comfortable with yourself for a little while, with who you are and the place you are in. Well, that's what I bought anyway; the others just splashed one another with their paddles and made figures of eight in the water.

I was paddling very slowly with Jim, away from the group, discussing the ups and downs of writing. When I started telling him my thoughts on seaweed, he pulled to the right and hauled up a long thread of sea spaghetti – as he called it – a piece about a metre long. Try that, he said. In the state of mind I was in, it was no challenge and I bit into it happily. It tasted fresh, light and only a little salty. I chewed away happily on it for a while, and imagined using it in salads and soups. This is how Jim gives things to you, simply and without fuss. If you get it, that's fine. If not, then maybe another time. For me and seaweed, it lasted only as long as I was on the water. Back in town, I couldn't move it on, I literally had no appetite for it. Some day perhaps, but not here and now.

Sea spinach

The shoreline is another matter. Without getting your toes wet, there are some delights to be found near the sea if not actually in it. Seakale is a wild plant that grows in shingle near the sea, but it is now more familiar as a cultivated plant, and that is how I have dealt with it elsewhere in this book. However, if you come across it, don't be put off by talk of its being suitable to eat only as a blanched plant. It is a wonderful green, especially the central young flower heads, just before they flower.

Sea spinach, or sea beet as it is also known, is a much more common plant. An ancestor of beetroot and chard, it grows in rocky areas and cliffs close to the sea and produces generous-sized leaves in late spring and into the middle of the summer before it starts to flower. The leaf is similar to spinach and can be cooked in the same way, though it is tougher and won't shrink or break down to anything like the same extent. Maybe 'tougher' is too strong and doing the plant an injustice. Let's just say that it's firmer and holds its shape better. Sea spinach is very useful for savoury pancake fillings and as a foil for egg dishes, where ordinary spinach might lack the character and structure you want. The flavour is similar to strong spinach but with some of the saltiness of the sea. Even though I pick or buy it as a wild food, I have read that it can be cultivated very easily.

We generally get sea spinach from June onwards and through most of July, although in a good year and with a bit of luck we might get a second crop in late September. I get sea spinach from two suppliers. One is a grower who does a little foraging in his spare time. The other is a woman who showed up one spring with sea spinach, watercress and nettles. Since I already had a good supplier for watercress, I took some nettles and the sea spinach, partly because I can always use another green vegetable, and partly because I was curious. With a new ingredient or a new source, it is never just about the product. I want to know about where it is grown, the variety, crop size, length of season. Also, I want to know about the person who supplies it and their feel for what they do. This isn't idle curiosity, and I'm not naturally a prying type, so I don't push it too hard, but I do like to know who I am buying from, hoping to weave together another strand in the fabric of the local food culture.

Because I already had a supply of sea spinach, the issue was really about why I would buy from the new source. We talked a little about wild foods in general, which was at that time just a tiny hint of a potential obsession of mine. Two things were soon obvious: this woman was passionate about wild foods, particularly those growing by the sea; but I wasn't going to find out anything about where they grew. I was to learn over the next while that this is a characteristic, and quite a grudgingly admirable one, of most serious foragers. They will give you the stuff, but the provenance is not part of the deal.

Samphire

After I had taken a couple of deliveries from the sea spinach gatherer, she asked if I had ever tried samphire, saying she could source decent quantities of it for summer. I was certainly interested. I had eaten samphire once before but had no idea how to source it and so had put it out of mind. Naturally, this cemented my commitment to taking sea spinach from her rather than from my previous supplier. I was already convinced by her dedication to foraging, but the prospect of samphire was certainly an additional incentive.

This is an intrinsic part of dealing with suppliers sometimes, and it is nothing like as cynical as it might appear at first. The supplier will give their best produce to reliable customers, the ones who buy a range of produce and pay on time. On the flip side, a buyer will have the good sense to occasionally take what the supplier needs to sell in the interest of getting the cream of the desired crop, too. Dealing with small producers, one of the trickiest things is getting the balance right between what you need in the

MARSH SAMPHIRE

kitchen and what they produce. If you have found this balance in, say, courgettes to be 5kg (11lb) twice a week, you can't phone in an order for 12kg (26lb) the night before delivery. Neither can you phone in and cancel the order in mid-season. What should the producer do? Tell the stupid things to stop growing? Well, you can if you want, but you won't be getting any asparagus next spring.

There are two plants known as samphire. Their names are descriptive: rock samphire, which grows out of cliffs, rocks and stone walls; and marsh samphire, which grows on the marshy area left by the sea at low tide. I have only tasted rock samphire once. This was on the first Sunday of September, the day of the double tragedy of Cork losing an All-Ireland hurling final, and a mushroom hunt turning up no mushrooms. However, leaning over a wall outside the harbour pub where I had watched the game with my grower, Ultan, we spied something resembling the samphire we had been cooking that summer. He insisted it was rock samphire, so we tried a bit. The first flavour-hit was familiarly sweet and salty, but then it developed into something quite aromatic, pungent and, finally, medicinal. As I spat it out, Ultan lectured me on the likelihood that the flavour of samphire changes after it has flowered, as is true of so many plants, and that it really shouldn't be eaten so late in the year. I promised to give it another try the following spring, but that taste won't leave my brain so easily.

Marsh samphire, however, is an exquisitely structured and flavoured vegetable. It grows in clumps which break up into little fingers or even hand-like groups. It is a vivid shade of green and has a crisp, juicy texture. The flavour is clean, refreshing and slightly salty and it is quite delicious eaten raw. Whether raw or cooked, it is a good idea to soak samphire in cold water for twenty minutes before using it. This leaches out some of the salt, but don't overdo it, the salt is part of the unique pleasure of eating it.

Cooking the samphire for a minute in boiling water brings out the colour without losing the flavour or texture. While still warm, toss it in a little olive oil and black pepper for a lovely side dish. A light tempura batter is another way to serve samphire simply. This also has the advantage of encouraging people to eat it with their hands. The fingers of samphire, especially the central ones of a bunch, can have a tiny root extending a little inside the flesh. Eating with your hands is a fun and practical way to deal with this, as you hold the base of the root and pull the flesh off with your teeth. Towards the end of the season the leaves become woody and you should let it go for a year. Of course, you don't, and instead persevere for a week in the hope it is just a blip, but in your heart, you know it's over.

Dipping a toe into the underworld of fungi

'Nothing more than mushroom identification develops the powers of observation' JOHN CAGE *Indeterminacy*

Mostly, the things we call mushrooms are merely carriers with the sole purpose of spreading spores for procreation. They come through the ground, pushed up by the parent life-form below, with the intention of releasing thousands of spores from the opening gills. Unlike fruit, most mushrooms do not try to attract humans or animals by making themselves pretty, obvious, tasty or sweet-smelling in any way so that we might carry its seed away.

It is quite possible that we have come to find mushrooms attractive despite their sly endeavours to hide from us. It is easy to understand why some mushrooms are poisonous – so that animals stay away while they open up their spore-bearing caps – but why do others taste so damn good? If it is not deliberate, if coy, seduction on the mushroom's part, is it mere accident or a human perversion? Other than slugs and maggots, animals don't bother them much, though apparently reindeers in Lapland like to chomp on a certain red one that gets them stoned, sometimes enough to fall over like students on happy-hour Thursdays.

There is a small percentage of mushrooms that will seriously trouble your stomach, poison you or even kill you. At the other end of the spectrum there is another small percentage that is delicious to eat. In between are thousands of mushrooms that are technically edible but really won't do much for the taste buds, being either plain dull or slightly bitter. Most edible mushrooms aren't a lot of fun to eat. However, in that tiny percentage at the delicious end of the scale are some wild mushrooms so sought after that hunting for them has become, in the minds of some, an obsession. Recently, my curiosity about that obsession overcame my careful nature, and I took a few steps down that shady path for the first time.

Amethyst deceivers

One Saturday morning in September, I was to teach a cookery class in a wooden house in a stunningly beautiful garden centre that specialises in wild grasses and their outrageous flowers. Over a bottle of wine the evening before, Jimi, the owner, suggested that there might be mushrooms for breakfast – if we both got up very early, of course, and if we had boots and raincoats, keen eyes and a good sense of balance. I wouldn't normally tick the boxes of many of those criteria, but then I thought – why not? Out of your comfort zone you might as well be out of character as well. You might find mushrooms, and you just might find out something about yourself in the process.

So we rose at the crack of dawn – well, not quite – but shockingly early anyway. There was a chill in the air I was unfamiliar with. What's more, it was Saturday. Saturdays I work the showtime service in Paradiso, almost without exception. Saturday is the hardest but the best night of the week. You could almost say it's the ultimate point of the whole week. Any decent restaurant chef will share that sense of anticipation and excitement building towards a busy Saturday night, the culmination of a week's work. When I think about that, I realise that I have become a chef almost against my intentions. I have been reluctant to admit this over the years, preferring to think of myself as an amateur, as a way of preserving my love of food in a business that can wear that love down. Too many professional cooks the wrong side of forty are cranky, grumpy, social misfits who can't remember why they chose to wear this uniform over another. I digress. All I meant to say was that I was up unusually early for one who works the moonlight shift.

We set off across the brightly coloured wildflower garden, through a gate that was designed to either keep giraffes in or terrible monsters out. 'Deer' was the unconvincing explanation. Unlikely, I thought, still a little nervous in the gloom. Nervous is my natural state in the countryside. Having passed through a field of nothing more dangerous than long grasses, I relaxed. Through the

AMETHYST DECEIVERS

misty half-light it was clear that we were heading towards the wood at the end of the semi-domestic field. At the edge, there was a descent to a thin muddy stream and a steep climb on the other side to a forest of oak and beech. As our eyes adjusted to the even lower light levels in here, it became obvious that in amongst the floor covering of rotting leaves, twigs and desperate but beautiful flowers, there was an abundance of mushrooms.

There were big brutish mushrooms that looked very tasty and all sorts of smaller ones varying in colour from cream to a golden beige and dark brown. I picked a short stubby thing that looked like dinner to me, but what do I know? We had two options at this stage: pick everything and check it later back at base, or pick only what we knew was safe. We didn't have a lot of time, so whenever I held up a fungus that looked too good to be left, Jimi said no, just stick to the ones we're looking for. The golden rule. He was no expert, but had learned that one of the varieties that flourished in his patch of forest made a damn good breakfast.

We were looking for tiny purple mushrooms going by the extraordinary name of 'amethyst deceivers'. Looking for mushrooms in a forest at dawn makes tactical sense, I'm sure, but it's bloody difficult in the half-light. Is this beautiful white one good? No, that's definitely poisonous. The ground was covered with mushrooms, most of them fleshy dark-gilled things that looked appetising, but definitely nothing purple. I started to wonder, 'Are there such things as edible purple mushrooms? What am I doing out here? I could be dicing onions or making marinades. I could be asleep, for heaven's sake. Oh God, there's one!' It was tiny, an inch of scrawny stalk with a tight hood, barely visible in the debris of leaves. Not one, but three or four, more, maybe a dozen. We were in pig heaven. They were definitely purple, beautifully and defiantly so, even in that dim place. When we found a patch, we would fall on it, picking every tiny mushroom, our faces close to the earth and our X-ray vision turned up to max.

As we moved further into the wood, I had a Red Riding Hood moment. I was almost completely obsessed with picking tiny purple mushrooms, blind to all other varieties, but a little voice in my head began calculating how far we had come and how much work I had to do to prepare for class. We had to turn back, but Jimi was convinced there would be a trove under the two large oaks at the top of this little hill. We went quickly, and he was right. We gathered all we could, then moved at a clipping pace back through the forest, trying not to look at the ground. In time-honoured tradition, we crossed the stream at a different point and made our way home by another route. Even in a hurry, it's best not to travel in straight lines.

While I picked over the mushrooms, Jimi burgled the chicken coop, and we had poached eggs and fried mushrooms for breakfast. Surprisingly, and pleasantly, despite their potent appearance, they tasted more like field mushrooms than the often earthier woodland ones, but in a satisfyingly intense way. This was a pleasant surprise to me, given that I was still a little tentative about eating fungi from the deep forest.

Some mushrooms are best cooked quickly over high heat, while others are better cooked in a way that retains their soft succulence, and this is true of the amethyst deceivers. Cook them in plenty of butter over moderate heat with a little garlic so they stew in their juices rather than fry.

Ceps (porcini)

Arriving home from the class at the garden centre, I realised I was developing a fascination for wild mushrooms. I knew where this could lead, I've seen it happen, and I knew my own tendency towards obsession. I needed to proceed cautiously – but one of those delicious-looking things I had had to leave on the ground back in the wood was bothering me.

Never having acquired a mushroom book, I decided to check the internet for photos. The authority on wild food, Roger Phillips, has a site with thousands of crystal-clear photos of mushrooms. It's easy to navigate so it took no time at all to realise that what I'd left behind was a perfect, if small, cep. Ceps, possibly better known as 'porcini' or the generic 'boletes', are the best loved of wild mushrooms right across Europe and America – and I had chucked away a decent specimen.

Of course, I began thinking about the other larger mushrooms that had looked so appealing in the early morning half-light of the forest. Could they have been ceps? They must have been. We were right not to pick anything we were unsure of, but how could we be so ignorant as to not know a cep? My curiosity was becoming rampant; I wanted to go back there, or somewhere, anywhere that I might have a chance to find some of those beauties.

For a couple of days, it stayed on my mind and I wondered who I might get to take me out. It's hopeless just blundering around in a wood on your own with a photograph like a missing-persons poster. I needed an expert. Somehow, I wasn't making the calls, though, and there were people I could have called. Instead I was just waiting and thinking about it. This is something I also do when I need to hire a chef: wait for one to show up. It almost always works. Last time, I lost my nerve and phoned the local paper to post an ad. In the hours between the phone call and the paper going to print, she showed up. I kicked myself for losing faith, and for the loss of a few hundred euros.

CEPS

This time, my faith held and things happened. Just two days later I got a phone call from a woman wanting to know if I could use 9kg (nearly 20lb) of ceps. *Excuse me? 9kg?* I did a quick mental visualisation, reckoning it to be three or four large punnets. *Of course I want them! I want the mushrooms and I want you to show me where you got them, and how to find them. I want you to tell me everything you know. I swear I won't steal your stock or divulge your locations. What I really want is to spend a few hours in a wood with a mushroom freak. Oh God, I'm becoming obsessed. I can feel it coming on, recognising the steady adrenaline increase and the empowering sense of mission.* I didn't say any of this, but it was a feat of self-control not to.

She arrived hours later with four boxes, three of which were piled high with mushrooms of all sizes, some with heads up to 20cm (8in) wide. Monsters! Poking through the boxes there were also some 'bay' boletes that she pointed out, of the same genus as the ceps and almost as good as the definitive version.

I asked why she had contacted me. After all, she must have driven past quite a few restaurants on the forty-mile trip to Cork. It turned out the mushrooms were for a chef close to her home, a man who sensibly always took what she delivered and found a place for it on his menu. This time, he was away for a week and the kitchen didn't want to take the responsibility. She called me because she wanted them to go to a cook with a passion for food who would appreciate them. It's not the flattery of this that interested me, but the fact that she reached out to connect with me while I was sitting and thinking about finding someone just like her.

Before I put the ceps on the menu, I took home a couple of small pale ones, and one giant: a martyr to the cause, as always. The little ones I ate as a raw salad, thinly sliced and dressed simply with lemon juice, olive oil and shavings of Parmesan. Then I roasted half of the monster, thickly sliced and lightly brushed with olive oil. When it was tender, I pan-fried some slivers of shallot in butter with thyme and chopped pine nuts and spooned this over the mushroom. The first course was delicate and light, but this was rich, intense and ... well, just one of the nicest things I've ever eaten. I confess I swore and blasphemed more than one 'god' out of sheer delight at the simple but ecstatic pleasure of it. I might have gone to bed happy then, but being a true pro I soldiered on, frying the other half in butter and garlic, finishing it with a splash of white wine and another piece of butter to make a sauce with the mushroom juices. I ate this with lazy country mash, where you break chunks of boiled potatoes on a plate with butter, or in this case the buttery mushroom sauce.

There are some things you need to watch out for with ceps. No matter how big and valuable they may seem, if they are very spongy it's not worth bringing them home. They simply won't push the buttons you expect. Ceps are also one of those fungi that slugs and maggots love. Don't be disgusted, these guys love a lot of the things we do. Always cut a cep in half and have a good look to see if one of these fellow enthusiasts has got there before you. Finally, ceps have foam-like spores under the cap instead of the usual mushroom gills. In young specimens, these are fine to eat but in older, bigger ones they are just not pleasant and have to be removed. Luckily, they peel off easily in your hands.

Chanterelles

Valued and loved almost equally as the finest of wild mushrooms, chanterelles and ceps also share their extraordinary way of living symbiotically with their host trees. While some fungi feed off dead or dying trees, those classified as 'mycorrhizal' actually live with the tree, breaking down organic matter in the soil for it to absorb and taking sugars in return. Both thrive in the relationship.

Chanterelles are easily recognisable because of their straw-yellow colour and their funnel shape with gills that run all the way down the stem. There are other closely related mushrooms that are also edible though perhaps not quite so exquisite. Most have funnel-shaped heads but usually with gills that stop at the top of the stem. Chanterelles are scarce where I live, except in pockets of woodland that are often the closely guarded secrets of foragers who could be considered professional given that they sell their finds in markets or to restaurants. In my limited experience of mushroom hunting, I haven't had the thrill of discovering a true yellow chanterelle, but I have found handfuls of some of the edible relatives. I was with a trusted mushroom expert at the time, who told me what was edible and what was not. Well, actually, what he told me was the difference between what was edible and what was worth eating. That is a very useful distinction.

Part of the reason for the popularity of chanterelles must surely be the range of our senses to which they appeal. Besides the taste and an elegant appearance, they have a faint but definitely exotic scent that is often compared to that of apricots. This is definitely a good reference to have in mind when thinking about how to cook chanterelles. With the first delivery of chanterelles to Paradiso, I thought about the apricot thing and decided to cook the mushrooms with shallots, brandy and sweet spices, just a touch of cinnamon, cloves and nutmeg, and then a little cream to hold the juices together. We served them like this, adding some simple potato gnocchi to mop up the sauce. Some sliced potato or even just toasted bread would serve the same purpose as the gnocchi if you're short on time. No matter how complex or simple the recipe, there is no denying that chanterelles have an affinity with potatoes.

Still, don't experiment with recipes until you've had chanterelles simply fried in a pan with garlic and butter at no more than moderate heat to preserve their lovely texture. Chanterelles are also wonderful with eggs, especially in omelettes and frittatas.

Puffballs

Puffballs are the joke fodder of the mushroom world; these lovable giants are seen by some serious mushroom-heads as merely a novelty, a fun find for the amateur hunter. Well, maybe psilocybin magic mushrooms get more sniggers at golf-club monthly committee meetings, but the sight of a giant puffball can make a grown man laugh out loud with a mixture of wide-eyed astonishment and hilarity. It's hard to believe that this football-sized, gleaming white thing is a mushroom, even more so to think that it is edible, and delicious. There are smaller varieties of puffball that grow to no more than the size of a tennis ball, some even as small as a golf ball. These have a more intense flavour, but with the same fantastic texture as their giant relatives.

One September morning when Ultan was delivering vegetables to Paradiso, he shocked a wheel-chasing dog by slamming on the brakes and reversing his lumbering van to check out the ball he'd glimpsed at the edge of a field. If it had turned out to be a football, we would have been happy enough. If it had been a giant puffball, white and unspoiled, we would have laughed out loud. It turned out to be a huge white puffball, but so pock-marked by the night-time feasting of slugs that it looked like a head with multiple rubber-bullet wounds. Still, Ultan brought it in and we recoiled in horror and peered up close in wonder all in one movement. The slugs, creatures often thought to be insatiable, had clearly gorged themselves on this monster and collapsed in defeat. I pictured them crawling away in the half-light of morning, bloated and sick but unwilling to leave such a treat. (A depressed, self-pitying slug is a nice thought.)

I checked some references for advice on how best to cook the thing, then went at it with a sharp bread knife, cutting slices 2cm (³/₄in) thick and brushing them lightly with olive oil – puffballs are very absorbent so you have to be careful how much oil you feed them. A classic way to prepare puffball is to coat the slices in fine breadcrumbs before frying them in olive oil, which does give a fantastic contrast of crispness outside and sublimely melting inside. However, I wanted to taste it straight up the first time, so I dropped the slices on to hot but dry, heavy iron pans, cooking them until browned on both sides. We ate them with nothing more than a little seasoning at first. The texture was wonderful, lightly crisp on the outside but meltingly soft inside, like a soft omelette or warm buffalo mozzarella. The flavour was of a very fresh field mushroom, which was surprising in such a bland-looking thing. Immediately, it was obvious that it would love a sharp dressing, so we tried it with a salsa of tomato, fennel and capers. Lovely. I can recall the taste of it even now.

With any kind of puffball it is important to cut it in half before thinking of eating it. If it is cleanly white right through, eat it. Otherwise chuck it out. It won't taste good and it won't do your tummy any good either. Puffballs are so-called because they build up spores as they stand in the ground, turning darker inside as they do so. Eventually they explode in a cloud of powdery spores. Seeing one that is clearly gone past being good food, it is hard to resist stomping on it, or swinging a boot, to release its puff. In the country you take your sport where you find it.

Cauliflower fungus

If the mushroom world were a freaks' circus, the cauliflower fungus would be the bearded lady with seven arms. It gets its name from its vague resemblance in shape and colour to a cauliflower, but could be said to be more like a cross between a sponge and a ruffled, frilly Christmas ornament. It is quite rare and therefore very exciting to a mushroom hunter. However, as a cook, I admit to initially being less than excited by it.

Because it grows at the base of a tree and has a loose texture, cauliflower fungus can be very dirty and requires a lot of careful washing or else you end up with a lot of small pieces and a few chunks of central core. The thicker pieces retain a firm, slightly sinewy texture when cooked. Whether this appeals or not is very subjective. For me, that's not a good thing.

I cooked some of the lighter frilly pieces in tempura batter, which worked very well. The texture was still firm but in a good way, and the subtle and slightly nutty flavour came through nicely. I tried it with a light rosemary aïoli and a standard soy-based tempura dip. The aïoli was better. Better yet was frying it in butter with a touch of garlic and chives. In the mouth, the small pieces of fungus felt like broken scraps of fresh tagliatelle cooked just al dente, a texture that was somehow very pleasing. Finally, I made some fritters with the last of the scrappy little pieces, binding them in a simple batter of egg, flour and milk, and then cooking them slowly in a heavy pan so that not only were the fritters cooked but the mushrooms themselves were, too. These were good, a lovely flavour and in fact the mushroom had become softly chewy.

Next time I come across a cauliflower fungus, either on the forest floor or in a delivery basket, it will trigger the pleasurable memories of taste and a sense of potential that have joined, if not quite replaced, the freakish image in my mind.

Hedgehogs and shaggy parasols

For restaurant owners and chefs, unless they have access to the services of a good forager – and even that will be erratic – it is a hit and miss business trying to get your hands on enough local wild mushrooms to use on a menu. Sometimes you may not even get enough of a variety to make more than a snack in the kitchen. Two such mushrooms that I had fleeting contact with are the comically named hedgehog fungus (or hedgehog mushroom, as I prefer to call it) and shaggy parasols.

I was once given about a dozen shaggy parasols, some small, closed and with ne'er a sign of shagginess, others half open and slightly ragged on top, and a couple that were wide open and truly shaggy. Whether fried or roasted, they have a wonderful and surprisingly intense flavour, sweet and nutty, and very appealing. There was no opportunity for experimentation here, so we simply ate the lot. It's no way to run a business, but on the other hand maybe it's one of the joys of trying to run one.

Even better was the hedgehog mushroom. It doesn't have a thorny back, nor is there anything remotely threatening about its shape or lovely cream colour. But it has soft spines underneath instead of gills, hence the name. Hedgehogs have something of the flavour of a chanterelle and some of the pleasing comfort-zone character of a field mushroom too. You may read that it has a tendency towards bitterness, leading people to sometimes cook it with sweet alcoholic drinks. We had some reduced cider to hand for an oyster mushroom dish already on the menu, so after eating some hedgehog mushrooms simply cooked with garlic and butter, I added the cider and some pecans just because they were nearby, boiled it off and added a little cream. This was delicious, but that's not to say the simpler version wasn't, too, and that the best thing in both versions was the flavour of the mushroom itself. The texture is firm and slightly chewy, which immediately made me think it would be good to showcase it in a salad. It's definitely a classy fungus, and one I wanted more of.

Reluctant to give up on them, I asked a local importer to see what wild mushrooms he could source. Amazingly, the one that he could get in the most dependable supply was the hedgehog. Possibly because it is so dry and hardy, the hedgehog mushroom stores well, and we had a supply right through November and up to Christmas. We mostly served them in a warm salad with leeks and hazelnuts, but also simmered them with cultivated king oyster mushrooms in a fragrant wine sauce that acted as a sauce for a cabbage and celeriac timbale.

Field mushrooms

Although it is often thought of as common and doesn't have the mystique of its forest-dwelling cousins, the field mushroom will remain unrivalled in my heart for a while yet. It has a flavour that is incredibly pleasing and lovely, in a way that seems benign, warm and comforting. For me, this flavour is evocative of childhood memories that are connected to the sense of home as a warm safe place. Blackberries were the sweet 'high' of late summer, often eaten as a snack without bringing any home to share, but picking field mushrooms was more of a collective thing. Adults and children went out together to find the mushrooms, and later at home we ate them together in a quietly ritualistic way, as the smell of them cooking filled the kitchen – a smell that would become a touchstone in the memories of everyone present.

I found myself talking mushrooms recently with an older relative. He was helping to repair a wall in the restaurant that had become ragged from repeated water leaks, and I was making rosehip syrup. The old-fashioned process fascinated him, and somehow we got to talking about foraging and memory. He told about a time, not too long ago, when he had eaten a field mushroom roasted on coals. It took him by surprise how the taste had seemed so perfect, and how it had transported him back to his childhood in another part of the country. His spontaneous exclamation of joy didn't greatly please his wife, mind you. For decades, he had been eating his mushrooms the way she cooked them, the way she was brought up to cook them – that is, boiled in milk with onion. It wasn't that he thought this wrong or unpleasant. In fact, he quite liked it and had simply forgotten about the other way, the one from his past, but the taste brought it all back, and it carried a pleasure that was more than flavour. At the moment of tasting the mushroom, he had remembered home, and his mother, how their food was cooked and God knows what else about the place and time in which he grew up. Even in telling it, he was remembering both the eating of the mushroom and the memories they evoked.

For me, it is the same story even if our tastes are opposite. I love roasted or grilled mushrooms, but boiled in milk is the way that connects me to my own personal nostalgia. To set off over a five-bar gate into a series of small cattle-grazing fields in search of mushrooms is also a journey back in time and, if I allow it, one into my own self too. In there, I am sure to meet family and friends, and even myself at different times and ages, seeing familiar small histories in a new light, in the way that the realities painted by our memories change with age. If I'm lucky, I might actually find mushrooms too.

On a recent day out, I went with a couple of friends to a field that had been reliably tipped as being bursting with mushrooms. It was also fairly heavily occupied by a bunch of very frisky young bullocks. Everyone in the countryside laughs at you if you even hint at nervousness around these lumbering beasts, usually adding that they mean us no harm ... but they weigh half a ton, and have that fatal combination of intense curiosity and a complete lack of grace. In their own deluded minds, they are elegant deer or young ponies. It would be little comfort to you to know that the one who bowled you over and trod all over your soft body was merely clumsy and over-excited, with the braking power of an elephant on ice.

Of course, they trotted over immediately and proceeded to follow us around like puppies. They were desperate to get up close for a nuzzle but were always prepared to turn and flee if the little voices in their prehistoric brains were right and we turned out to be hunters. They had also trampled a lot of mushrooms in their earlier meandering.

At two extreme ends of the field, we found concentrations of still untrampled mushrooms, enough to fill a couple of bags and hightail it before the beasts arrived to squash everything. There wasn't a lot of time for the contemplation of any childhood memories except those of being chased by various animals, including a pig and some geese, on an uncle's farm.

When we returned home, we gave a new airing to the old debate about whether mushrooms should be washed or not. There is an accepted wisdom that mushrooms should never be washed as they take on too much water and lose flavour. The reason we were pondering the issue at all was because our haul was quite dirty, with lots of grass stuck on the caps and muddy grit in the gills. A copy of Harold McGee's *On Food and Cooking* was produced, which settles most arguments of this kind. You can always count on science to knock the blind fun out of a good argument. According to his experiments, there is little appreciable loss of flavour. The water absorption isn't a huge problem, particularly if you're using them in wet dishes like soups and stews, although you wouldn't want to go soaking a puffball. The bottom line is that if the choice is between washing the mushrooms and throwing them away, you may as well wash them. Do it quickly but efficiently and pat them dry with kitchen paper afterwards if you intend to fry them.

Neither of the friends I was with was keen on the boiling-in-milk recipe (which is in *Paradiso Seasons* if you are turned on by the thought of it), so we fried and grilled some of the mushrooms to test the quality and compare results. Both methods were equally good, so we had a glass of wine and thought about what to with the rest. After much humming and hawing and growling of tummies, I decided on a gratin, pairing them with the mushroom's best friend, the potato. We layered slices of potato and mushrooms and baked them in the oven, then poured in some cream, topped it with breadcrumbs and cheese and baked it again until it became crisp, dry and richly earthy. Eating it afterwards, I thought it could have done with some onion to cut the richness. The recipe that follows later is the improved version.

Some unfinished business with ceps

As good as it was to have an occasional supply of ceps, I had realised that my fascination with them was really centred on the potential of finding some for myself. The season was moving on and I began to fret that it might not happen this year. So I signed up for an organised mushroom hunt not far from town and led by Jim, the man I had been buying oyster mushrooms from for years. I'm not much of a club-joiner, and my nervousness wasn't helped by the gathering of forty people in school-outing fashion, marching in single file down the lanes and into a wood. We wandered around, unsure and insecure about what we were meant to do. The half-hour of introductory information had told us that there were endless variations on countless varieties of mushroom out there, and that we were hopelessly equipped to tell good from bad. For a topic as wide and deep and full of mystery as mushrooms, every piece of information illustrates the iceberg of knowledge hidden beneath it, inaccessible to the toe-dipping amateur.

Gradually, we drifted apart in the forest of young beech trees and scraggy undergrowth. I was still thinking I couldn't possibly spot a mushroom here, this is ridiculous. Then I noticed that others were bending and plucking, so I focused, shutting out all other visual distractions and thinking only of mushrooms. They're all so different, so what image do you focus on? I decided to be one-dimensional and think only of ceps. As the ground cover thinned out and the forest became denser, it was obvious that there was a lot of fungus in here. A great deal of it was familiar from the display on the table back in the hotel, and therefore not much use to eat. They were pretty-looking, though, and good practise for spotting ceps. So, I picked, as everyone else was doing. They were tiny scraggy little things. Some were the amethysts that I had come to think of as friends, some that looked like chanterelles but disappointingly did not have the right gill patterns. My, I've come on a bit here, I thought, and moved towards the larger trees over by a stream.

Occasionally we stopped to share notes and peek into each other's baskets, and it was obvious we were all collecting interesting things to either make a disappointing dinner or kill our guests. Yet, when I found myself in the middle of a thicket of saplings and thorny bramble, hands scratched and trousers muddy, I realised I had crossed to another mode. I had seen something like a cep, or some boletus-type mushroom anyway, on the bank across the stream and had ended up in here wondering if it was possible to get to the other side. I decided against crossing the Ganges, but the sight of the mushroom made me certain I was in the right territory and I scoured the ground near every tree, ignoring the bramble scratches. I even stopped worrying about my new jacket. I forgot about everything in fact, my mind emptied in the way a meditation master would die for. I love finding this mode in any activity, when you are no longer thinking, but simply being. You hit the same spot at about 8.45 p.m. on a Saturday night in a busy kitchen. Others prefer to find it sitting on a board at the edge of the ocean or in the intense battle of competitive sport.

Eventually I spotted what my mind was obsessed with, and knew two things in the same split second: I had found my first bolete, but it was a spongy old useless thing. I picked it and put it in my bag. There was no real triumph in it and I chucked it away when we were called to regroup and find our way out. A little disheartened but chalking it down to experience, we traipsed through boggy scrubland, all thoughts of finding mushrooms gone, until we reached the lane again. When a further search of another field was suggested, we groaned but followed wearily. Coming to a large field with a tree-lined stream on two sides, I was first in with the guide. With a sly smile, he whispered that there were definitely ceps here. Clever. They had saved the best to pick up our sagging spirits on the way home. I was in like an excited schoolboy at a chestnut tree and had half a dozen decent-sized beauties in my bag before the rest got their bearings. Sorry, but my gut instinct was that all's fair in love and mushrooms.

There is only a second or two between seeing a healthy specimen and cutting it, but it passes in slow motion while your heart literally leaps and you take an internal shot of adrenaline. You do a quick visual scan of the prize, then inhale a deep snort of its scent, trying to get a sense of the pleasure to be had later from eating it. When you pop it in your bag with a sense of triumph, your eyes turn back to the ground like lasers on cep setting. Now you are wired to mushrooms and feel as though you were specifically designed to find the damn things. I think a lot of this feeling will be there every time because there is no perfect mushroom and no perfect day out, in the way the nature of bread makes every loaf an individual achievement but never a perfect one. But equally, none will ever be like the first.

I picked enough for a couple of meals, then walked away from the trees to the middle of the field, realising what a beautiful place we were in. An old meadow, a hazy autumn sky, and a trickling stream with large oak, chestnut and beech trees all around. As well as my stash of ceps, I also brought home a single conker, one beautiful shiny chestnut, just out of its split spiny shell. You should never leave a chestnut tree without pocketing one. It might be the best conker in the world.

Sweet and sour harvest of the hedgerows

If the golden rule about foraging is not to eat anything you're not absolutely certain is safe, the silver rule must be not to plan dinner around your find before you set out. There are no guarantees, even with the best reconnaissance and whispered leads. The first trip I made this year to find field mushrooms was incredibly fruitful. I mean literally fruitful, as in we came home with fruit but no mushrooms.

There is a lovely balance to a day spent in a combination of foraging for mushrooms and picking fruit. One part involves hopeful and concentrated searching with the potential for disappointment. The other is simply a matter of going to the source and picking the fruit. It is more relaxed and social. You can hold a conversation while picking fruit, while mushroom hunting is more of a furrowed-brow kind of experience with occasional giddy highs.

Sloes and crab apples

It was a perfect late summer Sunday morning, warm and sunny, though it had rained a bit over the previous days. I was to meet up with Ultan Walsh, the vegetable grower, who had done some research and was confident the day was long and fine enough to widen the brief to include sloes and crab apples as well as the mushrooms. In hindsight, he was ensuring that we came home with something for our troubles even if the mushrooms failed to show. But he was optimistic too, believing he had engaged the help and company of a man who knew the name, address and sexual preferences of every wild foodstuff in the area. When Ultan and I arrived at the guide's place, bearing offerings of freshly picked tomatoes, the man's attitude to the forthcoming expedition was clear from his outfit of vest, ancient overalls and no socks. Dressed for the couch, was my first and accurate impression. And, sure enough, his contribution to the day was to point in the general direction of a few fields we were perfectly capable of seeing for ourselves and

CRAB APPLE

to warn us about getting nothing more than soggy trousers today.

With an eye on the clock, Ultan and I (sans guide) set off quickly down a narrow track, leading to some small fields. Two hours later, we had at least learned that he did know his area because we hadn't seen a single mushroom. And, of course, our trousers were very soggy by now. There is a point in a day's foraging when the nagging sense that it might not be a great haul turns into the certainty that it is going to be a blank. Your mood goes flat for a while, then you suck it up and get on with the other pleasures of the walk. And you do a mental check on the fridge at home, hoping there is the makings of dinner in it.

Changing our focus, we remembered seeing some blackthorn trees heavy with sloes close to where we had started, so we circled round to them and filled our bags with the bitter fruit. Sloes are ancient plums but ones with no sweetness at all, or if they have any it is masked by the most mouth-drying astringency. The taste of sloe has been imprinted on my brain since childhood but it's impossible to believe they are so unpalatable. So I popped one in my mouth. The first second is okay, there is something vaguely plummy about it, then the astringent juice coats the mouth, leaving it dry and stuck together, as well as causing your face to contort into a lemon-sucking grimace. And, of course, you make a mental note to remember not to do it again next year. Fat chance.

Having switched our attention to fruit, we drove to a length of roadside hedging where Ultan knew there were some crab apple trees. Parking the car in the middle of the narrow lane, we filled another couple of bags there, feeling quite good about the day, happy to have put the infuriatingly unreliable mushrooms out of our system by switching our focus to fruit.

Sloes and crab apples are too sour for most of us to eat raw now, though they were certainly eaten in times before the development of processed sugars. Now, our easy access to so much food with concentrated sugars has given us a collective sweet tooth that makes some wild fruits taste almost shockingly sour. Still, they survive, partly through their own tenacity as plants and partly because they are nurtured to an extent by landowners who tolerate them, possibly even allowing for the place they still hold in society. There may be a declining amount of hedgerows and idle land for these trees to thrive in, but what is left is valued by people for whom it is part of the annual cycle of life to spend a day gathering fruit and another making jams and syrups.

The potential uses for sloes and crab apples are traditional, and I didn't feel it was my place to get too chef-like with them. So I made a jelly of the apples with a small amount of sloes and wild mint as flavouring. 'Use what you find' is a good approach to foraging. Sloes are far too bitter to make a jam or syrup on their own, and they have a large stone which would make them very troublesome in any case. But a small amount of sloes in jams made with other fruits, such as damsons and blackberries, can give them a new level of complexity. Crab apple jelly has a lovely mixture of tartness and sugar, so it works well both as a sweet spread on your morning toast and as a foil for sharp cheeses, especially mature hard ones.

With the rest of the sloes I had gathered, I made sloe gin. I searched for recipes in old books and new websites, and 95 per cent of them were for gin. Why fight it? Talking about it in the restaurant kitchen the following evening, one of the cooks said he had set about making sloe gin too; he gathered the fruit, bought sugar and found a recipe. Only then, to his horror, did he realise he would have to buy commercial gin and wait a couple of months for it to infuse before he could drink it. He gave up in disgust and chucked the sloes away.

As a gin lover, I think sloe gin is an interesting drink, with an agreeable sharpness, although it also has a lot of sugar, so I wouldn't waste any expensive brands on it. After a little experimentation, I got in the habit of using it in two different ways, one a variation on a classic martini, and the other a refreshing combination of sloe gin, fresh orange juice and tonic water.

Damsons

On a more successful mushroom hunt than the day of sloes and crab apples, we made a perfect circle through a number of fields and then back to the road we had come from, at the edge of which we had noticed a row of damson trees acting as a 6-metre (20-foot) tall hedge overhanging two fields. The fruit was a beautiful near-black colour with a powdery blue coating of wild yeasts. As with the sloes, we couldn't resist tasting them, though with less trepidation. Damsons are ancestral plums too, like sloes, but that's where the comparison ends. These were wonderful, their rich fruity flavour a balance of sweetness and acidity rarely found in cultivated fruit. We greedily filled our pockets and our hoods.

Damsons have been cultivated for quite a while, so it might be argued that they are not really a wild food any more. However, nobody has ever offered me cultivated damsons for sale, and if wild is the only type I have access to, then they are, by definition, wild. The fruit is small and intense, so to make dishes like tarts or crumbles it is best to mix them with apples or pears, both for volume and to tone down their acidity. They make wonderful jam, and most recipes suggest that you can scoop the stones off the top as it cooks.

Stoning damsons is an issue, it has to be said. Looking for a way to use a large quantity in the restaurant without having to stone them, we made a sweetened purée, sieving out the stones. There is a dessert of fruit fool on the menu that changes with the availability of seasonal fruit, so we tried out the damson purée. It was the best of the year, without question. It had a fantastic complexity of flavour and that wonderful sugar and acid balancing act to back it up. When I printed it on the menu as 'wild damson fool', it flew out the kitchen door. Did the word 'wild' sell it or do people love damsons? Our supply lasted two weeks, but I never got around to conducting the survey that would have solved the issue. I often feel like conducting such surveys, but the sane little voice at the back of my head says that some good things are best left unquestioned.

We also made a small quantity of damson cheese. 'Cheese' is an old word for what is really a thick, unclarified jelly similar to the classic Spanish membrillo made from quince. It is incredibly intense but a wonderful accompaniment to strong cheeses.

The elusive berries

From the middle of summer, the first wild berries begin to appear, though the real abundance only becomes obvious when the blackberries turn from red to black in August and September. Before that, you may come across patches of summer varieties like wild strawberries, raspberries and bilberries in your wanderings, but it is very unlikely you'll be bringing home bucketfuls. These are really treats to be enjoyed along the way, taste sensations to punctuate a walk on the wild side. The fruits you might find in hedgerows are more delicately flavoured and less sweet than their cultivated cousins, but in the context of a day out, they are exquisite. Each one found is like a jewel, and rarely seen in bountiful clumps. If you are lucky enough to come across a decent crop, don't get carried away with fancy recipes. Eat them slowly with a little sugar and cream and think about how lucky you are.

Bilberries look like small blueberries but are less juicy and more acidic, though they are just about sweet enough to eat raw. They grow in low heather and on scrubby hillsides, which makes them incredibly difficult to find. But, as with any foraging, when you find a couple your eye seems to re-focus and zooms in on every berry nearby as though it had an arrowed sign erected overhead. They certainly must have been plentiful once, or perhaps we used to have better eyesight, because the first Sunday of August was known as Fraughan Sunday, after the Irish name for the berries. There were many legends and rituals attached to the day: rituals of courting mostly, whereby boys and girls got paired off in the course of the day. In some, the potential lovers picked together, in others the girl found enough berries to make a pie, some mashed fruit with cream or a bottle of cordial for her target. Sounds like a very exciting day out, conjuring an image of previously unmatched couples suddenly lifting their heads from the heather and disappearing round the curve of the mountainside or down into a shallow dip. Imagine too the fevered planning and scheming that must have been going on right through the month of July. That's the stuff of long hot summers of childhood memories, for sure.

Blackberries

Blackberries are still amongst the most accessible wild food for most people. Despite the shrinking amount of hedgerows, the thorny brambles that produce the fruit thrive anywhere they can get a hold, including walls, waste ground and any hedging. Unless you're a demon with the weed-killer, it's likely there are some in your garden. At the very least, most of us know how to identify and where to find blackberries. Unlike some wild fruit, they are sweet enough to be eaten raw and plentiful enough to be used in many different recipes, from ice-creams and muffins to tarts and jams.

As always, the best thing to do with the first precious haul of the season is to eat them simply with sugar and cream. Let the memories settle back in, then take out the recipe book and start cooking. Blackberries are the only wild fruit that even the most urbane amateur can count on gathering in sufficient quantities to make whatever it was you had your mind set upon before you left home. To make a tart for dinner, get the pastry ready and pick the weight of fruit you need, allowing for snacking. You want jam for the winter? Stay out a little longer. There are no certainties in the wild, of course. There may have been a ferocious downpour which left the fruit soggy and bland, or you may have been beaten to it by the pig who got up early (your neighbour, that is).

Maybe we even take blackberries for granted. When we haul ourselves out of the sofa to take a casual walk during the months of August and September, they are in the hedges to be snacked. Just as often, they are in the supermarkets, big fat ones with more water, more sugar and no bugs. The usual deal: you can have it clean and dull and delivered, or you can go get it yourself. Take the 'leave it' option and pick your own. Picking blackberries is pure pleasure. For kids, there is no misunderstanding, no wondering what this nasty stuff we're collecting is about. The berries are sweet, and the slight thorny challenge only just enough of a problem to make them feel adventurous and appreciate the reward. Don't get preachy, but you will know that you are making future memories; building and nurturing connections and stretching them into the next generation. This is how traditions survive, with the merest fingertip contact with the past. If blackberry picking is the easy link, it may well be the portal through which another generation may pass in order to explore the wider possibilities of wild foods.

The bitter berries: rowan and elder

The rowan tree, or mountain ash, is about as handsome a plant as you will come across in the Irish countryside. Growing on the sides of hills and small mountains, it is short and wide with nicely spaced branches that let a lot of light through. The boughs are heavily hung with bunches of incredibly attractive bright red berries. There is a lot of folk mythology surrounding the tree, mostly relating to its powers of protection against evil spirits and its ability to release your own powers. Nailing a branch to your front door or growing a tree in your garden certainly won't do you any harm and its beauty will lift your heart every day.

But you will be put very straight when you bite a rowan berry, as you must. The suggestion in some books that the juice can be used in place of bitters when making martini is a mere hint of the taste in store. When we made a jelly from them at Paradiso, we added a little milk to soften the bitterness. Even so, we expect it to outlast the rest of the store cupboard. To be honest, as a vegetarian I think only the strongest cheeses would stand up to this stuff, and I'm not at all sure they would benefit from it. I was disappointed, but it wasn't the worst thing to happen to me that week.

Elder shares the rowan tree's aesthetic and reputation for protective power, and its branches hang heavily in autumn with dense clusters of black berries, where in spring it lit the countryside with a delicate floral lace. Unlike the über-friendly blackberries, these fruits are bitter to taste and mildly poisonous unless cooked. They do make a decent jelly and syrup on their own or mixed with other berries, and if you have an abundance nearby, you should not let it go to waste. But, as with rowan, I didn't care much for the jelly I sampled this year. Elderberries are said to make good wine, however, and I would always go along with the idea that if something can't be eaten, you might as well try drinking it.

Rosehips

Rosehips were a godsend when I was becoming a little bitter about wild berries. They are the hard, bright red fruit of certain varieties of rose.

ROSEHIPS

Although technically and historically edible, in practice they have long been treated as inedible in any simple way. The thin red flesh surrounds a mess of tiny seeds and short itching hairs which you would not want to get into your mouth in any way. Nor down the back of your jumper during class – a childhood prank that was as tormenting to the victim as it was hilarious to the bully.

While it is possible to clean out each one, I haven't met anyone who has ever bothered. As children we were warned to stay away from the things as they were poisonous. I suppose that's a simpler message to get across, and it cuts out any possibility of curiosity leading to experimentation. I remember cracking a few open as a child, and I have to say that the inside does look like trouble. But I never used them as a weapon.

But rosehips are well worth gathering for the fantastic syrup that you can make from their juice. I know this is said of lots of berries and the like, but in this case it's definitely true. This syrup has a flavour unrivalled in commercial or cultivated products, and that is one of the best reasons for persevering with any wild food. Nutritionally, it is loaded with vitamin C – more than ten times that of oranges. Because of this, the making of rosehip syrup as a substitute for oranges became a government strategy in England during the Second World War. It is because of this that it is still commercially available, though less obviously now. However, it's no bitter medicinal tonic, to be swallowed out of duty. Instead, it has a rich and complex sweetness which is a pleasure to take by the spoonful or diluted in water, and it is wonderful for flavouring ice-cream, yoghurt and custard or sponge-based desserts.

Rummaging in the past to enrich the future

For a townie with a naturally nervous disposition in the countryside, this year has been a revelation, a journey into an area of food I had been ignoring. And one into my own past and place too, in the way that foraging is about so much more than getting supplies for dinner. For anyone who has memories of searching for wild food in their childhood, returning to it can put you back into scenes from another time and connect you to the people in them, including yourself.

Foraging is rarely a solitary activity. At its best it is a day or a few hours out in the countryside in good company. Conversation is not really necessary, just the presence of someone with whom you are comfortable sharing the time and space. My father wasn't really one for wild food, but he walked a lot in a countryside he was comfortable in, and always said that the best walking companion was one who knew how to keep his mouth shut. That reads harshly in print, but he meant someone who was comfortable with you and with the simple pleasure of the walk without needing to chatter.

In a time when we are sufficiently well off to buy any food we want from the eager supermarkets who are more than happy to sell it to us, searching for food in the wild is up there with growing our own as the best way to put that unquantifiable value back into what we eat.

However, the dwindling amounts of hedgerows and woodland, and the increasingly intensive farming of land, means that there is less and less opportunity to indulge in the traditions of foraging. Farmers, too, are not always happy to see strangers traipsing around their property. So we can't all go barging out into the countryside in the hope of finding a few berries and mushrooms for tea. With some careful planning and research, and equally careful diplomacy, it is heartening to know that there is still a lot of edible food out there that costs nothing but time.

Nettle and Potato Gnocchi with Sage, Walnuts and Cratloe Hills Sheep's Cheese

You do need a floury potato variety to make gnocchi, to avoid it needing too much flour.

   If this recipe makes more gnocchi than you want to serve or eat, freeze the remainder uncooked, after you have shaped them and tossed them lightly in flour. They can be stored in the freezer for up to ten days and cooked straight from frozen.

For the gnocchi, chop the potatoes into even-sized pieces, then steam until tender. Mash the potatoes or pass them through a sieve. Cook the nettles in boiling water for 5 minutes, then cool them under cold running water. Squeeze out all of the water and chop the nettles very finely in a food processor, then stir them into the potato mash. Add 80g (2³/₄oz) of the cheese and both the egg yolks, and season well with salt and pepper. Add most of the plain flour and quickly work it into the potato. If the dough feels like it's not too sticky to roll out, nick off a small piece, roll it into a ball and drop it into boiling water to test. If it floats to the top and holds its shape firmly don't add any more flour to the dough. If it breaks apart add a little more flour and test again. Cut the dough into three or four pieces and roll each into a long tubular shape, about the thickness of your finger, and cut off pieces 2.5cm (1in) long. Roll each one into an oblong. As you go, keep the gnocchi on a tray, tossed in a little flour – semolina or rice flour are best as they won't be absorbed into the dough.

   To cook the gnocchi, drop batches into a large saucepan of boiling water, taking care not to overcrowd the pan or the gnocchi will stick. The gnocchi are done when they float to the top. Remove the cooked gnocchi with a slotted spoon and toss in a little olive oil.

   While the gnocchi are cooking, melt the butter in a pan with one tablespoon of olive oil, and fry the sage, garlic and walnuts for 1-2 minutes, then stir in the gnocchi.

   Share out the gnocchi and sauce between four plates, and sprinkle over the remaining cheese. Serve immediately or place under a hot grill for a minute to melt the cheese.

Serves 4
600g (1lb 5oz) floury potatoes, peeled
150g (5¹/₂oz) nettle leaves
120g (4¹/₄oz) Cratloe Hills or other hard sheep's cheese, grated
2 egg yolks
salt and pepper
120g (4¹/₄oz) plain flour
a little semolina or rice flour to coat
olive oil
3 tbsp butter
2 tbsp chopped fresh sage leaves
2 garlic cloves, finely chopped
2 tbsp walnut halves, sliced

Dandelion Salad with Quail Eggs, Almonds, Blood Orange and Sherry-orange Dressing

If you don't want to eat straight dandelion leaves or don't have enough, mix in some other wild leaves, some milder rocket or even frisée lettuce.

Bring a large saucepan of water to the boil, carefully lower in the quail eggs and boil for 2 minutes, then cool them in a bowl of cold water. Peel and halve the eggs.

     Whisk or shake the vinegar, orange zest and juice and the olive oil together to make a dressing.

     Peel the oranges with a knife and cut out the segments, leaving the pith that separates them behind.

     Toss the leaves, diced shallot and orange segments with the dressing, then divide between four plates. Scatter over the almonds and tuck some quail eggs into each salad.

Serves 4
12 quail eggs
50ml (2fl oz) sherry vinegar
zest and juice of ½ blood orange
150ml (5fl oz) olive oil
2 whole blood oranges
600g (1lb 5oz) dandelion leaves, washed
1 shallot, finely diced
2 tbsp flaked almonds, lightly toasted

Wilted Dandelion with Ginger and Sweet Pepper

Chop any large dandelion leaves in half and use only a little of the stalk below the leaf.

     Heat a little olive oil in a shallow pan, toss in the onion and pepper and cook for 2 minutes over a medium heat. Add the garlic, ginger, dandelion leaves and a pinch of salt and continue cooking for 5–10 minutes. Add a splash of water occasionally if the pan is getting too dry. When the dandelion is tender, remove the pan from the heat, stir in the balsamic vinegar and sugar and serve.

Serves 4 as a side dish
600g (1lb 5oz) dandelion leaves, washed
olive oil
1 medium red onion, thinly sliced
1 sweet red or yellow pepper, quartered, seeded and sliced
1 garlic clove, finely chopped
1 tbsp finely chopped fresh root or sweet pickled ginger
salt
1 tsp balsamic vinegar
1 tsp caster sugar

Potato, Wild Garlic, Feta and Pine Nut Tart

To make the pastry, put the flour and a large pinch of salt in a food processor and carefully pulse in the butter until you get a fine crumb texture. Transfer this mixture to a bowl and gently work in the water. Working quickly and handling the mixture as little as possible, form the pastry into a flattened ball. Wrap it in clingfilm and leave in the fridge for at least half an hour. Roll the pastry out thin enough to line the base and sides of a 23cm (9in) tart tin. Carefully lift the pastry into the tin, press it into the sides and trim off any excess. Prick the pastry all over with a fork and put it back in the fridge for another half hour.

Preheat the oven to 180°C/350°F/Gas mark 4. Blind-bake the pastry case until firm and lightly coloured.

Peel the potatoes and slice them thinly, no more than 5mm (1/4in) thick. Cook in boiling water for 3–4 minutes, until just done, then cool under cold running water before drying them on kitchen paper. Drop the wild garlic into boiling water for 30 seconds, then remove and cool. Squeeze the garlic dry and chop it coarsely.

Combine the garlic, feta and pine nuts. Beat the eggs lightly with the cream and nutmeg. Season lightly with salt and pepper.

Place a layer of the wild garlic mix in the pastry shell and cover it with a layer of potato slices. Repeat the layers, then pour in the egg mixture, allowing it to seep down through the layers.

Bake the tart for about 30 minutes, until it is set and the potatoes on top are lightly coloured.

Serves 6

FOR THE PASTRY

120g (4¼oz) plain flour

salt

60g (2¼oz) cold unsalted butter, diced

2 tbsp cold water

FOR THE FILLING

500g (18oz) firm potatoes, such as Nicola or Charlotte

150–200g (5½–7oz) wild garlic leaves

250g (9oz) feta cheese, crumbled finely

2 tbsp pine nuts, lightly toasted

4 eggs

150ml (5fl oz) double cream

pinch freshly grated nutmeg

salt and pepper

Wild Garlic and Walnut Pesto

This pesto makes a lovely sauce for pasta, tarts and egg dishes like frittata. Stored in a jar in the fridge with a thin layer of olive oil on top, it will keep for up to a week

Put the wild garlic and walnuts into a food processor and blend to a coarse purée. Pour in the oil and blend again for a few seconds. Transfer to a bowl and stir in the cheese. Season with salt and pepper.

Makes 300 ml (10fl oz)

100g (3½oz) wild garlic leaves
50g (2oz) shelled walnuts
200ml (7fl oz) olive oil
40g (14oz) Desmond, Parmesan or other hard cheese, finely grated
salt and pepper

Samphire, Pear and Hazelnut Salad with Rosehip Dressing

This salad is a lovely refreshing starter with its combination of sweet and salty flavours. Add some dollops of mascarpone for a richer salad if you are that way inclined, as I often am.

Trim away any woody stalks of samphire. Boil a large saucepan of water, add the samphire and cook for 30 seconds, then cool under cold running water.

Quarter the pears, remove the cores and cut the fruit into thin slices. Press the hazelnuts gently under a rolling pin to break them into large pieces. Put these in a bowl with the samphire, pears, lettuce and herbs.

Whisk the rosehip syrup with the lemon juice and olive oil to make a dressing. Pour most of this into the bowl with the salad and mix everything together gently to coat the salad. Divide between four plates and drizzle over a little more dressing.

Serves 4 as a starter or light meal

300g (10½oz) samphire

2 medium pears

3 tbsp hazelnuts, roasted and peeled

1 small head little gem or other crisp lettuce, chopped

1 tbsp chopped fresh dill or chives

2 tbsp rosehip syrup (see page 148)

juice of ½ lemon

6 tbsp olive oil

Nettle Risotto

Bring the stock to the boil in a large saucepan and drop in the nettles for 30 seconds, remove and cool them under cold running water, drain and chop them quite finely. Lower the heat and keep the stock at a low simmer.

Meanwhile, melt one tablespoon of the butter with one of olive oil in a large saucepan. Throw in the rice and stir it well to coat the grains with oil. Cook the rice gently for 10 minutes, stirring often, then add the spring onions, garlic and nettles and cook for 1 minute more. Pour in the wine and simmer until it is absorbed. Now add a ladle or cup of the stock, about 150ml (5fl oz), and continue to simmer, stirring often until it is all but absorbed. Add another cup of stock and carry on stirring until it is absorbed and adding more until the rice is just cooked and the dish is still moist. This should take about 20 minutes. Stir in the rest of the butter and most of the cheese. Season well and serve immediately with the remaining cheese sprinkled over once at the table.

Serves 4

1.2 litres (2 pints) vegetable stock

300g (10½oz) nettle leaves

60g (2¼oz) butter

olive oil

320g (11¼oz) risotto rice, such as arborio or carnaroli

1 bunch spring onions, chopped

4 garlic cloves, finely chopped

120ml (4fl oz) dry white wine

60g (2¼oz) Desmond, Parmesan or other hard cheese, grated

salt and pepper

Sea Spinach with Oyster Mushrooms and Soba Noodles in Miso Dressing

Mix all the ingredients for the dressing together and put to one side.

Cook the noodles in simmering water according to the packet instructions until tender. Cool them a little under cold running water to stop the cooking, but leave the noodles warm.

At the same time, fry the mushrooms in a little olive oil over a medium heat for 1 minute, then add the sea spinach and spring onions, and cook for 2–3 minutes more, until the spinach is soft. Remove from the heat and add two tablespoons of the dressing over the vegetables.

Add four tablespoons of the miso dressing to the noodles and toss lightly together until the noodles are coated. Place a little on each of four plates, and top with some mushrooms and sea spinach. Repeat the layers, and finish with a little more dressing and a sprinkling of sesame seeds.

Serves 4

100g (3½oz) thin soba noodles
200g (7oz) oyster mushrooms, sliced
olive oil
100g (3½oz) sea spinach leaves
2 spring onions, sliced
1 tbsp sesame seeds, lightly toasted

FOR THE MISO DRESSING

1 tbsp white wine or rice vinegar
1 tbsp soy sauce
2 tbsp miso mixed with 2 tbsp water
1 tsp caster sugar
1 tbsp sliced ginger, pickled or fresh
1 tsp sesame oil
1 tbsp sunflower oil

Samphire Tempura with Coriander Yoghurt

Mix together the ingredients for the coriander yoghurt and put to one side.

Sift the flour and curry powder into a large bowl, add the egg yolks, water and a pinch of salt, and whisk to make a batter.

Trim any woody stalks from the samphire and break it into pieces. Heat some vegetable oil in a deep saucepan or a deep-fryer to 190°C/375°F. If you are using a saucepan, put a few drops of the batter into the oil and if it floats quickly to the top, turn the heat down to hold the temperature. Drop the pieces of samphire into the batter and roll them around until they are completely coated. Lift them out one at a time and lower them carefully into the oil. Fry for 2 minutes until crisp and golden and drain on kitchen paper. Serve with the yoghurt.

Serves 4 as a starter

FOR THE TEMPURA

225g (8oz) plain flour
2 tsp mild curry powder
2 egg yolks
375ml (13½fl oz) cold water
salt
300g (10½oz) samphire
vegetable oil, for deep frying

FOR THE CORIANDER YOGHURT

150ml (5fl oz) plain yoghurt
1 clove garlic, crushed
2 tbsp finely chopped fresh coriander

Samphire, Red Onion and Potato Frittata

As with any frittata, how many people this recipe feeds depends on how you serve it. As a main course, it will satisfy four, but it will make a snack for six, and as part of a picnic or buffet, you might even get eight slices from it.

Trim any woody stems from the samphire and break the rest into bite-sized pieces.

Heat two tablespoons of olive oil in a wide, heavy or non-stick frying pan. Put in the onions and potatoes and cook, over a medium heat, stirring often, for 10–12 minutes or until the potatoes are cooked through. Add the samphire to the pan with the parsley, increase the heat and stir the vegetables for 1 minute. Tip the vegetables from the pan into the beaten eggs, and season with black pepper.

Wipe the pan clean and brush it with olive oil. Put the pan back on the heat, pour in the egg mixture and quickly spread it flat in the pan. Cook the frittata over low heat for about 6–8 minutes until the edges are set. Loosen it a little with a spatula and place the pan under a grill or in a preheated oven (if your pan is oven-proof) at 180°C/350°F/Gas Mark 4 until the top of the frittata is set. Cut into wedges and serve.

Serves 4–6 (see introduction)

200g (7oz) samphire

olive oil

200g (7oz) red onion, thinly sliced

300g (10¹/₂oz) firm potatoes such as Nicola or Charlotte, peeled and cut into matchsticks

1 tbsp chopped fresh parsley

6 eggs, beaten

pepper

Chanterelles in Shallot and Brandy Cream

Serve these as a starter or lunch with gnocchi or with crostini. It also makes a wonderful sauce for the cabbage timbale on page 276 or a spinach-stuffed pancake.

Melt some butter in a large shallow pan, then add the chanterelles, shallots and garlic. Fry over a low to medium heat for 5–7 minutes until tender. Add the brandy and spices, bring to the boil then turn the heat down and simmer for 1 minute. Add the cream, bring back to the boil, turn the heat down and simmer for a further minute.

Serves 4
butter
120g (4¼oz) chanterelles, cleaned
2 small shallots, thinly sliced
1 garlic clove, finely chopped
100ml (3½fl oz) brandy
1 pinch freshly grated nutmeg
1 pinch cinnamon
1 pinch ground cloves
150ml (5fl oz) double cream

Roast Ceps with Shallot, Pine Nuts, Lemon and Thyme

Serve this as a starter on its own or as a main course with risotto, potato mash or some soft polenta.

Preheat the oven to 180°C/350°F/Gas Mark 4. Trim the ceps, peeling away the foamy spores if necessary. Cut into slices 1–1.5cm (½in) thick including the stem. Brush lightly with olive oil and a sprinkling of salt and roast in the oven for 10–12 minutes until tender and lightly coloured.

In a shallow pan, melt the butter and cook the shallots, pine nuts and thyme for 1 minute only over a medium heat. Off the heat, stir in the lemon zest and juice, two tablespoons of water and a little salt and pepper. Pour this over the ceps and serve immediately, pouring the juices over the mushrooms on the plate.

Serves 4
4–6 medium ceps or similar boletes
olive oil
salt and pepper
2 tbsp butter
2 small shallots, thinly sliced
2 tbsp pine nuts, toasted and chopped
1 tsp fresh thyme leaves
zest of 1 lemon
juice of ½ lemon

Sorrel and Leek Fritters

Preheat the oven to 150°C/300°F/Gas Mark 2.
Quarter the leeks lengthways, wash them and chop
them finely. Melt the butter in a medium pan and
cook the leeks over a medium heat for 6–8 minutes
until tender. Add the sorrel and nutmeg, and continue
cooking for another minute until the sorrel softens,
then transfer the cooked vegetables to a bowl to cool
a little.

Beat the eggs until frothy, stir in the flour, then
add the vegetables. Stir until combined then season
well with salt and pepper.

Heat a heavy frying pan and brush with olive oil. Drop in a tablespoon of
the mixture for each fritter, cooking over a medium heat for 5–6 minutes until the
underside is lightly coloured. Flip the fritters over and cook until the other side
is coloured and the fritters are firm. Keep the fritters warm in the oven while you
cook another batch.

Serves 4

2 medium leeks	
1 tbsp butter	
60–80g (2¼–2¾oz) sorrel	
1 pinch freshly grated nutmeg	
2 eggs	
30g (1¼oz) plain flour	
salt and pepper	
olive oil	

Pan-Roasted Puffball with Plum Tomato and Fennel Salsa

To make the salsa, quarter the fennel bulb and cut out
the core, then remove the stalk and any tough or
wrinkled parts. Chop the rest into small dice. Heat the
olive oil in a shallow pan, add the fennel and cook over
a low heat for 1 minute. Add the tomatoes, garlic and
spring onions, and cook for 1 minute more. Off the
heat, add the lemon zest and juice and a little salt and
leave to stand for a few minutes. Use the salsa warm
or at room temperature.

Cut away any dirty or damaged parts of the
puffball and slice the rest into wedges 2cm (¾in) thick.
Cut the slices into large chunks. Heat a heavy frying
pan over a medium heat. Brush the puffball slices lightly with olive oil and cook
them on the dry pan for a few minutes on each side, until coloured and heated
through. Serve the puffball wedges with some salsa spooned over each portion.

Serves 4

1 puffball, about 500g (18oz)	
olive oil	

FOR THE PLUM TOMATO AND FENNEL SALSA

1 fennel bulb	
2 tbsp olive oil	
4 plum tomatoes, peeled and diced	
1 garlic clove, finely chopped	
2 spring onions, thinly sliced	
zest and juice of ½ lemon	
salt	

Puffball, Aubergine and Leek Casserole

This recipe calls for some water or stock to be added before it goes in the oven. The strained soaking water of a few dried mushrooms would be a good way to intensify the mushroom flavour of the dish. The casserole cries out for some potatoes as an accompaniment, and the basic version of the pancakes on page 295 would be perfect.

Preheat the oven to 180°C/350°F/Gas Mark 4. Chop the aubergines into large chunks and toss them in olive oil in an oven dish. Spread them out in a single layer and roast in the oven for 20 minutes, stirring occasionally, until tender and browned.

Cut away any dirty or damaged parts of the puffball and cut the rest into wedges 2cm (³/₄in) thick. Brush these lightly on both sides with olive oil and roast them in the oven for 10–12 minutes, until tender. The slices will shrink, but if they are still too large chop them into large bite-sized pieces.

Chop the leeks into slices 2cm (³/₄in) thick. Heat two tablespoons of olive oil in a large flame-proof casserole dish or oven-proof pan and fry the leeks and garlic for 10 minutes over a medium heat, stirring often. Add the tomatoes, wine, herbs and a little salt. Bring to the boil, then turn down the heat and simmer for 5 minutes until the tomatoes have begun to break down. Add the roasted aubergine and puffball chunks and 100–150ml (3¹/₂–5fl oz) of water or stock, enough to make a slightly wet stew. Bring the casserole back to the boil, cover it loosely with baking parchment and transfer the dish or pan to the oven. Bake for 20–30 minutes until the casserole has thickened and the leeks are tender.

Serves 4
2 medium aubergines
olive oil
1 medium puffball, about 500g (18oz)
2 medium leeks, trimmed and washed
4 garlic cloves, finely chopped
6 fresh tomatoes, chopped, or
1 x 400g tin tomatoes, chopped
150ml (5fl oz) red wine
leaves from 2 sprigs fresh thyme
1 tbsp rosemary leaves, chopped
salt

Chanterelle and Sea Spinach Tarts in Hazelnut Pastry

Serve these tarts with salad as a starter or add a potato dish to make a main course.

To make the pastry, put the flour, hazelnuts and ¼ teaspoon salt into a food processor and carefully pulse in the butter until you get a fine crumb texture. Transfer the mixture to a bowl and gently work in the water. Form the pastry into a ball then roll it out to about 2mm (¹/₁₆in) thick. Cut out 4–6 circles large enough to line the base and sides of 8cm (3¼in) tart tins. Press the pastry into the tins then chill in the refrigerator for 1 hour or more. Preheat the oven to 180°C/350°F/Gas Mark 4. Prick the pastry all over with a fork and blind bake for 8–10 minutes until crisp.

Bring a large saucepan of water to the boil, add the sea spinach and cook for 2 minutes. Cool under cold running water, squeeze out all the water and chop finely. Mix the spinach with the cheese, nutmeg and eggs. Divide the spinach mixture between the pastry cases and bake in the oven for 10–12 minutes until almost set.

Meanwhile, fry the chanterelles in butter over a moderate heat for 5–7 minutes until tender. Season and press onto the tarts, then return them to the oven for a few minutes more to warm through and set.

Serves 4–6

FOR THE HAZELNUT PASTRY

150g (5½oz) plain flour

40g (1½oz) hazelnuts, finely ground

salt and pepper

75g (2½oz) cold butter

40ml (1½fl oz) cold water

FOR THE FILLING

200g (7oz) sea spinach

50g (2oz) fresh soft cheese or ricotta

large pinch freshly grated nutmeg

2 eggs, beaten

80g (2¾oz) chanterelles, cleaned and shredded

butter

Raw Cep Salad with Lemon, Chives and Pecorino

Use only the freshest small to medium ceps for this or
for any recipe calling for raw mushrooms.

Slice the mushrooms thinly and toss them with the
olive oil, lemon juice, chives and a little salt.
  Arrange the rocket, mushrooms and cheese
shavings on each plate. Offer more oil and lemon juice
when serving.

Serves 4

150g (5½oz) ceps

2 tbsp olive oil

juice of ½ lemon

1 tbsp chopped fresh chives

salt

100g (3½oz) rocket

50g (2oz) Pecorino or similar
hard sheep's cheese, shaved

Wild Mushroom, Barley and Celeriac Soup

This is a very adaptable recipe, which will accommodate any combination of mushrooms you bring home. Add the drier, tougher ones such as hedgehogs and chanterelles to the pan sooner than light but sturdy field mushrooms, and throw soft delicate ones like the amethyst deceivers in just a couple of minutes before the end of cooking.

Using the strained soaking water of some washed dried mushrooms in place of some of the stock will give the soup a deeper mushroom flavour, as will using a mix of field and forest mushrooms.

Serves 4–6

olive oil
2 medium leeks, washed and finely chopped
200g (7oz) celeriac, peeled and finely chopped
4 garlic cloves, finely chopped
leaves from 1 sprig fresh thyme
2 bay leaves
50ml (2fl oz) sherry
60g (2¹/₄oz) barley
1.5 litres (2³/₄ pints) vegetable stock
150–250g (5¹/₂–9oz) mushrooms, torn, shredded or chopped
salt and pepper
1 handful chopped fresh parsley

Heat a little olive oil in a large pan. Add the leeks, celeriac, garlic and thyme and cook over a medium heat for 5 minutes. Add the bay leaves, sherry and barley and cook for 5 minutes more. Pour in the stock, bring to the boil, lower the heat and simmer for an hour or so until the barley is soft. Add the mushrooms according to their toughness and cook until all the mushrooms are tender. Depending on what sort of mushrooms you are using, this could take up to 15 minutes. Season well with salt and pepper and stir in the parsley just before serving.

Cauliflower Fungus Tempura with Paprika and Caper Aïoli

Preheat the oven to 150°C/300°F/Gas Mark 2.

To make the aïoli, snip the tops off the garlic cloves and roast for 10–12 minutes until soft and lightly coloured. Squeeze the flesh out of the skins. Put the garlic in a food processor with the egg, egg yolk and capers, and process for a full minute. With the motor still running, pour in the olive oil in a slow stream until the aïoli has a nice dipping consistency. Transfer to a bowl, stir in the paprika, a little salt, and a squeeze of lemon juice if you like.

Sift the plain flour into a large bowl with the turmeric and a pinch of salt. Drop in the 2 egg yolks, then whisk in the cold water to make a thin batter.

Quarter the cauliflower fungus, then slice or break the quarters into smaller, thin pieces. Make sure that any hard core pieces are thinly sliced or they won't cook through in the batter.

Heat some vegetable oil, in a deep-fryer or large, deep pan, to 190°C/375°F. If using a saucepan, put a few drops of batter in the oil and if they float quickly to the top, turn the heat down to hold the temperature. Put some pieces of fungus in the batter, roll them around to coat them, lift out one at a time, shake once gently to get rid of any excess batter, then lower them into the oil. Cook for 2–3 minutes until crisp. Keep these warm in the oven while you fry another batch. Serve with the aïoli as a dip.

Serves 4

250g (9oz) plain flour
1 pinch turmeric
2 egg yolks
375ml (13½fl oz) cold water
1 small cauliflower fungus, about 300g (10½oz), washed under running water
vegetable oil, for deep frying

FOR THE PAPRIKA AND CAPER AÏOLI

4 garlic cloves, unpeeled
1 egg
1 egg yolk
1 tbsp capers
200ml (7oz) olive oil
1 tsp sweet smoked paprika
salt
squeeze of lemon juice (optional)

Cauliflower Fungus Fritters with Mustard and Chive Yoghurt

Sift the flour and baking powder together, then stir in the milk, eggs and shallot and beat to make a batter.

Break the cauliflower fungus into small pieces and stir it into the batter. Season with salt and pepper.

Heat a heavy frying pan over a medium heat and brush it generously with olive oil. Drop dessert-spoonfuls of the battered fungus into the pan, and cook for 5 minutes until golden on the underside. Flip over to cook the other side for 5 minutes more. The fritters should be firm and lightly coloured. Keep them warm in a preheated oven if you need to cook a second batch.

To make the yoghurt sauce, simply mix all the ingredients together. Serve the fritters with the yoghurt sauce spooned over the top or on the side.

Serves 4

100g (3½oz) plain flour
1 tbsp baking powder
100ml (3½fl oz) milk
2 eggs, beaten
1 small shallot, thinly sliced
150g (5½oz) cauliflower fungus, washed under running water
salt and pepper
olive oil

FOR THE MUSTARD AND CHIVE YOGHURT

200ml (7fl oz) plain yoghurt
1 tbsp chopped fresh chives
2 tsp coarse-grain mustard
1 tbsp finely diced red pepper

Amethyst Deceivers with Scrambled Eggs

This recipe is for two only because it is almost impossible to get more than two people to agree on how they like their eggs.

In a shallow stainless steel bowl, beat the eggs lightly with the milk and add in one tablespoon of butter. Season well. Set the bowl over a pan of simmering water, making sure the bottom of the bowl is clear of the water, and cook the eggs slowly, stirring occasionally with a spatula, until the eggs are as you like them. Stir in the chives.

Meanwhile, melt another tablespoon of butter in a medium pan and cook the mushrooms and garlic over medium heat until tender, about 7–10 minutes. These mushrooms leak quite a bit of moisture, which makes a nice buttery sauce. If you are feeling up to it, add a splash of brandy, sherry or white wine during the cooking. Season with salt and pepper. Serve the eggs on toast (or not as you prefer) with the mushrooms and their juices spooned over. Open a bottle of prosecco and cancel the rest of the day.

Serves 2

5 eggs
2 tbsp milk
2 tbsp butter
salt and pepper
½ tbsp chopped fresh chives
100g (3½oz) amethyst deceiver mushrooms
1 garlic clove, finely chopped
splash of brandy, sherry or white wine (optional)

Warm Salad of Hedgehog Mushrooms, Leeks and Roast Beetroot with Hazelnut Dressing

Make the hazlenut dressing by whisking together the orange zest and juice, lemon juice, olive oil and hazelnut oil. Put to one side.

Preheat the oven to 180°C/350°F/Gas Mark 4. Cut the beetroots into wedges, toss them in a little olive oil and roast in the oven for about 10–12 minutes until beginning to caramelise at the edges.

Cut the leek in half lengthways, wash it and slice it on a diagonal. Heat some olive oil in a large frying pan, then fry the leek for 8–10 minutes over a medium heat until just tender. Remove the leek from the pan and set aside. Add a tablespoon of butter and another of olive oil to the pan and cook the mushrooms over a medium heat for about 7–8 minutes until tender. Season with salt and pepper.

Toss the lettuce leaves in a little of the dressing and divide between four plates. Tuck some beetroot wedges into each portion. Scatter over the warm leeks and some hazelnuts, then finally the mushrooms. Drizzle a little more dressing over the top and serve.

Serves 4

4 medium beetroots, cooked and peeled
olive oil
1 medium leek
1 tbsp butter
150g (5½oz) hedgehog mushrooms, broken into large pieces
salt and pepper
1 head frisée lettuce, leaves separated and washed
2 tbsp hazelnuts, roasted and halved

FOR THE DRESSING

zest of 1 orange
juice of ½ orange
juice of 1 lemon
150ml (5fl oz) olive oil
2 tsp toasted hazelnut oil

Field Mushroom and Potato Gratin

Preheat the oven to 180°C/350°F/Gas Mark 4. Boil or steam the potato slices for 3 minutes, then drain.

Brush a medium oven dish with the melted butter and cover the base with a layer of potato. Scatter over half the shallot, garlic and thyme, and season with salt and pepper. Next add a layer of mushrooms. Drizzle with olive oil and season again. Repeat the layers. Press down on the top mushrooms, then place the dish in the oven and cook for 15 minutes. Pour in the cream, and return the dish to the oven for another 15 minutes, or until the cream has been absorbed and the vegetables are tender. Combine the breadcrumbs and cheese, sprinkle over the dish and cook for 5 minutes more, either in the oven or under a grill for a crispier finish.

Serves 4

600g (1lb 5oz) firm potatoes such as Nicola or Charlotte, peeled and sliced 1cm (½in) thick
a little butter, melted
4 small shallots, thinly sliced
4 garlic cloves, finely chopped
leaves from 2 sprigs fresh thyme
salt and pepper
400g (14oz) field mushrooms
olive oil
200ml (7fl oz) double cream
50g (2oz) fresh breadcrumbs
50g (2oz) Gabriel or other hard cheese, grated

Rosehip Syrup

To preserve the high vitamin C content of rosehip syrup, it should be stored in a cool, dark place. Well-sealed and sterilised bottles or jars will keep for months, but opened bottles should be kept in the fridge for no more than one week.

Makes about 3 litres (5½ pints), 10–12 jars

3 litres (5¼ pints) water	
1kg (2¼lb) rosehips	
1kg (2¼lb) caster sugar	

Bring 2 litres (3½ pints) of the water to the boil in a very large saucepan. Chop the rosehips roughly in a food processor and add them to the boiling water. Bring back to the boil, then turn off the heat and leave to stand for 15 minutes. Strain well and collect the juice. Put the rosehip mush back in the pot with 1 litre (1¾ pints) fresh water, bring it to the boil again then turn off the heat and leave to stand again for 10 minutes. Strain again. Put all of the juice in a clean saucepan, add the sugar, bring to the boil, stirring frequently and scraping down the sides, then boil for 5 minutes. Turn off the heat and leave the syrup to cool a little before pouring, while still warm, into sterilised bottles or jars and seal immediately. Put the bottles in a very large pan with cold water, bring it to the boil and simmer for 10 minutes. Remove the jars and store in a cool place.

Minted Crab Apple and Sloe Jelly

Stored in well-sealed sterilised jars, this jelly will keep right through the winter, though it is too delicious to last that long. Use it on toast, scones and muffins or to sweeten a breakfast yoghurt.

Makes about 2.2kg (4¾lb), 8–10 jars

200g (7oz) sloes	
2kg (4½lb) crab apples	
2 litres (3½ pints) water	
1kg (2¼lb) caster sugar	
1 bunch fresh mint	

Partially crush the sloes with a rolling pin. Slice the apples and put them in a very large pan with the sloes and the water. Bring to the boil, then lower the heat and simmer for 10 minutes. Mash the fruit with a potato masher, then simmer for a further 10 minutes. Strain this mash through a jelly bag, pressing down on it, to collect the juice. Put this juice back in the pan with the sugar. Bring back to the boil, reduce the heat and simmer, stirring, until the sugar is dissolved. Toss in the mint and stir for 5 minutes, then remove it again with a slotted spoon. Bring back to the boil for 1 minute. Test it by pouring a spoonful onto a plate and allowing it to cool. If it isn't quite as set as you want, boil the juice for a further minute. Pour the jelly into hot sterile jars and seal.

Rosehip, Almond and Orange Breadcrumb Cake with Cinnamon Yoghurt

Preheat the oven to 180°C/350°F/Gas Mark 4. Grease the base of a shallow rectangular baking tin, 20 x 30cm (8 x 12in) – preferably a loose-bottomed one – with baking parchment.

Mix together the caster sugar, breadcrumbs, almonds and baking powder in a large bowl, then stir in the sunflower oil, eggs and orange zest. Mix well and pour the mixture into the tin. Bake for 20–30 minutes until the cake is lightly coloured and just about set. It should still be a little wobbly when you remove it from the oven. Leave for 10 minutes or so to cool a little.

Gently warm the rosehip syrup and orange juice in a small pan over low heat, then pour it over the cake. Allow the cake to cool to room temperature before slicing it.

Whisk the cream and icing sugar together until they form soft peaks and fold in the cinnamon and yoghurt. Taste and add a little more cinnamon if necessary. Lift the cake slices out of the tin and serve with a dollop of the cinnamon yoghurt on each portion.

Serves 8

FOR THE CAKE

butter for greasing

300g (10^1/$_2$oz) caster sugar

75g (2^1/$_2$oz) stale breadcrumbs, preferably brioche

225g (8oz) ground almonds

2 tsp baking powder

200ml (7fl oz) sunflower oil

5 eggs, lightly beaten

finely grated zest of 1 orange

100ml (3^1/$_2$fl oz) rosehip syrup

juice of 1 orange

FOR THE CINNAMON YOGHURT

100ml (3^1/$_2$fl oz) whipping cream

2 tsp icing sugar, sieved

1 large pinch ground cinnamon

200ml (7fl oz) plain yoghurt

Elderflower Fritters

Cut the elderflowers just above the main stalk so the flower heads separate into individual florets.

Sift the flour and cinnamon into a large bowl, add the eggs, orange zest and juice and the sparkling water and whisk together to make a batter.

Heat the vegetable oil to 180°C/350°F in a deep saucepan or deep-fryer. If using a saucepan, put in a few drops of the batter to test the temperature. If the batter floats to the top quickly, sizzling but not too vigorously, reduce the heat to hold the temperature. Dip the florets in the batter to coat them and lower them carefully into the oil. Fry for 2–3 minutes until the batter is crisp and golden brown. Drain the fritters on kitchen paper and sprinkle liberally with icing sugar.

Serves 4

4–6 heads elderflowers

160g (5^3/$_4$oz) plain flour

1 large pinch cinnamon

2 eggs, lightly beaten

finely grated zest of 1 orange

1 tbsp orange juice

200ml (7fl oz) sparkling water

vegetable oil, for deep frying

2 tbsp icing sugar

Carrageen, Honey and Sheep's Milk Yoghurt Pannacotta with Blackberries

The addition of yoghurt to this classic Irish recipe makes it richer and creamier, as well as masking the potentially overpowering flavour of the carrageen itself. Use a good, thick, natural dairy yoghurt if the sheep's milk variety isn't available.

Serves 6

200g (7oz) caster sugar
1 tbsp water
300g (10½oz) blackberries

FOR THE PANNACOTTA

300ml (10fl oz) double cream
1 vanilla pod, split
100g (3½oz) runny honey
150g (5½oz) sheep's milk yoghurt
300ml (10fl oz) milk
8g (¼oz) carrageen, rinsed
butter, for greasing

For the pannacotta, put the cream, vanilla, honey and yoghurt in a medium saucepan and bring slowly to the boil, stirring occasionally, then remove from the heat.

In another pan, bring the milk and carrageen to the boil, lower the heat and simmer very gently until the milk becomes slightly viscous, about 7–9 minutes. It is important not to make the milk too thick at this stage to avoid setting the pannacotta too firmly. Remove the vanilla pod, then combine the liquids. Pass the mixture through a fine sieve three times to remove all the carrageen.

Lightly butter six dariole moulds and line the bases with baking parchment. Fill the moulds with the cream and milk mixture and chill for 8 hours.

Put the sugar and water in a pan and bring to a boil. Add the blackberries, bring back to a boil and simmer for 2 minutes. Remove from the heat and leave to cool to room temperature.

To serve, run a knife around the edges and carefully unmould the pannacotta and place one on each plate. Spoon some blackberries and their syrup around the pannacotta.

Damson Membrillo

This is adapted from an old recipe for damson 'cheese'.
I use the word 'membrillo' because it is probably now
a more clearly understood description. As the old name
suggests, this is a fantastic accompaniment for strong
cheeses.

Makes 100 squares

2kg (4¹/₂lb) damsons

250ml (8fl oz) water

caster sugar (see method for quantity)

sunflower oil, to grease

Put the damsons and the water in a large saucepan, bring to the boil, cover, lower
the heat, and simmer gently until the fruit is reduced to a pulp. Pass the pulp
through a coarse sieve to remove the damson stones and weigh the pulp – there
should be about 1.6kg (3¹/₄lb). Pour the pulp into the pan, return to a low heat and
cook again until the excess water has evaporated and the pulp is thick.

Weigh the sugar, allowing 350g (12oz) for each 400g (14oz) of pulp. Add the
sugar to the pulp and continue cooking over low heat, stirring frequently, until
it is very thick. The old way to test this is to draw a spoon along the bottom of the
pan – if the pulp is thick enough there will be a clean line through it.

Line a rectangular cake tin, about 20x30cm (8x12in), with baking parchment
and lightly grease it with sunflower oil. Pour the hot pulp into the lined tin and
leave it, uncovered, for 24 hours to cool and dry out. Cut the membrillo into
2cmx3cm (1inx1¹/₂in) rectangles, wrap them well in baking parchment and store
in an airtight container for up to a month.

Damson Fool

The three different sugars here might seem overkill.
However, the toffee flavour of muscovado sugar goes
very well with damsons while the icing sugar adds
a sweet note to the finished dish. The damsons seem
to absorb any amount of sugar that is added during
cooking.

Serves 6–8

100ml (3¹/₂fl oz) water

50g (2oz) caster sugar

100g (3¹/₂oz) muscovado sugar

500g (18oz) damsons

1 large pinch freshly grated nutmeg

1 large pinch cinnamon

300ml (10fl oz) whipping cream

20g (³/₄oz) icing sugar, sieved

Bring the water to the boil in a large saucepan with the
caster and muscovado sugar, then add the damsons.
Bring back to the boil, then lower the heat and simmer for 8–10 minutes until the
fruit is soft. Pass this through a coarse sieve to remove the damson stones, then
purée the rest in a blender or food processor. Leave to cool. Stir in the spices. Whip
the cream and the icing sugar together until they form soft peaks, then fold this
into the fruit purée. Serve with shortbread or sponge fingers.

Sloe Gin

Traditionally, the sloes are each pricked many times with a pin to aid the release of their flavour. It didn't sound like a fun evening to me, so I use the lazy method described below, and it works just fine.

Makes 1.5 litres (2¾ pints)
450g (1lb) sloes
225g (8oz) caster sugar
1 litre (1¾ pints) gin

Clean the sloes, put them in a freezer bag and leave them in the freezer overnight. Next day, bash the bag with a rolling pin to bruise but not split the sloes. Put the sloes in a clean vessel, such as a large preserving jar or a few wine or gin bottles. I use two 1 litre (1¾ pint) gin bottles. Add the sugar and gin, dividing it equally if you are using more than one container, seal and shake well. Leave in a cool place and shake the bottles every two days for a week or so. Then shake them only once a week for two months. The gin is ready after two months but will keep for much longer, depending on how much you like it.

...and a Damn Fine Martini

Despite the innate sourness of sloes, sloe gin is sweet and so this martini needs the balancing character of the vermouth, bitters and lemon.

3 parts sloe gin
1 part dry vermouth
3 drops of Angostura bitters per serving
lemon peel twists, to garnish

Put the ingredients into a cocktail mixer with some ice and shake briefly. Pour into glasses, leaving the ice behind. Add a lemon twist to each glass.

A passionate pursuit

The beginning of agriculture is one of the most critical points in our history. It might even be said that it defines the beginning of civilisation. When we humans stopped going out searching for food and instead began the process of learning to produce it from seed, we took a step away from the wilderness. That step opened up all sorts of possibilities, not least in terms of time made available for other activities. With the food supply sorted, we turned our minds to other domestic skills such as shelving and plumbing, and then, ultimately, to matters of high culture. When we got so far as to delegate growing to those best suited to it, the rest of us were free to become whatever we wished. Freed from the need to produce or find our own food, we could specialise in an endlessly expanding array of professions and hobbies. There might be time to write a play, perhaps, or form a pop group. Agriculture may also be the root cause of domestic strife. Think of the consequences of the change at home when the men stopped going AWOL for days at a time to 'find food', and took to pottering around in the garden instead, even coming inside to do a little cooking. Is it going too far to suggest it also caused the invention of golf, as a means of getting rid of them again for a day, perhaps even a whole weekend on the Algarve?

Indeed, agriculture might ultimately be blamed for causing the appearance in the 1970s of the career guidance counsellor. Still, these all reflect intrinsic human weaknesses that would no doubt have emerged even if we were still foraging for food and living in caves, and agriculture remains at the heart of civilisation no matter how ridiculously we behave.

Growers, the good ones at any rate, have an intense affinity with their crops and a huge respect for the miracle of the food that nature provides. Then they start messing with it. It may seem like a surprising thought, but it is the essential nature of a grower to manipulate – they can't afford to just sit around watching the plants grow, hoping things turn out well. While respecting the almost unbendable season of asparagus, growers will nonetheless stretch that of spinach, courgettes or broccoli as far as they can, and at both ends if possible. As good as last year's crop might have been, they are constantly on the lookout for the seed of a variety that is reputed to have better flavour, bigger yields or an impressive natural resistance to disease. Everything that a grower does, and the timing of it, is focused on the ultimate goal of producing the best crop possible for as long as there is demand. It involves a constant process of trial, experimentation and hard, painful work, but let's not encourage the moaning.

The careful nurturing and manipulation of plants starts with seed selection and protective germination, often in a warm, controlled

environment. It carries through to the field, where pruning, weeding, thinning, spacing and feeding give the plant every chance to produce to the best of its potential. There are some extreme practices such as protecting vegetables from the light to encourage them to grow white instead of green. Even that is nothing compared to talking to the damn things, which I know people do, probably more than is suspected or admitted. Some encourage with kind and gentle words, while others prefer to take a firm, school-masterly line. I imagine cabbages respond best to this.

In the cooler climate of northern Europe, probably the greatest manipulation lies in the use of glasshouses and, more recently and commonly, plastic polytunnels. Where the glasshouse has for centuries given the aristocracy access to exotic foods of foreign climes, the polytunnel has democratised that access. Tunnels are used to create a space with higher temperatures and protection from wind. In them, plants thrive and ripen fully that might otherwise struggle outside. Tomatoes are particularly successful, as are beans and summer herbs, along with grapes, strawberries and other fruit that need long hot days to ripen. Salad leaves that would have a short season outside can be produced all year round.

From the viewpoint of advocating local produce, it might seem improper to grow things that are not indigenous to the area, the culture and the environment, but that would be to deny the history of vegetable growing and the movement of vegetables since ancient times across continents and between hemispheres. This is the outer edge of growing, reaching for the limits of possibility, driven by curiosity and a desire to widen the palette of foods we have to work with in the kitchen.

We humans are inquiring by nature, always looking for the new and undiscovered, curious about what we don't already know or haven't seen. Explorers may have wooed wealthy sponsors by disguising the purpose of their travels using the language of economics, but you can be sure that their own motivation would have been due just as much to a fierce inquisitiveness. When this innate curiosity is applied to food, it becomes a search for pleasure, for new flavours and new variations. Food (after water) is our most essential need, but it is also our greatest sensory indulgence. We think about food more often and with more longing than anything else, sex included. Well, most of us do. We love to eat and we take pleasure from food in so many different ways. Depending on our mood, we can enjoy the comfort of the familiar or the sensation of novelty, sometimes even in the same meal, if we are so inclined. Food pushes our sensory buttons by appealing to all the senses simultaneously – taste, smell, texture and colour – in an incredibly complex and satisfying way; and it acts as a catalyst for so much of our social interaction, including the conviviality of good company and, yes, sex too. Food leads to sex, it's true, but you hardly need me to tell you that.

The history and development of what we eat is a story of trial and error driven by curiosity, but food is too serious an issue, too vital to our wellbeing, for it to exist in some kind of laboratory of cheap thrills. The discovery and distribution of staple foodstuffs such as potatoes, wheat and rice was all about providing cheap and consistent sustenance, but the foods that excite us are the peripherals, the ones that add the pleasure of intense flavour to the staples. Tomatoes, chillies, sweet peppers, herbs, spices, pungent leaves, even artichokes, are all foods that stimulate our taste buds but they can't sustain us on their own. Most fruits also fall into this bracket. Though they can have great nutritional qualities and are important for all-round health, we eat them and value them primarily for the pleasure of their flavours. Spices may have medicinal qualities, applied since ancient times, but they don't feed us, don't fill us up, and they were never likely to replace spuds or rice on our plates. That hasn't prevented us from going to extraordinary lengths to get hold of them, not even stopping short of war. Chickpeas may be a very important staple around the rim of the Mediterranean, but when you have enough chickpeas to be beyond worrying about starvation, it is the mint, basil, cumin seeds and cardamom, the pomegranate and aubergines, that make dinner more than just an exercise in survival.

It's a good thing that, as a species, we produce enough adventurous individuals to go out and find the new, to keep us all from boredom. Even when we think we know with absolute certainty what we like to eat, and we are satisfied that we have it in reassuring abundance, culinary curiosity and experimentation will see to it that what we like to eat keeps on quietly evolving.

The living traditions of an evolving food culture

This constant search for the new in food might seem to be anti tradition, and yet the new and the old often sit happily alongside each other. Because if there is one thing we value as highly as this month's new sensations it is the comfort of foods that are part of our history. That includes the history of the culture we belong to in the wider sense, as well as the personal histories we inherit and create.

The traditional and the innovative are seen as opposing ideas only by people entrenched in extreme camps. This faux battle plays out in other cultural areas too, especially music. For every bold young pup who wants to break the mould – play a jig at twice the speed with half the notes, and on a theremin – there is another for whom the only way is the one passed down by his father's father. While one is consciously thrashing tradition to see what will happen, the other is blindly refusing to allow his personality to affect his culture. One is trying to knock down walls that the other is desperately holding together with old mortar. Perhaps both are essential, creating a balance between them.

A living tradition, one that is grounded in the past but alive in the present, with a value and relevance to both the producers and consumers within it, must include the innovative and the new. And the momentum that drives it must be in the hands of active practitioners who bring their own personalities to it.

Is this relevant to food? I think it's obvious that it is. Certainly, here in Ireland, this is a debate that quietly simmers away all the time. For all I know, it may be a hot topic in Greece, Denmark and Estonia too. It certainly is in Sweden. I spent ten days working at a country hotel/cookery school there where the students were given a wonderful education in modern European cooking, at the same time as learning how to prepare the food peculiar to their own country. This involved, amongst other weird obsessions, a unique use of fruit in savoury cooking, often reduced, stewed or caramelised. And a voracious appetite for mustard. I sat down to a first lunch in a tiny village 300 kilometres west of Stockholm, during which the two chefs I was meeting put away in just one meal a timid Irish family's weekly supply of intensely hot mustard. But they and the younger staff and students were equally aware of their place in modern Europe. They were eager to cook with fashionable produce and recipes, while holding on to their own traditions. It's a juggling act, but one that they were approaching with the open, curious minds of people who know they want to engage with the rest of the world while still confident in their own culture.

The debate that simmers here in Ireland, coming to the boil from time to time, is whether we have a worthwhile food history, and whether much of what goes on in domestic and professional kitchens is part of any live tradition. Essentially: have we dumped our food history and are we now mostly cooking 'foreign' food? We love this kind of stuff. Navel-gazing, self-absorbed, often drink-fuelled discussion, about our Irishness and the nature of Irishness is a national sport. I waded naively into it with a comment I made in the introduction to my first book, The Café Paradiso Cookbook. A comment with which I have been flogged once or twice since.

I said our supposed food tradition was really just a scrappy collection of dishes, only some of which were worth eating or cooking; and that

I regarded our culture as a blank page to be developed in any way that we wanted. I saw this as an exciting prospect that cooks in deep-rooted food cultures such as Italy and France don't have the same freedom to do. Being a little older now, I regret the lazy negativity of the first half of that statement. I was reacting to the endless trotting out of cabbage 'n' spud combinations as 'Irish' dishes worthy of attention. God spare us, though I like cabbage and potatoes as much as the next native. Putting it down in ink may even have been subconsciously, if not deliberately, provocative. But I accept that I was also closing my eyes and my mind to the strong traditions of local produce, market gardening, wild foods and milk products of extraordinary quality.

Nonetheless, I stand by the second part of the statement. When I wrote it, I was thinking only in terms of restaurant cooks, in the belief that this is where our new food culture would evolve from. And it is happening there, in our restaurant kitchens, to some extent. The real action, the driving energy, is coming from the public and from the food producers. So much has changed in the intervening years, including the ethnic make-up of the population. Not only has the potential begun to blossom, but that potential has itself grown exponentially.

When I fantasised about a self-inventing food culture, I had only a vague idealistic notion of how it might come about. Shortly after, it was obvious that the opportunity that was opening up before us wasn't about new recipes that might be invented in restaurant kitchens. Instead, it was about the possibilities for connecting, possibly even re-connecting, with the food itself and with the producers, and to let this dictate how we cooked and ate. Seasonal eating, paying attention to the potential of the produce, engaging with producers, buying local: these are all the elements. It is here, between the producer, the retailer and the public, that the real growth of a food culture is taking place. And it is in the kitchens of food lovers that the living tradition is being nurtured.

But visitors and some curious natives still ask the same question: what is Irish food and where is it going? The answer is the same, but the details are more exciting than ever. Irish food is food produced, cooked and consumed on the island by people who live here, irrespective of their own birthplace, the ethical origin of the recipes they use or the supposed cultural home of the ingredients. The food that my grower, Ultan, produces is no less Irish for being pak choi rather than cabbage, purple potatoes rather than Kerrs Pinks, or aubergines rather than parsnips. The way that swede turnips from a stall in West Cork can be used in an obviously Indonesian-style recipe is as Irish as the soft summer rain. We can grow aubergines now, and plum tomatoes too, which means we can cook Mediterranean dishes without importing the produce. Did I say Mediterranean? I wonder if there is a hardcore of southern Italians who refuse to accept the tomato as native, since it was imported from the Americas as recently as the sixteenth century. Unlikely, I imagine. The issues of origin are largely irrelevant, whether they relate to the producer, the produce, the cook or the recipe. The vibrant, living tradition that is Irish food in the twenty-first century is being fuelled by those who are most aware of the importance of food in their lives. And that is a rapidly growing and very engaged section of the population.

My current passions

The vegetables and fruit covered in this chapter might appear to be a disparate, unconnected bunch, but – trust me – there is a connecting thread. Maybe it's more than a single thread, more of a small web, spun around the relationship between grower and cook. For the most part, the vegetables here are ones that might not be seen as indigenous to the place where I live and work; some might be thought of as exotic and many would not crop successfully in the outdoors. I am fortunate to work with a grower, Ultan Walsh, who doesn't yet know his own limitations or those of his terrain. Long may his optimism last. I think he often becomes quietly infuriated when he sees me using produce he believes he could grow. At other times, I have asked him to try growing something when I am frustrated with the quality available from other sources. Or it might be that I can get what I want but not in the exact size, freshness or specific variety I would like.

There are a few vegetables here too that are old and familiar ingredients, native to the climate, that have fallen out of favour due to being uneconomical to grow or perceived as old-fashioned. All, however, are fruit or vegetables that I would source somehow because I couldn't imagine working without them. This is the essence of it – finding ways to not only replace imported crops but also to source varieties that work well here and which can be obtained in the freshest state possible and at the right stage of maturity. Even the seemingly mundane, such as courgettes, broad beans or gooseberries, take on a renewed value when they are locally sourced from a grower who harvests them to your specific needs. The selection is, of course, both very personal and specific to a year in my life. Chances are that if I were to put this collection together again at another time, the content would be somewhat different, which is how it should be. All cultivated vegetables and fruits need nurturing to some extent, but these are ones that have been a central focus of the experimentation and consultation between kitchen and producer over a period of one intense year.

Mr Pak Choi and his sidekick Tofu cross the cultural borders

One evening, early in the life of Café Paradiso when every rare and precious spare minute was still greedily grabbed for experimentation, I tried marinating tofu in red wine and herbs. The idea was to move it away from its natural Eastern styling and create something 'European' with it. I wanted to do something elegant with slices of tofu, hoping they would absorb the flavours of red wine and herbs as well as they do soy sauce-based marinades. It worked, in so far as the flavours went in, but it tasted truly disgusting. The tofu soaked up the red wine and then released it again in the mouth. Not nice. Maybe I'd done something wrong, maybe a few adjustments would have given the result I was hoping for, or even a completely unexpected result that was nonetheless edible. But after one attempt, I went back to thinking of tofu as an Eastern food that needed appropriate flavouring. Even now, as I write this, the part of my mind not engaged in typing and remembering is actively pursuing the possibilities again. Hmm ...

Anyway, the point is that I gave up on doing tofu à la européenne. Phew! Europe sighs with relief. Now, I don't claim to have any inside information on specific Asian cuisines. Sure, I've got the cookbooks, like most of you, and I've travelled a little, but I've always been more of a magpie, taking a little of this culture and that cooking style to make dishes that are somehow coherent but not necessarily faithful to a historic culture.

It may have something to do with the influence of the often maligned 'fusion' cooking that made quite an impression on me in its early years. The best fusion cooking combined the flavours and ingredients of East and West in a way that could sound alarming on paper but worked on the plate and, more importantly, in the mouth. The general style was often criticised by the food press, particularly in the UK, where it was wrongly seen as simply a new trend. In the Pacific countries of New Zealand and Australia – and in California too – fusion cooking was less a trend and more an expression of their evolving populations and the way that they saw themselves.

These countries were shaking off their colonial heritage and coming to terms with the physical reality of their locations on the globe. The young chefs, brought up on both Anglo and classical European (read 'French') cooking, were becoming interested simultaneously in fashionable Italian food and the dishes and ingredients of their nearest neighbours in Asia. Fusion cooking was an expression of growing individuality and self-confidence. Some of the food was awful, but so is a lot of professional cooking. (If you don't believe me, take a stroll into town and have dinner at, say, the fourth restaurant you come across. Chances are you won't go back.) Fusion was no worse than any pioneering venture. There were,

MR PAK CHOI (MAI QING VARIETY)

and still are, a few great chefs doing it and there were cocksure cowboys. Nothing new there.

Right now, as for the past few years, there is a dish on the Paradiso menu consisting of tofu briefly marinated in a very hot and sweet marinade based on the Indonesian chilli sauce *sambal oelek*. The tofu is then seared in a frying pan, the marinade is added back in and cooked over a high heat so that it forms a glaze on the outside of the tofu slices, leaving the centres relatively bland. We serve it on some pak choi that has been briefly cooked in a broth of coconut milk flavoured with lemongrass, ginger, basil and coriander. It's a mild and soothing base for the spiced tofu. Just so you don't get bored over dinner, there is also a little mound of fresh noodles with sesame and some deep-fried wonton filled with mashed aduki beans flavoured with tomato and ginger.

The dish is clearly Asian, isn't it? Not specifically or authentically belonging to any one cuisine, but in the general sense. This might well be due to my inherent laziness about research, but I prefer to think of it as acknowledging the fluid nature of food styles across cultures and times. Not everyone agrees. Jing Li is a young man from China who is in Ireland to study the English language, amongst other things. Li does some dishwashing to earn a few euros and keep himself out of the pubs. When it comes to dinner time, he is as predictable as rain in April. The tofu dish, every time. Sure? Fancy a change tonight? No, the tofu, please. After a few weeks, I asked him about it, whether he liked the dish, suggesting I could improve it for him. Under a little pressure, he admitted he didn't like coconut milk. The rest – tofu, chilli, sugar, soy sauce, pak choi, noodles, wonton filled with aduki beans – all of that was good, but coconut he didn't really fancy, seeing it as alien to the other tastes in the dish. Now we're not arguing here; I'm confident the dish works, though in my head it's mostly Thai/Indonesian with some Chinese influence. To Li, however, who is very traditional in his tastes, it is decent Chinese food with a dodgy south Asian coconut thing going on. So I came up with a version for him that flavours the pak choi with the tastes he prefers. One or two of the other staff have taken to it too but some find it heavy on soy and chilli.

As Asian as the dish seems, it's worth looking at where the produce actually comes from. The tofu is produced in England, the noodles are freshly made in Cork by Iago, the wonderful cheese and pasta shop. By day the same noodles are 'tagliolini' on the lunch menu, by night they dress up as 'Asian egg noodles'. I like the multiple ironies of it all. As our palates and our repertoire of recipes become more and more internationalised, the challenge in maintaining a local element to the food lies in its production.

In the definition of a living food tradition, it matters not that the recipe is intrinsically Asian when the primary ingredients are local. Now, how do I convince someone to try growing coconuts?

The pak choi I use, as often as not (and it annoys me when it's not), is from Ultan's farm ten miles south of Cork. Ultan is still in experimental mode with pak choi so there are gaps and crop shortfalls. Sometimes I resort to a local Chinese shop. The woman behind the counter once admitted that she's unhappy with the imported stuff, too. It comes from Holland the slow way around and is bad as often as it is good. You could never actually guess that from what she puts in the bag for you because she always angrily trims all the dodgy leaves off with a cleaver and sells the decent hearts of pak choi by weight. She asked if my guy would grow for her as well. I had to tell her that it wasn't going to happen, what with the supply still erratic and the price probably too high. In a market that is always looking for the lowest price, the small and local can't compete. On the other hand, low price isn't always best value, as evidenced by the amount of stuff she chucks out, unable to bring herself to pass it on in the European way – buy cheap, sell cheap, waste is the buyer's problem.

Pak choi, bok choi, and all the other names you might encounter for Chinese brassicas (I call them all pak choi to cut down the confusion) may be as alien to Europe as ET on a bicycle, and we may indeed almost always cook them in Asian-style dishes. But the thing is that they grow easily and well here. Pak choi is essentially a cool season plant, producing best from early autumn through to early summer, though it is possible to produce it year round in an unheated polytunnel. It grows quickly, too, which is a nice change from the long wait needed for European cabbages, and most varieties like to be watered frequently. Welcome to Ireland, Mr Pak Choi! There are risks of bolting and of crop failure, but isn't that all part of a grower's lot?

Of the great many varieties of pak choi, there are a few that are best suited to our climate. After a few trials, Ultan settled on a green-stemmed one that goes by the name of Mai Qing, declaring it to be the best he'd ever tasted. So he grows what he likes, as always. That's good enough for me. This one grows well in this climate and many experts say it has the best flavour, being less watery in the stem and with a slight touch of mustard in the leaf. Like most pak choi that has been picked while still quite small, it can be cooked whole, or cut in half lengthways, or you can cut the base off and use the individual leaves. Pak choi needs very little cooking, and is best stir-fried, lightly steamed or braised quickly with a little soy sauce. It also works wonderfully either lightly cooked in warm salads or served raw in cold ones.

Of obsession, curiosity and the mythical artichoke farm

Back when my grasp of local food culture was barely more than a pup, I would hear occasional talk among those who know such things that there was an artichoke farm down in Allihies in West Cork. A *what* farm? In those days, artichokes seemed unbelievably exotic, if vaguely ridiculous, something that the untrustworthy Continentals dabbled in. What's more, Allihies is not the West Cork of softly rolling hills and vividly green fields scattered with grazing cows bursting with rich milk. No, Allihies is way out on the end of the Beara Peninsula, one of the most remote and rugged extremities of the whole island. It is visually stunning, certainly. There is a sad, tragic beauty in the landscape of rocky, barren hills and wild seas. Although the area was once heavily populated, the land mostly looks like it could never have produced much more than rock and thin grazing for tough, mountainy sheep and goats.

Over the years, this by now mythical artichoke farm still came across my radar from time to time. A combination of shortage of detail and the distance from Cork city meant that tales of its existence remained sketchy.

I have been to Allihies a few times on short holidays to the edge of the Atlantic, soul-cleansing weekends in the wild west and all that, but I never saw an artichoke. It's true to say I wasn't looking for one, but it worries me that this undermines my fantasy. Because, somewhere in my mind, I have been carrying an image of one of the many recognisable stony hills of the area covered in thousands, maybe millions, of artichoke plants.

More recently, and even while working with Ultan, a grower who has a passion for the vegetable, I rarely hear tell of the artichoke farm any more. Indeed, I had forgotten all about it until it came up in conversation with a friend, another vegetable grower, who swears she visited and even filmed with a TV crew there some years back. Even then, the details were vague, not enough to demythologise the place for me. Maybe I like it that way: holding on to my illusion of a huge field sloping from the horizon to the small cliff over the sea, with thousands of green and purple artichoke heads swaying just a little in the fierce Atlantic wind. Only a true obsessive could think of creating such a thing, someone who was afflicted with a need to grow the plant, but wouldn't move from the glorious location. And what would become of the fruit in a country that preferred turnips? Suddenly the image in my head changes and all the heads have sprouted fabulous flowers of blue and purple. Beautiful flowers but wasted vegetables.

My dilemma in thinking about it again was how much, if any, research to do. In the interest of at least approaching the truth of it, I decided to do a little. It wasn't hard because the place and the obsessive creator existed all right. But I'll say no more in case you've formed your own mental image. Except that the location wasn't mad at all. The mild year-round climate and softly damp sea air mirror the conditions of coastal Brittany, where artichokes thrive. Obsessives aren't mad; it can just look that way to the mere hobbyist.

When talk turns to the issue of how humans took to eating certain foods, artichokes will always make an appearance among the most unlikely vegetables. Indeed Jonathan Swift's quip that it was 'a bold man that first ate an oyster' could just as easily apply to an artichoke. Take a good look at one. Many of us have them in our gardens as decorative plants, tall thistles that they are, with their strikingly beautiful pink or purple flowers bursting out the top. How did anyone decide to eat that? Think of the determination required to go in there, pulling off the tough leaves to see, just to see, if there might be something worth popping in one's mouth. Then to find that in the centre there was a mess of hair, the 'choke' as it is now known. And to doggedly wade through all that before coming to – finally – the wonderful jewel that is the base, the heart, of an artichoke? And how ecstatic might that person have been when he or she first tasted it? Surely this has to be one of the most heroic acts of perseverance in food history. The motivation could only have been a combination of curiosity and a dedicated epicurism. Artichokes are almost a definition of pleasure as reward for effort.

Of course, artichokes didn't just recently spring out of the ground, putting out baseball-sized shiny green heads. It's generally thought that they probably developed in North Africa or Sicily, from the cardoon, a coarse cousin with a much smaller head. The cardoon is a vegetable that still survives and makes occasional revivals in the food fashion stakes even now. Both the small head and the stalk of a cardoon are eaten and they were considered a delicacy by the Greeks and Romans. (Now, there are two cultures who knew a thing or two about the pleasures of the table.)

In Siena a few years ago, I ate a plate of mixed artichokes and cardoons. The highly rated restaurant had an atmosphere of mild eccentricity combined with a serious love of food. In a room of random pieces of furniture and shelves crammed with cookery books were seated a mixture of earnest, out-of-town foodies – me included – and families of natives, including kids still doing their homework, having the best supper for miles around. Seeing this dish on the menu seemed to present the perfect opportunity to compare these two related vegetables. When I actually tried them, however, the pairing only served to highlight the superiority of the artichoke, in my view, in taste, texture and appearance. Maybe they weren't the best cardoons in the world, so I'd like to say my mind remains open to at least giving them another chance one day. That evening I would have gladly swapped all my cardoons for one more artichoke.

In Italy there is a preference for the small, usually purple, variety of artichoke, which can be eaten whole or with minimal preparation. If people had become accustomed to eating these relatively accessible treasures as they evolved from cardoons, then the mystery of the impenetrable and unlikely vegetable evaporates. By the time we had moved on to those hairy green monsters tamed for consumption at Francophile dinner parties, the information was out there that these things were definitely edible. Not only that, but it was no secret that the heart was worth going after. Hold on to that thought while you learn to trim an artichoke.

With the exception of a small number of restaurants and the homes of dedicated fans, artichokes are still rarely eaten in Ireland. In France, they have made a ritual out of the long, slow process of eating the artichoke from the outside in, one leaf at a time, each leaf a little more succulent and generous with the scraping of soft flesh against teeth. Eventually, when the leaves are all off and strewn around the table, the choke is scooped out and disdainfully discarded before the heart is greedily consumed. This is undoubtedly a sensual ritual, and in the right company you might well see why artichokes are sometimes thought to be an aphrodisiac. Oh, those French, I hear you say, and notice the eye-rolling that goes with it.

To prepare artichokes in this way requires no more than slicing off the top inch or so and steaming or boiling the rest until a leaf comes away easily. Usually a little aïoli, vinaigrette or softly melted butter is used as a dip for the leaves. As if there wasn't enough excitement! In the restaurant, we carve out the base, the heart. This is nobody's favourite job: the large artichokes are tough and nothing comes off them willingly or straightforwardly. We boil the hearts and often roast them afterwards, before using them in many different ways, including stuffed or sliced, coated in breadcrumbs and fried.

In Italy, and especially in the south, you will see graded piles of medium, small and tiny artichokes on sale in the markets. Often the stall-holder will be armed with a sharp paring knife and a bowl of water with lemon juice in it. He or she will prepare the artichokes for you at a speed that makes nothing of the chore. And with these artichokes it really isn't a chore at all. When the buds are young, there is no hairy choke, and almost all of the leaves and much of the stem are perfectly edible. With even the biggest, it's simply a matter of trimming away the toughest part of the outer leaves to expose the tender yellow/pale green part, and peeling the stalk and the 'shoulder' of the base. When the artichoke is then cut in half lengthways, you can see that it is indeed wholly edible. The business of the

IMPERIAL STAR ARTICHOKES

lemon water is to stop the vegetables discolouring, and is essential whenever you work with artichokes.

The perception of artichokes as being difficult to prepare persists for a number of reasons. By and large, we don't come across them often enough, and when we do it is usually in the form of the green monsters. There is no denying that these guys are intimidating if you want to do any more than eat them leaf by leaf. Yet if we had a better supply of the smaller varieties, I think a lot of the fear would disappear.

Ultan has been cultivating a number of varieties over the past few years, as his obsession with artichokes grows. The smaller Italian purple varieties are great for an early cropping of succulent buds. But a favourite for both of us is a medium-sized green variety called Imperial Star. This beauty can grow up to 10cm (4in) long without getting to the stage of producing a choke, which means it has a high proportion of fleshy leaf and edible stem. It is a joy to work with, and a good chef can get through a crate of them almost as fast as a Sicilian market seller, and without frowning or swearing too much. In any case, ours is a civilised kitchen, so I always assume that any invoking of deities is in fact prayer and not swearing.

Once you have prepared smaller artichokes by trimming and peeling them, they can be used in many ways. My favourite at the moment is to fry them with garlic and thyme, and a touch of lemon, either by simply adding the juice and rind at the end of cooking or by serving them with a lemon-flavoured sauce. Artichokes also go well in a stew with carrots, borlotti beans and some tomato. The medium-sized ones are great stuffed, either whole or cut in half lengthways. Olives, pine nuts, soft cheeses and herbed breadcrumbs make good stuffings, if not necessarily all together. Artichokes are good in salads, too, warm or cold, sliced or shredded, boiled, grilled or roasted. Raw artichoke salad is a classic dish, with lemon, olive oil and some shavings of Parmesan, on its own or mixed with rocket leaves.

Renewing the ancient cult of broad beans, a communion of souls

One day in early spring, strolling through infant broad bean plants, Ultan asked me a blunt but deceptively complex question: 'Why do you buy broad beans?' I tried to pass it off with a smartass 'Because you grow them', but he pointed out that he loves broad beans and, to occasionally have them for his supper, he must grow his own, because he would never buy them. Like many growers, he doesn't buy vegetables. Well, perhaps the odd onion or two when he runs out, or some clementines to keep the sniffles at bay in winter, but he always goes to town disguised as an old lady in case the other growers doing the same thing spot him in the local M&S.

What he meant by the question was that they are expensive to buy fresh and involve a certain amount of (expensive) labour, which reduces the 10kg (22lb) you bought to about 2kg (4^1/$_2$lb). And all this while there are packets of perfectly fine broad beans sitting in the freezer of the local supermarket for some cheap price I don't even want to think about. Freezing does for broad beans as it does for peas, interrupting the process of the plant's sugar turning to starch, so that when you take them out of the freezer to eat them, the beans are as close to fresh as they could be. In fact, this is what we do in Café Paradiso during the height of the broad bean season. A couple of 10kg boxes come in every day, and they are podded by various people through the day until all are done before the last chefs on the evening shift get a sip of beer. Well, truth be told, the last of them are often done with a beer in one hand. That way, the chore is closer to the domestic version glorified in the image of a family sitting on the porch, podding beans and sipping beer or iced tea. The beans we don't use immediately go in the freezer and a stock is built up, all as fresh as on the day they arrived.

Podding broad beans is easily the most sensual pleasure of all the repetitive kitchen chores. The dark green pod splits easily, and inside you find anything from four to eight beans nestled in a soft cushion of white fur. A broad bean's early days are the most luxurious and pampered of any vegetable. The first time you see this, it is at once surprising and quite moving. Though you become used to it, every time you split a fresh broad bean pod, there is still a twinge of delight at the careful, mollycoddling beauty of it all.

I admit that broad beans are one of those vegetables for which I stretch the season. While local beans are the heart and core of the season for me, I can't say no when I am offered a box of Italian beans at a time when local broad bean plants are only flowers with good intentions. At the other end of the season, when Ultan's are almost gone, another source from further west kicks in with his first crop. This is an unusual approach to the issue of stretching seasons. By planting later and praying harder for an Indian summer, some growers avoid the high-season rush. Instead of feeling jealous on seeing that your neighbour's crop is a week ahead, you can relax in the smug assurance – or hope – that the market will be all yours when you're ready to sell. It does take a little faith, but what is a farmer without faith?

Behind it all, there is a fundamental reason why I buy fresh broad beans – quite simply, I love them. Frozen beans, no matter how close they come, just don't do it for me, maybe because of their uniformity of size and character. The first fresh broad beans of the season, tiny green babies in their cotton-wool pods, are delicate and sweet harbingers of summer.

They are equally delicious raw or very lightly boiled. Throw a few into a pasta dish, a risotto or a salad. Do no more than toss them in lemon juice, olive oil and salt and eat them as a snack. Through the season, the beans get bigger, the texture becomes denser and their skins may need to be peeled off for some dishes. Mostly, the recipes remain the same, though the bigger beans can take stronger flavouring, such as garlic, summer herbs and even a little chilli. The denser texture also makes the beans suitable for mashing and for stew-like summer soups.

It bothers me how broad beans have become a peripheral vegetable in the general scheme of things. They are thought to be one of the oldest crops, and were an important staple for millennia in Europe, North Africa and the Middle East. Even now, the broad bean still has a strong role in many parts of the world. In Europe, however, it seems as though the vegetable is simultaneously seen as an old-fashioned garden plant from another time, and a highly fashionable ingredient, the latter mainly due to the attention it gets in some restaurant kitchens.

The most bewildering thing about it is the range of emotions that the broad bean can elicit from people. For everyone who thinks the taste is worth the trouble to prepare, there must be a hundred who disagree. While they are loved by a minority and ignored by many, there are plenty who will tell you straight up that they hate broad beans. Now, I don't understand people who can muster up such disgust for vegetables in general or for one in particular. I just don't see what it is in a vegetable, in terms of taste, texture or colour, that can cause such a strong negative reaction, though I can accept that people might not actually get excited by particular vegetables. When it comes to broad beans, I assume I'm too close and like them too much to understand.

So, I get to thinking it must be something traumatic, a bad experience from childhood, perhaps, that makes people hate broad beans so. Or maybe there is something else I've been missing. According to Alan Davidson's *Oxford Companion to Food*, the ancient Egyptians and Greeks ate loads of broad beans but, in a weird paradox, thought them unclean and that the souls of the dead might be contained in them. Pythagoras forbade his followers to eat them. Davidson quotes from a Roman writer, one Diogenes Laertius: 'Beans are the substance which contains the largest portion of that animated matter of which our souls are particles.' What can you make of that? Is it possible that modern bean-haters are tuned into some ancient dread that they themselves are unaware of and could never rationalise? A fear of consuming dead souls? Or is it that beans were perceived as consisting of living matter similar to that which makes up our own human souls, making

their consumption a form of cannibalism? Either way, it must have been a challenging dichotomy for those who insisted on consuming the beans. And if you're going to miss out on one of the finest vegetables, it should be for a damned good reason, such as protecting your soul. That way, too, I can accept the fact that broad beans are likely to remain a cult, with a devoted minority of fans, for some time yet. And perhaps, deep down, it is why those of us who advocate them continue to campaign for broad beans to be rescued from their fate and hauled back into the mainstream.

Borlotti, mottled beauties of the bean world

Like broad beans, borlotti attract a cult following, though not for any spiritual reasons that I've heard of. Though they are available in canned, dried and frozen form, none of these compare to the beautiful fresh beans, picked at just the right stage of maturity. Therein lies at least part of the reason for their relative scarcity. Borlotti grow in long, fat pods of a striking mottled pink colour. The beans inside have the same shading, often with a light green background. The vines are slow growing, and when they do eventually produce those elegant pods, the yield is a relatively small one for the input involved, though each pod is bursting with fat round beans. At this stage, you need to go carefully through the vines, picking the pods that are clearly full and mature. If you don't get to them, the beans will begin to dry on the vine. This is all very handy if you want dried beans, but if you want fresh ones, some vigilance is needed.

So why bother? The answer is the usual one – simply because the beans are unique and irreplaceable. After a trial year, Ultan has produced two further crops, each a little bigger than the previous one. If any of the crops had been unsuccessful or if the beans had proved disappointing, he might have abandoned the idea. But now, well, it's a case of no turning back. Borlotti have become a promise at the end of the summer. When the crops of other, more delicate vegetables are fading away, when we have stuffed our last courgette flower, but before pumpkin time, the borlotti are like the last rays of summer sunshine.

Borlotti do lose their beautiful shading when cooked, but make up for it with a sweet, nutty taste and an ability to absorb other flavours too. A fresh borlotti bean has the texture of a tiny potato, which makes them wonderful in stews and rustic, chunky soups. As a side dish, they are delicious, infused with citrus and herbs like marjoram, oregano and basil. The salty tang of feta is a great partner for borlotti, though other cheeses are good too, especially sheep's cheese. It is best to simmer them slowly in plenty of water, testing frequently. How long they take to cook depends on size to an extent, but more so on how dry they were coming off the vine. There are two ways to infuse borlotti with other flavours: by simmering them in water and then pouring on a warm olive oil marinade containing fresh summer herbs; or by simmering the beans in stock with ingredients such as garlic, chillies and herbs.

Three winter squashes: a treasure trove of stored sweetness

When asked what my favourite vegetable to work with, I often hum and haw a bit, as a collection of cooked dishes and raw vegetables shoots across my internal screen. How to choose? Sometimes I think I should just say anything, it doesn't matter. But it does! At first I can't see beyond what I'm working with at that particular moment. Of course I love asparagus, but it's often a distant memory in the seasonal calendar. Then I think further back to winter, when roots and leeks are the chief material. In the end I get there and it always comes out the same: pumpkins. When I say 'pumpkin', I use the word to cover most of the many varieties of squash that are harvested in autumn to be stored through the winter. It is true that all pumpkins are squash while not all squash are pumpkins. The Sweet Dumpling, featured here, is harvested in autumn but would never keep for very long, so in my mind that one is not a pumpkin. There is a form of logic to it, believe me.

A good pumpkin is just about the most adaptable ingredient in the winter store cupboard. I adore them as a food, for their rich, sweet taste, their vivid colour and a texture that absorbs other flavours beautifully. And as a cook, I love to work with them because they are so damn useful. Start by hacking up a pumpkin and you can make soup, mash, endless variations on stews and curries, gnocchi, ravioli, risotto, gratins, pies and tarts both sweet and savoury, cakes, mousses, sauces and broths. I've probably left something out, but you get the point. Most useful of all, you can chuck wedges of it in the oven – after first drizzling them with olive oil or dotting them with butter and sprinkling over some herbs or spices – for a side dish to rival roast spuds. And the fact that they store so well means they are there for us right through the worst of winter, adding their versatility and colour to our culinary arsenal.

I feel a bit protective about pumpkins in fact, because it seemed to me there were no pumpkins in Ireland when I came back from New Zealand in the early nineties, having developed a passion for them. Saying this is on a par with the adage that there was no sex in Ireland before television – specifically *The Late Late Show*. By the stealth of courageous current affairs coverage, the programme introduced a couple of generations to all sorts of perversities and sinful pleasures for free throughout the sixties and into the early seventies. To get the info you had to stay home on a Saturday night rather than go to the pub, but there certainly wasn't anything more exciting going on down town. By the time the show had fulfilled its purpose, we'd figured out the logistics of sex, though it took another couple of decades to become comfortable with it all.

I digress. Of course there were pumpkins. Carving them into demonic faces was a Halloween ritual, but, if anything, those bland orange giants have held back the cause. Anyone who has ever made a pie or soup from the scrapings of the insides of a Halloween pumpkin would have quickly sworn never to repeat the mistake. There were also a scattering of people through-out the country growing edible varieties for their own use. Inevitably, they found each other, to swap seeds, pies and recipes, and just to feel that they weren't alone in the desert. A solo pleasure is never far from a perversion, yet the same one shared is a celebration.

I knew that fellow devotees were out there because two of them found me. A Canadian country singer and her English bass-playing husband were ensconced in an idyllic hollow a few hills inland from Clonakilty. Despite being intelligent, sophisticated and culturally and politically aware, Kim and Ian good-humouredly accepted the tag of the 'Hillbillies' and gave the impression of living the life of dropouts. It must have been their fondness for performing raucous country music that earned them the nickname. They were producing a lot of interesting food, including cheese, butter, yoghurt, eggs and a very cosmopolitan range of vegetables. As well as watercress, rocket, beetroot, beans, chards and kales, they had a crop of Whanga Crowns or Crown Prince, a favourite pumpkin from New Zealand. They hooked me in with their pumpkins and their unique watercress pond. The damp eventually got to Kim, however, and she took off back to the wide open prairies of the Canadian Midwest, cowboy boots, songbook and husband in tow. Luckily, I have never been without Crowns because Ultan was already a pumpkin fan when we began to work together, and was easily convinced to switch to Crowns for his main crop, which has doubled in size in each of the last three seasons. For sure, the word is now out on pumpkins.

Pumpkins grow so well here that, had they become popular sooner, they might easily have been a longstanding regular in traditional Irish cooking. Instead, because they are such a recent arrival, they bring with them the culture and cooking styles of the places where they have always been popular. This ranges from all the shores of the Mediterranean to the Pacific, via Asia and North America. So the influences are very wide. Precisely because their culinary use is so well established in other cultures, pumpkins are the most unlikely 'new' vegetable in the British Isles.

There are so many varieties of pumpkin that if you were to try to figure them all out, you would either go mad with frustration or be forced to devote your life to the pursuit. I tend to take a practical approach to this. Or maybe I should say two approaches. When I find a variety I really like, I try to make sure I can persuade someone to grow it for me and stick with it. In return, I try to get to like the ones the grower has a fondness for. This year, we are using three winter squashes, and he is winning two–one, maybe three–two. He is growing Crowns because we both love them; and I am using Sweet Dumpling and Muscade de Provence because he likes to grow them.

Crowns I have eulogised many times before, and I don't think I will ever change my mind about them being the best pumpkins in terms of richness of flavour, density of texture, longevity and sheer elegance. Crowns are the staple of the winter kitchen, the basis for almost every pumpkin dish.

I was a reluctant convert to Sweet Dumpling, but this year I really began to see its qualities. At about twice the size of a tennis ball, its ridged shape is covered in a green-and-yellow striped skin that is just the good side of edible if picked at the right age and size. When cooking Sweet Dumpling, and any other squash with a dense flesh and potentially tough skin, it is a good idea to keep it moist. Especially when roasting, splash with a little stock or water regularly. The flavour is as sweet as the name, with a lovely nutty tone. You can stuff the smaller pumpkins as an individual dish or roast the bigger ones in chunks. I like to dress the roasted pieces in olive oil and spices or lemon juice and herbs.

Muscade de Provence is a monster of a pumpkin, but lighter than it looks. Inside the green-turning-orange skin, the flesh is a deep orange. Unusually for such a strongly coloured pumpkin, the flesh is moist, with a good intense flavour that is less earthy than that of other pumpkins, almost fruit-like, with a hint of melon. Where most good pumpkins make heavy, nourishing soups, this can be made into a wonderfully light and elegant one, but without any loss of flavour. When I first took delivery of this variety, I was told that it was edible raw and would make a good salad. Trying not to be sceptical, I gave it a go. On first tasting, I had to agree the thing was edible raw, but I wouldn't go so far as to say I would *want* to eat it raw. I tried a few more times, though it isn't really my style to persist after an initial disappointment. One evening, it came together like a dream, however, and all made perfect sense. But here's the thing – the pumpkin must be a moist, sweet, very ripe and flavourful one; it must be sliced to just the right thickness; and it needs a citrus dressing to draw out the fruity quality. For heaven's sake, don't try eating a raw Crown or Halloween pumpkin doused in mayonnaise.

The rampant biology of summer squashes

Summer squashes are eaten fresh rather than stored, and they are as varied as winter ones. There are tens, twenties or hundreds of varieties, depending on how deep you want to go into the subject. As a cook, I skim the surface and trust my grower. I use everything he trials, and we generally agree on the ones to use as main crops. In recent years, I have come to love the small yellow one with the fluted edge, which we call scallopini. It also goes by the name of 'patty pan', and kids of all ages call it 'spaceship', for the very good reason that it looks just like how you would have drawn one at school when you were either scared or excited about the probability of your little town being invaded by aliens. Picked at the size of a golf ball, double that at most, scallopini has the rich, sweet and nutty flavour that courgettes dream about (although never attain) when they are mere matchsticks feeding a flower.

Most summer squashes, and especially courgettes, are a gardener's delight, which could explain their popularity. Indeed, it could be argued that we grow them more than we eat them, and end up having to compost those we can't get around to eating, or find other uses for them. Years ago, I used a giant courgette as a doorstop for most of the following winter. Now, I hope I'd be smart enough to make a chutney from it.

Courgettes grow relatively quickly and easily and produce vast quantities of food. Every summer, a new grower shows up in the restaurant with a slightly manic look in his eyes that I have come to recognise as a need to sell off a glut of courgettes. Control your wanton plants, I say, taking on the tone of an over-churched auld wan eyeing the way-too-young pushing their prams along without a care for their shame.

As familiar as courgettes may be, there has been a change in how we perceive and use them. With an eye more on flavour, texture and even the impact of the unusual, growers are changing the market. By choosing courgette varieties with better flavour potential; by taking care of the crop so it is harvested at the optimum size and sold in the best condition. The way that we buy and use squash is shifting from the 'fodder' end of the scale closer to the exotic. If that sounds like a pitch too far, look at it from this angle: Ultan grows hundreds of kilos of courgettes and scallopini squashes every summer. He manages his crop brilliantly, culling fruit and flowers in a careful ratio and at slightly different sizes, depending on who's buying. Even so, within that juggling act, he is eating as many as he can. He looks forward to the summer squash season the way the rest of us look forward to ... well, name your pleasure. Some people might find that unbelievable, but you'd have to see his eyes pop the week before the squash are due to know the man doesn't lie about his passion for vegetables. As always, I suspect he's

MUSCADE DE PROVENCE

been eating the things for a week before he sells any. In this state, he tends and nurtures them, manages and sells them, as though they were asparagus or rare seakale. For Paradiso, he picks courgettes the size of a finger, and scallopini squashes the size of the afore-mentioned golf balls.

Each week, too, he delivers about 150 courgette flowers. This is usually a mix of male and female. I was hopeless at biology in school; actually no, it wasn't that I was stupid, the truth is we had a science teacher in early secondary level who made it clear he was actually a chemist and who 'taught' reproduction by handing out one afternoon a slim booklet while blushing furiously. End of lesson for three years. Somehow I've come to know about the sexing of squash flowers, and I didn't learn it at school: the females have courgettes attached, so you have to leave plenty on the plant to allow them to mature a little more; the males are mere showy flowers on stems and you can take most because it only requires a few to do their business. Yes, I know, it's horribly familiar. I prefer females because they look better – stop sniggering, it's no wonder old Redface couldn't teach the stuff – but the producer has to find the right balance. Throw in the fluctuations of the erratic summer weather and it becomes a tricky matter of physics, not to mind biology. This is about as far removed as it gets from throwing a couple of courgette plants in the garden and making ratatouille and chutney from the monster harvest. I don't mean to give the impression we are the only people doing this. Quite the opposite. The point is that growers are pushing the agenda on this, turning a fodder crop into something of value, and thereby adding to the value that we consumers and cooks place on it. Changing the way we buy it changes the way we use it, and the way we perceive and value it. Everyone wins. And no more courgette gluts? Hmm ... we'll see.

The globally conquering tomato moves indoors

The tomato is probably the most successful and commonly grown indoor vegetable. Naturally requiring a long hot summer to produce fruit with the right combination of sweetness, acidity and juiciness, it has long been a staple of gardens and even commercial farms in unlikely colder climates due to the use of glasshouses and polytunnels. Fresh tomatoes are imported from sunny countries where they ripen happily outdoors in the hot summers. And it is true, too, that their global dominance is due to how successfully and cheaply the tomatoes have been canned and bottled. But there is a great pleasure to be had nonetheless from growing your own, or from sourcing freshly picked local tomatoes, and it is due to their ability to soak up the sunshine from behind glass that they have become so beloved of growers everywhere.

In the context of how common the tomato has become, it is chastening to remember that it didn't have an easy time gaining its first few rungs on the ladder to global dominance. Arriving from America in the sixteenth century, it was treated with the same suspicion as its cousins the potato, capsicum pepper and aubergine, all members of the nightshade family (though, confusingly, the aubergine came from the East), which scared the pants off the constantly spooked middle Europeans of the time. Southern Europe took to it slowly at first, but at least took to it, whereas it wasn't until late in the nineteenth century that England let its guard down fully. At this stage, the tomato was trading shabbily as an aphrodisiac of sorts, the 'love apple' no less. God help us, the levels to which the ambitious will sink. All worth it in the end, the erstwhile *pomo d'amore* would argue, from its current position of power and ubiquity. Ireland, being more petrified than most of the risk of sin in taking on anything new, didn't accept tomatoes until the Dutch had made them resemble turnips in flavour and size, removed any hint of sex, and three consecutive non-Italian popes had personally okayed their consumption. Some of that sentence is a joke – there have never yet been three consecutive non-Italian popes.

But think about this: all the time the tomato was trying to gain a foothold in European food culture, the physical year-by-year, century-by-century reality of that struggle would have been manifested in growers testing seeds, cross-breeding, experimenting and constantly developing something they believed had potential for popular usage. The same is true of the potato, but that had the potential to be a staple that could feed a population. The tomato was never more – or less – than a taste sensation. I may be anthropomorphising the tomato here for fun, but while inanimate itself, it certainly had ferociously dedicated human advocates. Businessmen for sure, people who expected to profit from the trade, but, more importantly, growers who worked on the evolution of the tomato until its rise became unstoppable. While this development of a hugely popular vegetable focused on finding a crowd-pleasing version that had a smooth red skin and a nice balance of acidity and sugar, there were always enough mavericks in the game to see to it that other versions of the tomato survived and evolved too. Not for noble historic reasons, but simply because other varieties are wonderful on their own account and ideal in dishes in which the standard tomato would appear bland. There are hundreds of varieties of 'heirloom' tomatoes, all worthy of their place on the table. None are saved purely out of sympathy or nostalgia. This is food after all.

Ultan has developed a pattern of trialling different varieties of

THE GLOBALLY CONQUERING TOMATO

tomato every year, and taking a few into the ongoing crop selection. This might be due to their success rate, their usefulness or simply because of personal taste. One of the biggest successes is the orange-skinned Sungold, a small cherry-tomato type with a wonderful balance of acidity and sugar that changes through the season, starting out quite tart and becoming sweet by August. Everyone who tastes them has a point in the summer when they would declare the Sungold to be perfect. Strangely, in the little research I've done on this, it rarely coincides with their partner's evaluation. People should take more notice of these things before bedding down together.

We use Sungolds in just about everything. In fact, they practically define the complex game played out to balance the crop coming in against the diners' demands on dishes. No matter how well I manipulate the menus to make sure every guest is getting their share of tomatoes, there is a two-week period every summer when the kitchen staff have to personally gobble a few handfuls to keep up with the glut. It's no hardship, because at that point they are at their absolute best – according to me. Although Sungolds are used to add a sweet, raw kick to a wide range of dishes, my favourite way to prepare them is to soften them over gentle heat with a little olive oil and garlic, sometimes finished with a splash of balsamic vinegar if they are at the sweeter end of their season. Like this, they become a sauce to accompany so much summer food, and are especially good as a barbecue condiment.

In contrast to the luxuriant vines of the Sungolds and most other tomato varieties, plum tomatoes grow on low bushes, the fruit often touching the ground, hidden under the green leaves of the plant. These densely fleshed tomatoes are the backbone of the tinned-tomato industry, the basis of every pizza and spaghetti sauce you've ever had. Even when grown in small precious volumes, they are best when cooked, which is not to say they are not fit for a raw salad. When perfectly ripe with the heat of the sun still on their tight skins, they have the character to keep company with cheeses, herbs, garlic and olive oil in a salad, but put them in the oven with a little olive oil and salt, maybe a splash of balsamic vinegar, until they begin to caramelise a little, and you have a very different beast. It's in the intensity of flavour – a taste sensation that you would never have imagined before you turned on the oven. Because they hold their shape so well when cooked, plum tomatoes can be used in many different ways, from a simple side dish to stews, warm salads, pasta sauces and pilafs.

Introducing the tomatillo, sour cousin of the global ruler

Almost as popular in Central America as the tomato itself, and at least as old, the astonishing tomatillo got a run-out in the polytunnels of South Cork this year. We thought we might get a handful to play with, but the few plants produced what would be described in the local vernacular as a 'langerload', enough to have them on the Paradiso menus for a couple of weeks, and way beyond expectations. Even if they had never ripened or if they'd tasted awful, tomatillos would have been worth growing for the extraordinary way in which the fruit is hidden in a papery husk. Everyone who sees them for the first time simply can't help letting out a sigh and an 'Aw, they're so cute!'. The vegetable is ripe when green, though some turn purple in time. Even on one comparative tasting, it's obvious that they are best if picked while still green, as the sweetness they develop later is dull and the texture flabby. The green ones have a dense texture, and a flavour that is mildly fruity and definitely acidic, but in a good way, making them perfect for use in a raw or barely cooked salsa. We made one with stubby green jalapeno chillies that were still mild at the time, though they later became quite ferocious as their colour turned to red. This salsa goes really well with cheese and egg dishes and anything that has enough sweetness to stand up to it.

Sweet peppers pushing out the boundaries of possibility

There are some things that the industrial-scale vegetable world does well – the frozen pea being probably the best example. Peppers might well be another. By peppers, I mean the capsicum or bell pepper, those bright red, yellow or green ones on shop shelves with which we are so familiar. They are a success on a number of levels: ubiquitous year-round supply, consistency of flavour and texture, and low cost. Peppers generally do what they promise. The red and yellow ones are crunchy and sweet in a one-dimensional way, the green ones have a nicely tart edge, and the occasional other colours make you laugh. As with other vegetables that have shifted over the recent decades from the exotic end of the spectrum to the mundane, it is easy to forget the wonderful potential that peppers have to bring a burst of summer to the kitchen. In restaurants and at home, the pepper has become a consistent and unremarkable staple rather than a seasonal treat. Even my grower, Ultan, had occasionally remarked over the years that he didn't think it worth his while cultivating the things as he could never match the price of shop-bought peppers, and in any case it was unlikely his would be any better. He would also have been worried that they wouldn't ripen to their full potential of sweetness in our undependable Irish summers.

Then he trialled some Hungarian wax peppers in a polytunnel. Even with our average temperatures sneaking up year by year, it would be pointless trying to grow peppers outdoors in Ireland. The modern polytunnel, being relatively inexpensive to set up, has exponentially increased the range of produce that can be grown in this climate. There is an argument to be made about the aesthetic effect of too much plastic covering the countryside, but this is far outweighed by the benefits of the system for the diversity and quality of local food supplies. The glasshouse might be a more handsome sight but it is prohibitively expensive for small producers. The polytunnel, on the other hand, makes it possible for anyone with an acre or two and an appetite for work to grow food to sell. But it is in the broadening of our food range that the most dramatic benefit of tunnel growing can be seen. Where before we had to do without or import so many of the vegetables with which we have become familiar, there is now little that we can't at least have a go at cultivating.

The first crop of peppers that emerged was of a longish type with a subtly yellow-green colour, a thin skin and a delicate, sweet flavour. I had sourced these many years before for just one season from a since-retired grower, and had been frustrated at losing them without getting to know them properly. So, naturally, I was delighted when Ultan decided to give them a go. We roasted and stuffed the handsome ones with cheese and pine nuts, and used the chaotically shaped ones in stews. The following year, he also produced a long cayenne pepper, which was meant to be sweet with a mild kick. In the random nature of peppers and chillies, some were mild and most were ferociously hot. By the third year, Ultan's farm, or at least one tunnel on it, had become a festival of peppers. Right now as I write, we have two large sweet peppers, both with silly marketing names I won't embarrass them by using, as well as the hot cayenne and another large pepper with the mild kick that the cayenne promised. The larger of the sweet ones grows up to 25cm (10in) long and is ripe when yellow-orange with hints of sunrise red. It has a lovely juicy flesh and a rich fruity sweetness that completely wipes out my opening statement about its industrially produced siblings. This might be the consequence of a rare long hot summer rather than something we can depend on every season, but in the vegetable business you have to take what comes and maintain an optimistic outlook.

It is late summer now, the last days of August, and the fields and tunnels are bursting with the fruit of all those long hot days. Seasonal vegetables are always the backbone of our menus, but this time of year there are almost more than I can deal with. To celebrate, I've just put a stew on the dinner menu. It's not exactly a stew in the grand tradition of chucking stuff in a pot and leaving it for a couple of hours. The basis of this one is a combination of sweet and hot peppers, which are stewed with garlic and herbs before the other vegetables – aubergines, scallopini squashes and borlotti beans – are added, having been roasted or braised separately. When the vegetables are brought together, they are heated and moistened in an intense, reduced broth made from onions, tomatoes and more peppers. The effect is to give the dish a rich background flavour full of summer sweetness, but which allows the individual vegetables to retain their own distinct characters. I see the stew as a celebration of the field that the produce comes from. I serve it with gnocchi made from semolina and soft sheep's cheese, then finish it with a dusting of Cratloe Hills, a mature, hard cheese, also made from sheep's milk. This stew won't be around for long, and by the time it's gone we will be getting out our warm jumpers and thinking of things to do with leeks and pumpkins.

Playing with fire in a cool climate

Taking up about a third of the tunnel where the peppers grow, are some chilli plants – half a dozen varieties producing fruit of different colours, sizes and heat levels. As is the case every year, some are experiments and a few are serious crops. The short and stubby jalapenos are the first to come on stream, delicious when green and mild, and quite a more ferocious beast when a fully ripe red.

This year we were pottering along comfortably, using about a kilo a week, the kitchen and garden nicely in tune. Then suddenly, within the space of a very sunny few days, not only did the output shoot up but the peppers also ripened to a very hot level. Almost without warning, the balance had tipped, the garden was getting a little anxious and the kitchen distinctly nervous, unable to use large quantities of a very hot chilli. In a very short time, we knew there would be no catching up, so in the interest of peace I started looking into the options of preserving chillies. Or at least I talked about it. Eventually, my head chef, Johan, came up with a lovely way to pickle jalapenos that preserved their colour and texture as well as the fiery heat. Further, Ultan, in fear of seeing his beautiful crop rot on the vine, gave me the basics of a recipe for zhoug, a Middle Eastern pesto of sorts, which had the extra benefit of combining the chillies with a lot of fresh coriander, something that also needed to be cleared from the tunnel. Not only did this give us two new products to use in the coming months, it completely removed all future stress about over-producing chillies.

My favourite chillies this year are cayennes, one orange and one red.

The orange one is called 'Topaz', the red 'Garden Salsa' – two very different styles of name. Indeed, this illustrates the problem with the naming of varieties, not just chillies or peppers, but right across the board in the fruit and vegetable business. One name is exotic and evocative, the other rather more mundane, suggesting to me an unpromising jar of tomato-based sauce. I don't use the seed category names of vegetable varieties on the menu unless they are so appealing that I think they will help to encourage people to try a dish. Even then, to use some names and not others would be inconsistent, with the result that I hardly ever bother. Many of the names are embarrassing or ridiculous, some inappropriate, some a shameless egotism on the part of the originator of the variety. A very occasional one is actually so attractive you would want to write it down or say it out loud, but this is very much the exception.

The aubergine – a mysterious Eastern nightshade transplanted to West Cork

Of the four members of the nightshade family that have found their way into our hearts and on to our dinner tables, the aubergine is the most unlikely and still the only one treated with any degree of suspicion. Potatoes have become one of the most important staples in the world, while the tomato must be the most commonly used and best-loved flavouring, and peppers score with their easy sweetness. In hindsight, all were sure to be hits. The aubergine, on the other hand, has a weirdly spongy texture when raw and needs to be properly cooked to reveal its charms. Besides, it comes in a coat of shiny purple, hinting at its relationship to the dreaded purple nightshade, as well as being a rare enough colour in the food world to arouse suspicion. A suspicion that still lingers, it would appear.

Just a week before I sat down to write this section of the book, I came across one of the most bizarre instances of phobia/intolerance in a diner. Although the woman in question was sitting at the table closest to the open kitchen, we never actually met, never even made eye contact, remaining throughout our brief relationship separated by the high counter that divides the kitchen and dining room. I'm generally a calm and polite cook, not given to cheffy fits, but even so I have once or twice been grateful for the height and width of that counter. I've had to remind myself that to cross that barrier in a bad mood is more than a physical act, it is a psychological one too, and to cross it once is to tear off a veneer of civilisation that I might find eventually slips away altogether. In other words, do it once and you'll be out there too often, too fast and too unnecessarily.

This was a Saturday night between Christmas and New Year, chaotically busy in the unstructured way holiday evenings can be. The kitchen staff were tired, getting a minor hammering, but coping in the sullen tone of those used to being whipped. It will end, goes the mantra, it always does. Then we had a little fire on one of the kitchen stoves. I call it a little fire because we managed to put it out, so it can't be called a major conflagration. But there was a moment, just before we figured out where and how to shut off the gas, when our hearts were pumping a lot faster than our falsely calm faces would betray. In the spirit of the evening, we then turned our collective attention from fire fighting back to ... well ... fire fighting of another kind, to the increasing array of order dockets and the next round of torture, now short two of the stove burners that we had heavily smothered in salt. Please don't misunderstand: most nights are highly organised, sweet-flowing events where we have almost as much fun as the diners. But this was one of those times when you know it's going to be rough and you adjust your mindset accordingly. Just as we were beginning to make headway, the manically smiling face of a waiter told me that a funny order was on its way. 'Don't shoot the messenger' was the clear plea of his crooked smile.

'What is it this time?' I asked, resigned to the worst, given the general tenor of the evening, and thinking I could cope with any 'worst' that might be imminent.

'See the woman on table 14? The one in the filthy mood who has clearly had a few stiffeners in the pub next door? The one snapping loudly at waiters and "friends" alike? Well, she's vegan and wheat intolerant.' Oh God, bad combination, but we can do that, no problem, just need to get the head right to do it in a good spirit. 'And she doesn't eat any of the nightshade family ...'

At this point, my brain fried. I gave way to a little rant, not even an angry one, more bemused and mind-boggled, about how many centuries it had been since we had got over our Dark Ages fear of the nightshade family. I've been in commercial kitchens for over twenty years, some of them in places that actually cater to any food paranoia you might be inflicting on yourself. But this woman got me with one I had never even heard of, couldn't have foreseen and probably will never encounter again.

The waiter was still smiling, the smile so cracked by now that I recognised it as a cry for help, but I was merciless. 'Sorry,' I said, 'that's not my job, she's all yours – give her the menu and let her figure it out for herself. My sanity is on the line here. She could probably survive a trace of tomato in her dinner, but I am unlikely to be still standing at midnight if I have to scan the menu for dishes without dairy, eggs, wheat and the entire nightshade family when I should be cooking someone else's meal.'

Somehow, the scene lifted the evening into the realm of surrealism and we managed to see out the night in slightly crazed good humour. We fed her something; she didn't care much for it, though her friend whispered that it was unlikely anything would have pleased her. Some time later, after one long slug of the first beer from the freezer, I realised that, in the dishes we could have cooked for a vegan with wheat intolerance, there wouldn't have been any tomatoes, potatoes, peppers or aubergines. Later still, I was tempted to do a little internet surfing to see if this was a common affliction and whether there was anything concrete behind it. But I couldn't bring myself to go there, to face down the big food scare of the Middle Ages, and find it was still active. Still haven't. Please don't write in.

If 'pumpkin' is the usual reply to the question of what my favourite vegetable is, and if asparagus remains, for me, the most eagerly anticipated herald of seasonal change, then the aubergine is probably the most useful all-year-round vegetable in the Paradiso storeroom. For *most* of the year, I should say; there is a period after the new year begins when even the industrial crops of Holland and Spain are too poor to be of much use. But that aside, because of the aubergine's ubiquity and relative uniformity of texture and flavour, I've never given much thought to where they came from or what variety I've been getting. Aubergine, usually sliced, brushed with olive oil and roasted until browned and tender, is simply the best material in the kitchen for so many dishes that need wrapping, layering, rolling and the like. Calling it a 'material' seems a bit unkind, suggesting something that is merely useful and with little else going for it. But it is true to say that, in its raw state, aubergine has very little flavour; that is it would have if raw aubergine was even edible. Cooked in a hot oven or under a grill, however, aubergine either takes on a new character or simply becomes what it was always meant to be, depending on how you want to look at it.

Besides its textural role, aubergine makes wonderfully smoky soups and dips, delicately moist tempura inside crisp batter, and a rich relish with tomato and red wine. In fact, there is hardly a dish in Paradiso that aubergine hasn't strayed into now and then, including pasta and risottos, tarts and pastries, warm salads, couscous and stews. One week, it might feature as a finely diced flavouring for chickpeas, while the next the aubergine itself might be accompanied by a few fried chickpeas mixed with lemon juice and cumin.

For the past couple of years, the aubergine has been moving into new territory for me. It started when Ultan trialled a small, matt-skinned variety and agreed to pick it as a baby – or perhaps more accurately, as an adolescent – about 13–15cm (5–6in) long. For the first time, I was faced with the challenge of a locally produced aubergine with all that that entails – a limited and slightly unpredictable crop of a vegetable which now demands to be treated with individual respect, placed at the heart of a dish with the recipe built around it. I need to ask what does it taste like? How does it behave when cooked? Is the texture soft, firm, seedy? Is it bitter or subtly sweet? This is something I do all the time with vegetables, but never before with an aubergine, despite aubergine being one of my favourite ingredients. In the end, I decided to simply cut it in half lengthways, roast it carefully, covered with parchment to keep the skin soft, then serve it as a starter propped up on slow-roasted plum tomatoes and dressed with lemon basil, chilli, caperberries and shavings of any one of three local hard cheeses currently in the storeroom. The flavours are classic and the aubergine has room to breathe and the chance to shine.

The following year, we were presented with trials of two more varieties. One was a long Oriental variety, which we used in thin rounds in a warm salad, and also in a stew, this time cut in long, thick slices, dictated by its shape. The other was Rosa Bianca, a very beautiful bulbous variety, white with pink shading. The flesh is soft and sweet, richer and more luxurious than that of any other aubergine I have ever encountered. When you get small quantities of new vegetables, it's always best to cook and eat them simply first, before you start any messing about. After a tasting of Rosa Bianca sliced into thick rounds and roasted, I cut one in half and roasted it cut side down. Just as it was almost done, I broke up the flesh coarsely and loosely pressed in a simple filling of breadcrumbs, cheese and herbs, enough to enhance the aubergine but not drown it. Mmm ... I look forward to a lot more of those next year.

Nurturing unlikely fruit

When you think of fruit growing naturally in this climate, the ones that immediately spring to mind are likely to be the cultivated 'staples' such as apples and pears, in addition to plums and the various currants and berries, or the wild fruits such as blackberries or damsons. But for centuries people have pushed at the limits of what fruits from sunnier climes we can produce, usually in the south-facing ends of walled gardens or in greenhouses.

The tree of hope and dreams ... and the occasional peach

When I first visited Hollyhill Farm near Clonakilty in West Cork, it was owned by a couple known as Kim 'n' Ian, aka the 'Hillbillies', whom we've already met a few pages back. The farm has changed hands a few times since, but in the Hillbillies' era it was run along more 'alternative', self-sufficient lines.

On my first tour of the garden, it was obvious that these people were producing a wider range of vegetables than they needed just for sustenance.

Alongside the quarter acre of store potatoes, there was a trial crop of a waxy French variety; with the curly kale, there was a stand of Tuscan cavolo nero. Growing next to the carrots, there were tiny beetroots to brighten summer salads, and – as I've already mentioned – they had the first Crown pumpkins I'd ever seen outside New Zealand. You can tell that growers are cooks, and gourmets too, when it is obvious that their crops are grown for the pleasure of the table as much as for the fundamental business of providing fuel for the body.

Eventually I was walked through their polytunnel to see the beans (three varieties), tomatoes and salad leaves. Bang in the middle, taking up way too much space, was a beautiful tree. A peach tree, and no ordinary peach tree either, but one that produces delicate white peaches. 'Produces' might be too strong a word. Two years previously, the tree had given the Hillbillies more than ten, whereas this year only two were forthcoming, and these had just been eaten. Was the tree a textbook gardening folly, planted in ground where more prosaic cash crops could be grown? Or was it a symbol of hope and possibility? To dig it out would be to give up the dream element of their lifestyle, and admit that they should really stop messing around and just grow more spuds.

The peach tree was planted in the same spirit that has motivated many others in a long tradition of growing exotic fruit under glass in the cooler climates of northern Europe. Behind this motivation there is a basic desire to produce beautiful things, coupled with the curiosity to find out what is at the outer edge of possibility. If peaches can be grown, what else might be feasible? I know people who have grown banana, avocado and pineapple trees ... *in Ireland!* Not with the expectation of replicating the amazing fruits of those trees as grown in their native environment, but to see how close they might come to achieving this. Only the truly optimistic would bother with this foolhardy carry-on, but this is the essence of the experimental nature of food production. Growers have to constantly adjust their tactics, and often their basic thinking, on what they produce and how they go about it. One year's results provide the basic blueprint for the next, but chances are that the conditions will change, bringing with them new things to learn.

Growing what shouldn't really be possible represents an irresistible challenge to some. Peach trees will grow in colder climates, and they will produce fruit, but to ripen the fruit needs a long hot summer. Polytunnels and glasshouses can bridge that gap sometimes, except during those summers when the cloud cover just refuses to lift, no matter how much we swear at it or pray to the relevant cloud-lifting saints.

FIGS

Some people have had success by training the trees into a fan or espalier along a south-facing wall in a sheltered corner of a warm part of the country ... one that doesn't get frost in winter. That might rule out a lot of Ireland, though it suggests hope for West Cork, where there are still many Victorian walled gardens and the climate is mellowed by the warm air of the Gulf Stream. Perhaps this will be a brief beneficial side effect of the increase in temperatures caused by global warming: we will have glorious crops of sweet Irish peaches for a few years before the predicted disappearance of that warming stream of air leaves us contemplating growing cloudberries.

Conjuring up Greek idylls with homegrown figs and a vivid imagination
Figs, those other iconic fruits of the Mediterranean, are marginally easier than peaches to produce in a temperate climate. The same method of training the tree to grow along a south-facing wall is used. Again, you need a perfect location and a good summer to have any hope of harvesting the kind of figs that your imagination is feeding on before you bite – ripe, juicy and sweet, with an intense and heady flavour that can be evocative of endless sunny days in the heavily scented air of a tiny Greek island; even if you only ever holiday in the windy chill of Ballybunion.

I once spoke to a lover of figs who had spent long summer holidays in Greece as a child and I asked whether it was possible then to put your hand in a box of figs and take one out with absolute confidence that it would fulfil your expectations. She said 'of course' without hesitation. In my experience, this hasn't been true, however, and I suspect that mine is the more common. Being a bit more obsessive than most about food, I will go on trying figs every time I get the chance because the good ones are worth it, but I can understand why people would put them out of their minds after one or two misses; an under-ripe fig is about as underwhelming an experience as can be had, gastronomically speaking. This is as true of imported figs as it is of those occasionally snagged from a tree in a country house garden. I haven't spent enough summers – precisely none, in fact – lolling about on Greek islands to test their produce in situ.

The good news about disappointing figs is that they cook really well and any lack of sugar is easily compensated for by a syrup or a sauce. I like to use grilled figs in savoury salads with peppery leaves such as rocket and watercress, some soft cheese and a citrus dressing. In desserts, figs are lovely when poached with spices such as ginger, cinnamon, cardamom or star anise, whether in a red wine or simple sugar syrup.

The stoic bearded gooseberry

Gooseberries hardly belong in the company of exotic fruit. They are as native to the colder extremities of Western Europe as turnips and parsnips. Yet, in way, they too need nurturing if they are to survive. In an age where we like our fruit to be sweet and sexy, gooseberries suffer from an image problem, being perceived as frumpy hangers-on from a bygone era.

But there is much to recommend in this staid and stoic berry. Its sugar levels are more than balanced by acidity, while its armour of thorns and hairy skin are formidable and off-putting to casual foragers. The gooseberry has no time for the heat of the midsummer sun, the source of sweetness for most other berries and currants, instead producing its fruit in the meekest warmth of early summer as though it frowned on the frivolityoof the coming season. The warmer countries have either given up on them or never bothered much in the first place. It isn't that the French and Italians don't love berries and currants, but below a certain latitude the gooseberry simply doesn't take on the complex characteristics it is capable of. A very northern fruit indeed.

Besides, and this is very important in my world, gooseberries make a great fool. There is something charmingly old-fashioned about fools, including the peculiar and titter-inspiring name. They are the simplest of desserts, the basis of which is a pulp of cooked fruit folded into whipped cream. It is said that the name comes from the French word for 'to crush', fouler, which is a pretty dull explanation and a sorry-looking word in its own right. I'm sorry I mentioned it now, sorry I ever learned it.

The menu in Paradiso usually includes a fool for as much of the year as there is fruit from which to make it. It begins with rhubarb in early spring, then gives way to gooseberries when the fruit arrives in early summer, then on through the sequence of blackcurrants and blackberries. Rhubarb has its advocates, including me, but the tart berries, those with a high level of acidity in their flavour, make the best purées for fool.

There is always the temptation to buy extra fruit and freeze it, to extend the life of one or other variations on the fool, but the force of the seasons takes over and the momentum is to move forward rather than hang on. Last year, I was so keen to stretch out gooseberry time that I asked my supplier to try to source some from France. I needed just a few kilos or whatever he could get hold of, to make one last batch of fool purée and a few jars of chutney. He looked at me askew – at least I got the impression he did, we were actually talking by phone – and pointed out that the French didn't grow gooseberries. Or if they do, they produce small quantities of the large juicy reddish-coloured varieties, too sweet for our needs. *Quelle horreur!*

I was aghast, then a split second later I realised that I knew this already. Time to let the gooseberry go for another year.

The gooseberry has a complexity that makes it outstanding in fools, and in jams and chutneys too. I like to serve gooseberry fool with a swirl of elderflower syrup. These two flavours bring out the best in each other in that exquisite way that expresses this wonderfully optimistic time of year when summer is about to burst and everything is possible. There is a gooseberry fool recipe in *Paradiso Seasons* that has a shockingly large amount of sugar in it. This has been pointed out to me by occasional e-mailers, most of whom spotted the mistake before ruining their dessert. To make up, I am including a new version here, one that contains a more reasonable level of sugar.

It's a useful reminder that you should always think about the sugar level in a recipe using tart or acidic fruits – and I'm not just saying that to get myself and my proofreader off the hook. The sugar is there to sweeten the dish, but in a way that balances the acidity of the fruit. This can vary quite a bit depending on the variety of fruit and its ripeness, as well as the amount of sunshine in the particular year. There are gooseberry varieties that are more sweet than sour when fully ripe, and some which aren't even green, ripening to a wine red colour. The sweeter ones are best for eating raw or in dishes where they are only lightly cooked. For longer cooking, required in jams, chutneys, purées and the like, you will get a better flavour with green gooseberries, even slightly under-ripe ones if you are using a sweet variety.

Using slightly under-ripe gooseberries has an advantage that other berries and currants can't claim. It means you are picking the things before the birds descend on them. Sometimes growing berries and currants can be like running a bird charity. Most of the time, they like theirs just a day or two less sweet than we do, and they like them a lot. In fact, they've been waiting all year just as excitedly as you for berry time. Birds probably think that growers of uncovered currant bushes are minor earthbound gods. Or God's gardeners, perhaps.

One year's experiments, next year's crops – growing a cycle

Most of the vegetables in this chapter are ones I have been working with for many years, but which have been made new again to me recently by local producers with whom I work closely. Of all the positive aspects of working with fresh, local produce, this is the most rewarding. While it is always encouraging when someone new grows some carrots and spuds to sell, it is downright exciting when they start to experiment beyond their known capabilities.

The combination of the curiosity of growers and the appetite for inspiration on the part of consumers and cooks is what powers a thriving food culture. Experiments that fail teach the grower a lot about his location and its potential. The ones that work open up new possibilities. In the kitchen, every newly successful variety sparks off multiple new ways to cook with them. When the food culture is interactive, with contact along the chain between producers, cooks and consumers, the process of experimentation that begins in the field carries on into the kitchen, and the information goes back out so that we are only growing what ultimately works well in the dining room.

Next year, while we are cooking with the successful produce of this season's trials, the growers will be pushing the edges out a little further.

Pak Choi and Rice Vermicelli Salad with Egg, Apple and a Peanut Dressing

This is a recipe I threw together for a late lunch one summer afternoon when there were people to be fed and not a lot of food in the house. When I put it on the restaurant menu the following week it quickly became a standard. I thought about messing with the dressing ingredients to replace the chilli sauce, but decided to leave well alone.

For the dressing, put the chilli sauce and peanut butter in a bowl and whisk in the water to get a thick pouring consistency. Add the ginger, lemon juice, sugar and soy sauce and whisk again to combine. Add a little more water if necessary.

Bring a large saucepan of water to the boil, drop in the rice vermicelli, turn the heat off and leave for 5–10 minutes (or according to the packet instructions) until the noodles are tender. Drain and cool the vermicelli under cold running water.

Heat a crêpe or frying pan, brush it lightly with vegetable oil and pour in enough of the egg to make a slightly thick omelette. Cook for about 1 minute, until the underside is lightly golden, then flip and cook the other side for another minute. Repeat with the rest of the egg. Roll the omelettes up, then slice them into strips 1cm (½in) wide.

In a large bowl, mix the vermicelli with the egg, pak choi, apple, spring onions, celery and herbs. Pour in enough of the dressing to coat the salad generously, mix it well, and serve in deep bowls.

Serves 4

200g (7 oz) rice vermicelli

vegetable oil

2 eggs, beaten

4–6 small heads pak choi, thinly sliced

1 apple, cored and thinly sliced

4 spring onions, thinly sliced

1 stick celery, thinly sliced

1 handful fresh coriander, chopped

2 tbsp chopped fresh mint leaves

FOR THE PEANUT DRESSING

125ml (4¼fl oz) sweet chilli sauce

100g (3½oz) peanut butter

3–4 tbsp water

1 tbsp grated fresh ginger

juice of 1 lemon

25g (1oz) caster sugar

4 tbsp soy sauce

Li's Pak Choi with Ginger, Chillies, Fennel and Sesame

Serve this with some fried tofu and noodles.

Depending on the size of the choi heads, either cut them in half lengthways or cut off the ends and separate the leaves.

Heat the olive oil over a high heat in a wok or large frying pan. Add the spring onions, chillies, garlic, ginger, fennel seeds and pak choi. Stir-fry for 2 minutes, then add the soy sauce and stock or water. Bring to the boil, then lower the heat and simmer for 2 minutes. Dress with the sesame oil before serving.

Serves 2 as a main dish, 4 as a side dish

4–6 heads baby pak choi

2 tbsp olive oil

4 spring onions, sliced diagonally

2 fresh mild green chillies, halved and sliced, seeds included

2 garlic cloves, sliced

2cm (³/₄in) piece of fresh ginger, chopped

1 tsp fennel seeds

3 tbsp soy sauce

4 tbsp stock or water

1 tsp toasted sesame oil

Broad Bean and Purple Potato Salad with Knockalara Cheese

To give this salad an extra textural dimension, make some purple potato crisps according to the recipe on page 296–298, and scatter a few around each serving of the salad.

Combine the dressing ingredients by shaking or blending them together.

Drop the broad beans into boiling water to cook for 3–5 minutes, until just tender. Cool them briefly under cold running water, then drain, leaving the beans slightly warm. Boil or steam the purple potatoes until tender, then cool them under cold running water and drain. If they have lost their purple colour, squeeze a little lemon juice over them.

In a large bowl, mix the broad beans, potatoes, lettuce, spring onions and herbs. Add most of the dressing and toss gently. Season with salt and pepper. Share out the salad between four plates. Crumble some cheese over each portion and drizzle with the remaining dressing.

Serves 4

300g (10½oz) podded broad beans
200g (7oz) purple potatoes, peeled and diced
1 head little gem lettuce, sliced
2 spring onions, finely chopped
1 bunch fresh basil leaves, chopped
1 bunch fresh mint leaves, chopped
salt and pepper
120g (4¼oz) Knockalara fresh sheep's cheese or other soft fresh cheese

FOR THE DRESSING

zest of 1 orange
juice of ½ orange
juice of 1 lemon
200ml (7fl oz) olive oil
1 garlic clove, crushed

Broad Beans with Paprika, Mint and Yoghurt

Put the red pepper under a hot grill or over a flame to blacken the skin, turning as necessary. Put it in a bowl and cover with clingfilm to cool. When the pepper is cool enough to handle peel off the skin and discard the stem and seeds. Chop the flesh into small dice.

Heat two tablespoons of olive oil in a pan and fry the onion over a medium heat for 2 minutes. Add the garlic, cumin and mustard seeds and fry for 5 minutes more. Add the tomatoes and broad beans and continue cooking for 5–10 minutes more until the beans are tender. Add a little stock or water if necessary to keep the dish moist.

Take the pan from the heat and leave it to cool for a few minutes, then stir in the roasted pepper, mint, paprika and yoghurt. Season with salt. Serve warm.

Serves 4

1 red pepper
olive oil
1 medium red onion, finely chopped
2 garlic cloves, finely chopped
1 tsp cumin seeds
1 tsp mustard seeds
2 tomatoes, peeled, seeded and diced
400g (14oz) podded broad beans
1 tbsp chopped fresh mint leaves
½ tsp sweet paprika
100ml (3½fl oz) thick plain yoghurt
salt

Baked Artichokes with Olive Stuffing and Tomato-caper Salsa

While this highly flavoured artichoke dish makes a lovely starter, it can also be served as part of an antipasti or buffet.

Preheat the oven to 180°C/350°F/Gas Mark 4. Trim the artichokes by snapping off a few of the outer leaves until the visible ones are more soft yellowish flesh than tough green or purple. Cut off any tough tops and peel around the widest part of the base and down the stem. Now cut the artichoke in half and remove any hairy choke that may be in the centre. Squeeze the juice of two lemons into a bowl of water and drop the prepared artichokes into this as you go.

Bring a large saucepan of water to the boil and cook the artichoke halves in it for 5–10 minutes, until just tender, then cool them in a bowl of cold water.

Combine the olives and cheese, and press a little into the cavities of the artichoke halves. Brush an oven dish with olive oil and place the artichokes in it, open side up and close together.

Put the bread and parsley in a food processor with a pinch of salt and blend to get fine crumbs. Scatter these over the artichokes and drizzle generously with olive oil. Bake in the oven for 15 minutes, until the crumbs are crisp.

While the artichokes are baking, put the tomatoes, garlic, capers and thyme in a small saucepan with a tablespoon of olive oil. Heat them gently for a minute over a low heat, then remove the pan from the heat and season with salt and pepper.

To serve as a starter, place three artichoke halves on each plate and spoon some warm salsa over them. To serve as a side dish or as part of an antipasti, spoon the salsa over the artichokes in their baking dish.

Serves 4 as a starter

6 medium artichokes

juice of 2 lemons

60g (2¹/₄oz) black olives, stoned and finely chopped

40g (1¹/₂oz) cream cheese or ricotta

olive oil

80g (2³/₄oz) day-old bread

1 tbsp chopped fresh parsley

salt and pepper

4 tomatoes, peeled and diced

1 garlic clove, crushed

1 tbsp small capers

leaves from 1 sprig fresh thyme

Pan-fried Artichokes with Lemon Cream and Baked Semolina Gnocchi

This recipe calls for two different types of sheep's cheese. I use Knockalara, a fresh mild cheese from Cappoquin in County Waterford, as the soft cheese in the gnocchi. Any soft cheese, even commercial cream cheese, will give gnocchi a lovely contrast of crisp skin and meltingly soft insides, but a sheep's cheese, if you can get one, will add a piquant note that artichokes love. The hard sheep's cheese that I use over the top of the finished dish is Cratloe Hills from County Clare. This is a classy cheese, usually about six months old. An Italian Pecorino works very well, but do make sure you get one with clean, sharp flavours, nothing too farmyardy.

Serves 4

FOR THE GNOCCHI

750ml (1¼ pints) vegetable stock
180g (6¼oz) fine semolina
salt and pepper
120g (4¼oz) soft sheep's cheese

FOR THE PAN-FRIED ARTICHOKES

8 small purple artichokes
juice of 2 lemons
olive oil
2 garlic cloves, finely chopped
leaves from 1 sprig fresh thyme
1 tomato, peeled and diced
1 bunch spinach (about 150g/5½oz), chopped
80g (2¾oz) hard sheep's cheese

FOR THE LEMON CREAM

100ml (3½fl oz) vegetable stock
100ml (3½fl oz) white wine
300ml (10fl oz) double cream
zest of 1 lemon
juice of ½ lemon

To make the gnocchi, bring the stock to the boil in a large saucepan, whisk in the semolina and a little salt and pepper. When it returns to the boil, lower the heat and simmer over a very low heat for 15 minutes, stirring frequently. Stir in the soft sheep's cheese and remove from the heat. Line a swiss roll tray with baking parchment and spread the semolina on it to a thickness of about 2cm (¾in), then leave it to cool. When cool, cut the semolina into square slices, about 3cm (1¼in) wide. These are your gnocchi.

Trim the artichokes by snapping off a few of the outer leaves until the visible ones are more soft yellow than tough green or purple. Cut off any tough tops and peel around the widest part of the base and down the stem. Now cut the artichoke in half and remove any hairy choke that may be in the centre. Squeeze the juice of two lemons into a bowl of water and drop the prepared artichokes into this as you go.

Bring a large saucepan of water to the boil and cook the artichoke halves in it for 5–10 minutes, until just tender, then cool them in a bowl of cold water. Preheat the oven to 200°C/400°F/Gas Mark 6.

To make the lemon cream, bring the stock and wine to the boil in a small pan, then reduce the heat and simmer for about 5 minutes until the quantity is reduced by half. Add the cream and reduce again to get a slightly thickened pouring consistency, about 7-8 minutes more. Stir in the lemon zest and juice and a little seasoning.

At the same time, line a baking tray with baking parchment, place the gnocchi

continued overleaf

on it and bake in the oven for 8–10 minutes, turning once, until they are crisp and lightly coloured.

While the gnocchi are baking, heat 2 tablespoons of olive oil in a frying pan and cook the artichokes with the garlic and thyme over a medium heat for 5 minutes. Add the tomato and cook for 1 minute more. Season with salt and pepper.

In another pan, heat a little olive oil over a high heat. Add the spinach and cook for 3–4 minutes until soft, adding a splash of water if necessary. Season with salt and pepper.

Divide the softened spinach between the serving plates, and put two or three gnocchi on top of each. Pour some lemon cream around the edge. Place four artichoke halves against each portion of gnocchi and shave or grate some of the hard sheep's cheese over the top.

Fresh Borlotti Beans with Lemon and Marjoram

Put the borlotti beans in a large saucepan of cold water to cover them generously. Bring the water to the boil, then lower the heat and simmer gently for 15–20 minutes. Drain and return the beans to the pan. Add in the olive oil, garlic, lemon and marjoram and mix well. Season with salt and pepper. Leave to stand, off the heat, for at least 30 minutes to allow the flavours to develop. Serve at room temperature or reheat gently.

Serves 4 as a side or part of an antipasti

400g (14oz) podded fresh borlotti beans

4 tbsp olive oil

1 garlic clove, crushed

zest and juice of 1 lemon

2 tbsp fresh marjoram leaves

salt and pepper

Borlotti Bean Mole with Roast Winter Squash and Black Kale

This is a variation on a Mexican classic that Ultan Walsh loves to serve after a hard day's toil in the fields. The borlotti beans soak up the flavours beautifully during the long slow cooking. If you don't have fresh borlotti to hand, use dried or frozen ones, or even the more typically Mexican pinto beans, which have a similar mealy texture, but don't forget to adjust the cooking time accordingly.

Serve this rich, spicy mole with the classic accompaniment of tortillas or some polenta, mashed potato or potato cakes.

The heat level of fresh chillies can be unpredictable, so I have given an approximate quantity here. Adjust to your own taste.

Serves 4

200g (7oz) fresh borlotti beans
200g (7oz) peeled and seeded Crown pumpkin or other winter squash
olive oil
100g (3½oz) black kale (cavolo nero)
50g (2oz) butter
1 medium onion, chopped
2–4 red jalapeño chillies, halved, seeded and chopped
2 garlic cloves, chopped
500g (18oz) fresh plum tomatoes, chopped (or good quality tinned tomatoes)
2 tsp paprika
25g (1oz) almonds, dark roasted and finely ground
50g (2oz) 70% dark chocolate, broken into pieces
salt

Preheat the oven to 180°C/350°F/Gas Mark 4. Bring a large saucepan of water to the boil, add the borlotti beans and boil for about 10–15 minutes until they are just cooked or even slightly undercooked. Drain and cool under cold running water, and set aside.

Cut the squash flesh into good-sized chunks, about 2cm (³/₄in) square, place them in a roasting tray and toss in olive oil. Roast them in the oven for about 20 minutes until caramelised on the outside but still firm. Reduce the oven temperature to 130°C/250°F/Gas Mark ½.

Without removing the central stem, cut the black kale across the leaf into 2cm (³/₄in) slices. Melt the butter in a casserole dish and fry the onion and chillies gently over a low to medium heat for 20–30 minutes, until caramelised. Add the garlic and fry for 3 minutes more. Add the tomatoes and paprika, bring to the boil, reduce the heat and simmer gently for 15 minutes. Add the ground almonds, chocolate, squash, borlotti beans, black kale and a teaspoon of salt. Stir until the chocolate has melted. Cover the casserole and put it in the oven to cook gently for 2 hours.

Zhoug

I first made this well-known Middle Eastern condiment to deal with a glut of chillies, over 10 kilos (22¹/₂ pounds), ~~that~~ Ultan had produced and some fresh coriander that was going to seed. Being insecure about how long a fresh pesto-type sauce would survive, even if properly packed in sterilised jars, I decided to boil the sauce before jarring it. It does alter the flavour, though not in a bad way, and the green colour is diminished, but the result is a relish that keeps for months. If your chillies are not too hot, it will be a very useful condiment for sandwiches, grilled haloumi and egg dishes, to dollop onto soups or to use as an instant complex flavouring for rice and couscous dishes, noodles and curries.

Makes 2.5kg (5lb 8oz), about 10 jars
2kg (4¹/₂lb) fresh green or red chillies
400g (14oz) fresh coriander
1 tbsp coriander seeds, ground
1 tbsp cardamom seeds, crushed
4 garlic cloves
400ml (14fl oz) olive oil

In a food processor, pulse the chillies, coriander, coriander seeds, cardamom and garlic to a coarse paste. Add half the olive oil and process again. Continue adding the rest of the olive oil, a little at a time, and processing until you get a thick pesto-like consistency.

This can be jarred now, with a thin film of olive oil on top, and kept in a fridge for a week or so. To keep it longer, put the zhoug in a saucepan, bring it to the boil, then lower the heat and simmer for 10–15 minutes. Store in sterilised jars.

Scallopini Squash with Garlic, Basil, Pine Nuts and Cherry Tomatoes

I like to serve this squash dish to accompany a simple risotto or frittata. To serve it as a starter, add some shavings of Parmesan or hard sheep's cheese.

Cut each scallopini into four, six or eight wedges, depending on their size. The fat end of the wedges should be 2cm (³/₄in).

In a large shallow pan, heat the olive oil, add the red onion and scallopini and fry for 1 minute over a high heat while stirring. Lower the heat to medium, add the garlic and continue frying for a further 5 minutes. Add the basil and cherry tomatoes and cook for 2–3 minutes more, until the tomatoes begin to break down and the squash is tender. Season well with salt and pepper. Transfer to a serving dish. Crush the toasted pine nuts by pressing on them with a knife or rolling pin, then scatter them over the squash.

Serves 4
1kg (2¹/₄lb) scallopini squash
2 tbsp olive oil
1 medium red onion, halved and thinly sliced
3 garlic cloves, sliced
1 small handful fresh basil leaves, coarsely torn
200g (7oz) cherry tomatoes, halved
salt and pepper
1 tbsp pine nuts, lightly toasted

Grilled Courgette and Fennel Salad with Apricots, Almonds and Feta

Soak the apricots in warm water for 20 minutes, then chop them into thin slices.

Blanch the fennel by dropping it into boiling water for 30 seconds. Drain, then cool in a bowl of cold water and drain again. Toss the fennel with the red onion and a little olive oil on an oven tray and grill under a hot grill for 3–4 minutes until the fennel starts to colour.

Brush the courgettes with olive oil and cook them in the same way as the fennel. Put the grilled vegetables in a large bowl with the apricots, cumin seeds, fresh coriander and lemon juice. Toss the salad, then sprinkle over the almonds and feta.

Serves 4
4 dried apricots
1 fennel bulb, quartered and thinly sliced
1 medium red onion, halved and thinly sliced
olive oil
800g (1³/₄lb) small courgettes, halved lengthways
1 tsp cumin seeds, lightly toasted
1 handful fresh coriander, chopped
juice of 1 lemon
30g (1¹/₄oz) whole almonds, roasted
100g (3¹/₂oz) feta cheese, crumbled

Courgette, Pea and Chive Risotto with Courgette Flower Fritters and Tomato-basil Broth

Although it goes against received thinking on risotto, I sometimes like the finished dish to be more firm than soupy, so it just about barely stands in a mound on a plate. I then surround it with an intense oil or broth to bring an extra flavour dimension as well as providing the extra liquid that will soften the texture of the dish. In this recipe, the liquid is an oily tomato broth.

    The quantity of courgettes in the risotto is based on those attached to the flowers being about 6–8cm (2–3in) long, about 250g (9oz) in total.

To make the tomato-basil broth, heat the olive oil in a wide pan. Add the onion and fry it over a high heat for 5–7 minutes, until it is beginning to colour. Add the garlic, tomatoes and basil and continue frying for about 10 minutes until the tomatoes have broken down. Add the stock, lower the heat and simmer for 5 minutes, then remove the pan from the heat and set it aside.

    Cut the flowers from the courgettes, split the flowers in two lengthways and remove the pistils. Slice the courgettes into thin rounds. Put to one side.

    To make the risotto, bring the vegetable stock to the boil in a medium saucepan, then lower the heat and keep it at a simmer. In a large saucepan, melt one tablespoon of butter with one of olive oil. Add the shallots and fry gently over a medium heat for 5 minutes. Add the sliced courgettes and the rice, toss them well in the oil, and continue to fry gently for 7–8 minutes, stirring often. Add the wine, bring to the boil, then lower the heat and simmer gently, stirring, until it has been absorbed. Ladle in enough hot stock to cover the rice and continue simmering and stirring until this has been absorbed. Repeat this with more stock in batches until the rice is almost tender, about 20 minutes. Add the peas with the last ladle of stock. Simmer for a minute or 2 until the rice is tender. Add the chives, cheese and the remaining butter and season with salt and pepper.

    While the risotto is cooking, finish the other parts of the dish. Press the tomato-basil mix through a sieve and put the liquid in a small saucepan to reheat gently. Season with salt and pepper.

Serves 4

FOR THE TOMATO-BASIL BROTH

4 tbsp olive oil

1 medium onion, chopped

2 garlic cloves, finely chopped

5 ripe tomatoes, coarsely chopped

1 handful fresh basil leaves

200ml (7fl oz) vegetable stock

FOR THE RISOTTO

8 courgette flowers with small courgettes attached

1.2 litres (2 pints) vegetable stock

60g (2¼oz) butter

1 tbsp olive oil

2–4 small shallots, finely chopped

300g (10½oz) carnaroli or arborio rice

120ml (4fl oz) white wine

100g (3½oz) fresh peas

2 tbsp finely chopped fresh chives

60g (2¼oz) Desmond, Parmesan or hard sheep's cheese, finely grated

salt and pepper

FOR THE BATTER

225g (8oz) plain flour

2 egg yolks

350ml (12fl oz) sparkling water

vegetable oil, for deep frying

Make the batter by putting the flour in a bowl with the egg yolks and a pinch of salt, and whisking in the water. Heat some vegetable oil in a deep-fryer or deep saucepan to 180°C/350°F. If using a saucepan, put a few drops of batter into the oil and if they float quickly to the top reduce the heat to hold the temperature. Dip the courgette flowers in the batter to coat them, then take them out one at a time and lower them gently into the oil. Fry for 2 minutes until crisp, then remove the fritters and drain on kitchen paper. Fry the flowers in batches if necessary to avoid overcrowding.

Serve the risotto in shallow bowls with the courgette flower fritters on top. Pour some broth around the risotto in each bowl.

Raw Muscade de Provence Pumpkin Salad with Baby Spinach and Avocado

The plating of this salad makes for a pretty picture, with the contrast between vivid green and bright orange. If you're not bothered about the design aspect, the salad will still taste great simply tossed together.

Slice the pumpkin thinly, using the first or second thinnest setting on a mandoline. Alternatively, do this very carefully with a sharp knife, or by using a wide peeler, pressing firmly to get a slice a little thicker than a normal peeling. Put the slices in a bowl. Combine the ginger, lime juice, orange zest and sugar, pour it over the pumpkin and toss briefly. Leave this for 10 minutes or so while you make the rest of the salad.

Halve the avocado, remove the stone and the skin, and slice the fruit into thin wedges. Mix these gently with the spinach, coriander and chilli. Add the lemon juice and the oil, season with salt and toss to mix everything well.

Arrange the pumpkin slices on a plate so that they form an appealing pattern, leaving the centre of the plate uncovered. Drizzle over a little of the dressing from the bowl. Place some of the spinach and avocado salad in the centre of the plate, and serve.

Serves 4

250g (9oz) peeled and seeded Muscade de Provence pumpkin

2 tsp grated fresh root ginger

100ml (3½fl oz) lime juice

zest of 1 orange

2 dsp caster sugar

1 avocado

250g (9oz) baby spinach

1 small handful fresh coriander leaves

1 fresh mild chilli, halved, seeded and thinly sliced

juice of ½ lemon

2 tbsp toasted pumpkin seed oil, or olive oil

salt

Pumpkin, Pistachio and Sage Ravioli with a Saffron Cheese Sauce

I had this one evening at Ultan's and asked him for the recipe even before I finished. He's a generous host and it was in my inbox before I got home.

    The pasta recipe calls for one whole egg because Ultan has amazingly rich eggs from his own chickens, which give a wonderful colour to the pasta. If using shop-bought eggs, even free-range ones, you might want to use two yolks instead. If you don't have a pasta rolling machine, you can roll the dough by hand with a rolling pin. Or, if you're really lucky, you might live close to a shop that sells good quality fresh pasta sheets.

    The recipe makes four generous starters or two main courses.

You might want to make double or more of the pasta and cut the rest into noodle shapes such as tagliatelle or linguine for the next day.

    To make the ravioli, sift the flour into a bowl with a good pinch of salt, add the egg and 2 teaspoons of water and bring them all together with your hands to form a dough. Knead for 1 minute, then leave the dough to rest under a cloth.

    Cut the pumpkin flesh into 1cm (½in) cubes. Heat the olive oil in a large saucepan and add the diced pumpkin. Fry over a medium heat for about 10 minutes, until slightly caramelised. Add 3 tablespoons of water and the sage and cook for a few minutes more, then remove from the heat and mash the pumpkin in the pan. Add the pistachios and the cheese, and season well with salt and pepper.

    The pasta dough should be soft and easy to roll. Flatten it out and pass it through a pasta machine with the rollers at the widest setting, then fold it and pass it through again. Do this three or four times. Cut the dough in half and fold it until you have two equal sized pieces approximately 2cmx10cm (¾inx4in). Continue to pass through the pasta machine, reducing the thickness of the sheet each time by adjusting the rollers. After the lowest setting you should have two sheets of equal length and about 7cm (2¾in) wide. Arrange twelve separate teaspoons of filling on one sheet with 3cm (1¼in) between each teaspoon of filling. Dampen the uncovered edges of the pasta with water. Place the other sheet of pasta on top, pressing down around the mixture to form rough ravioli shapes. Make sure not to leave any air pockets. Cut into twelve individual ravioli and cover them with a damp cloth while you make the sauce.

Serves 2–4 (see introduction)

FOR THE RAVIOLI

100g (3½oz) very fine durum wheat flour
salt and pepper
1 egg
2 tsp water
150g (5½oz) peeled and seeded Crown pumpkin
1 tbsp olive oil
3 tbsp water
2 tsp coarsely chopped fresh sage leaves
15g (½oz) shelled and skinned pistachios, coarsely chopped
25g (1oz) hard cheese such as Desmond or Parmesan

FOR THE SAFFRON CHEESE SAUCE

25g (1oz) butter
25g (1oz) plain flour
400ml (14fl oz) milk
1 large pinch saffron threads
80g (2¾oz) mature cheddar
50ml (2fl oz) double cream

To make the sauce, melt the butter in a medium saucepan, add the flour and cook over a low heat for 2 minutes, stirring. Add the milk, stirring to incorporate the butter and flour, bring it to the boil and whisk for 1 minute. Add the saffron, reduce the heat and simmer for 15 minutes, stirring occasionally. This time it is necessary to fully cook the flour in the sauce and to bring out the full flavour and colour of the saffron. Stir in the cheddar and the cream. Season with salt and pepper, and keep the sauce warm over a very low heat while you cook the ravioli.

Bring a large saucepan of water to the boil and drop in the ravioli. Return to the boil, lower the heat and simmer for 3 minutes until cooked, then drain.

To serve, divide half the sauce between warm plates, arrange the ravioli on top and pour the remaining sauce over them.

Roast Sweet Dumpling Squash with Lemon, Sage and Cannellini Beans

Preheat the oven to 180°C/350°F/Gas Mark 4. Chop the squash into large bite-size chunks. Toss them in a little olive oil and a little salt in an oven dish, and roast in the oven for 15–20 minutes until tender. Turn the squash occasionally, and if necessary splash it with a little water to keep it moist.

While the squash is roasting, melt a tablespoon of butter and one of olive oil in a pan. Over a medium heat, fry the shallots, garlic, thyme and sage for 2 minutes, then add the cannellini beans, lemon zest and juice and the stock or water. Bring back to the boil, turn down the heat and simmer for 10 minutes.

Take the roasted squash from the oven and put it in a serving dish. Add another tablespoon of butter to the cannellini beans, season with salt and pepper, and pour the contents of the pan over the squash. Serve immediately.

Serves 4

1 kg (2¼lb) Sweet Dumpling squash, halved and seeded
olive oil
salt and pepper
2 tbsp butter
4 small shallots, finely chopped
2 garlic cloves, sliced
leaves from 1 sprig fresh thyme
8 sage leaves, coarsely chopped
6 tbsp cooked (or canned) cannellini beans
zest of 1 lemon
juice of ½ lemon
100ml (3½fl oz) vegetable stock or water

Roast Sweet Dumpling Squash with Mushroom and Kale Stuffing (and Gravy)

This is a variation on the filling for a massive stuffed pumpkin that was served at a Thanksgiving dinner hosted by a New Yorker in the Irish countryside. I wanted to change the delicious gravy to something more obviously modern but was told that Thanksgiving means gravy even for vegetarians.

Preheat the oven to 150°C/300°F/Gas Mark 2. Cut the bread into 1cm (1/2in) dice and bake in the oven for about 10-12 minutes until is dry and crisp. Turn the oven temperature up to 180°C/350°F/Gas Mark 4.

Cut the tops off the squash and scoop out the seeds. Cook the squash, including the tops, in boiling water for 5 minutes, then cool under cold water.

Remove the mushroom stalks and set aside to be used in the gravy. Brush the mushroom caps with some of the butter, sprinkle with salt and roast them for 10–12 minutes in the oven until tender. Chop the cooked mushrooms into small dice.

Cook the kale in boiling water for 8–10 minutes until tender. Drain and cool under cold running water. Squeeze the kale to dry, then chop it finely.

In a large saucepan, fry the onions in the remaining butter over a medium heat until soft. Add the garlic and herbs and fry for 2–3 minutes, then fry the kale for 2 minutes.

In a bowl, mix the mushrooms, the kale mixture and the bread. Season with salt and the green peppercorns. If the filling seems dry, add a little stock or water.

Fill the squash with the stuffing and replace the tops. Place them in an oven dish and bake for 30–50 minutes, until a knife slides easily through the flesh of the squash. Check occasionally to ensure the squash skin isn't becoming too dry, splashing on a little water or stock if necessary.

To make the gravy, heat a little olive oil in a pan and fry the onion, carrot, garlic, celery, fresh mushroom stalks and herbs over a high heat for 7–8 minutes until the onion is soft and golden. Add the soaked mushrooms and their water, the wine and tomato purée. Bring back to the boil, then lower the heat and simmer for 30 minutes. Strain through a sieve and discard the vegetables. Put the stock back in a pan and bring back to the boil. Mix the cornflour with a little water and stir it into the stock. Lower the heat and simmer for 5 minutes, stirring, until thickened.

Serves 4

FOR THE ROAST SQUASH

100g (3 1/2oz) stale bread
4 small Sweet Dumpling squash
200g (7oz) field mushrooms or Portobello
60g (2 1/4oz) butter, melted
salt
150g (5 1/2oz) kale
2 medium red onions, finely chopped
3 garlic cloves, finely chopped
4 sage leaves, chopped
leaves from 1 sprig fresh thyme
10 green peppercorns, cracked

FOR THE MUSHROOM AND RED WINE GRAVY

olive oil
1 medium onion, chopped
1 carrot, chopped
4 garlic cloves, finely chopped
2 stalks celery, chopped
leaves from 1 sprig fresh thyme
1 handful fresh parsley, chopped
small handful dried porcini or mixed mushrooms, soaked in 500ml (18fl oz) warm water for 1 hour
200ml (7fl oz) red wine
1 tbsp tomato purée
1 tbsp cornflour

Gazpacho of Tomatillo and Cucumber with Avocado and Almonds

Cut the cucumber in half lengthways, scoop out the seeds, and chop the flesh coarsely. Put the cucumber, tomatillos, spring onions, chillies, garlic and coriander in a food processor. Add half the water, and pulse to get a coarse purée. If you prefer a smoother finish, blend the vegetables for longer.

Transfer the purée to a bowl and add the juice of half a lime, the sugar and the rest of the water, and mix together to get a thick soupy consistency. Season with salt and chill the gazpacho for an hour or more.

To serve, ladle the gazpacho into bowls. Halve the avocado, remove the stone and the skin and chop the flesh into small dice. Spoon some avocado onto each portion of gazpacho. Sprinkle on some almonds, and squeeze a little lime juice over the avocado.

Serves 4–6

1 cucumber
500g (18oz) green tomatillos, halved
4 spring onions, chopped
2 fresh mild green chillies, halved, seeded and chopped
1 garlic clove
2 tbsp chopped fresh coriander
300ml (10fl oz) water
juice of 1 lime
1 tsp caster sugar
salt
1 avocado
2 tbsp flaked almonds, lightly toasted

Tomatillo Salsa

This hot and sour salsa is an excellent foil for rich dishes such as pancakes, frittata and cheese-filled wraps, as well as most Mexican-style dishes. When serving it with spiced dishes adjust the chilli levels so that only one of the dishes is hot. It also makes a lively dip for corn chips or pitta bread.

Combine everything except the coriander, season with a little salt, and leave to stand for at least 30 minutes at room temperature to allow the flavours to develop. Just before serving, stir in the coriander.

Serves 6–8, makes about 500g (18oz)

500g (18oz) green tomatillos, finely chopped

1–2 fresh jalapeño or other green chillies, finely chopped, seeds included

1 small red onion, finely chopped

2 garlic cloves, finely chopped

juice of ½ lime

salt

1 small handful fresh coriander, chopped

Gingered Pumpkin Chutney

This sweetly spiced chutney is a very versatile condiment. Serve it with cheese and crackers, in sandwiches or with hot rice dishes and curries. It will store for months in well-sealed and sterilised jars.

Makes about 3kg (6¹/₂lb), 8–12 jars

2kg (4¹/₂lb) peeled and seeded pumpkin
500ml (18fl oz) white wine vinegar
1kg (2¹/₄lb) caster sugar
80g (2³/₄oz) fresh ginger, grated
2 tsp coriander seeds, ground
1 tsp fennel seeds, ground

Chop the pumpkin flesh into 1cm (¹/₂in) dice. Bring a large saucepan of water to the boil and cook half of the pumpkin pieces for 5 minutes. Drain.

In another large saucepan, bring the vinegar and sugar to the boil and add in the cooked and raw pumpkin, the ginger and spices. Bring back to the boil, lower the heat and simmer, stirring often, for about an hour, until the chutney has thickened. Store in sterilised jars.

Gingered Gooseberry Chutney

As above, this is great with cheese plates or cooked cheeses dishes, and particularly with grilled haloumi.

Makes about 1.2kg (2³/₄lb), 4–6 jars

1kg (2¹/₄lb) gooseberries, topped and tailed
100g (3¹/₂oz) grated fresh root ginger
¹/₂ tsp mixed spice
300g (10¹/₂oz) sugar
juice of 2 lemons

Put everything in a large saucepan, bring to the boil then lower the heat and simmer for 30–50 minutes, stirring occasionally, until the gooseberries have broken down and the chutney has thickened. Store in sterilised jars.

Aubergine and Cime di Rapa with Chillies, Feta, and a Citrus and Pomegranate Dressing

I serve this warm salad as a first course but it is also good as part of an antipasti or even as a light lunch with some crusty bread. You can use spinach, chard or almost any green if you can't get cime di rapa, though bitter greens are a better foil for the combination of spice, salt and sweetness in this salad.

Preheat the oven to 180°c/350°F/Gas Mark 4. Make a dressing by combining the lemon zest and juice, orange zest and juice and the olive oil. Quarter the pomegranate and scoop out the seeds, saving them along with any juice.

Slice the aubergine into rounds about 1cm (½in) thick. Brush these on both sides with olive oil and roast them on a baking tray in the oven for about 8–10 minutes until lightly coloured, turning once if necessary. Quarter these slices and set aside.

In a shallow pan, heat a little olive oil over a medium heat and put in the shallots, chillies and cime di rapa. Cook for 3–4 minutes, stirring, then add the aubergine pieces. Stir briefly and remove the pan from the heat. Add some of the dressing, and divide the vegetables between four plates. Scatter the feta over and around each dish, then do the same with the pomegranate seeds and a little of their juice. Finally, sprinkle some more of the dressing over everything, and serve.

Serves 4

1 medium aubergine

olive oil

2 small shallots, thinly sliced

2 fresh mild red chillies, halved, seeded and thinly sliced

400g (14oz) cime di rapa

120g (4¼oz) feta cheese, crumbled

FOR THE CITRUS-POMEGRANATE DRESSING

zest of 1 lemon

juice of 1 lemon

zest of 1 orange

juice of ½ orange

200ml (7fl oz) olive oil

1 pomegranate

Sweet and Hot Pepper Stew with Squash, Aubergine, Tomatoes and Borlotti Beans

This stew was put together to celebrate the late summer produce of Ultan Walsh's farm. It seems complicated to read through, but essentially it's about cooking the vegetables separately in large pieces so they hold their individual flavours in the finished dish. I have given approximate quantities for the peppers, aubergines and squash, in case you want to make it with more readily available varieties of the vegetables.

Serve the stew with something to soak up the juices, such as potato mash, polenta or foccaccia.

Serves 4
8 long sweet peppers, about 800g (1³/₄lb)
4 fresh red chillies, halved and seeded
8 plum tomatoes, halved lengthways
olive oil
2 medium red onions, halved and sliced
1 bunch fresh basil leaves
200ml (7fl oz) vegetable stock or water
120g (4¹/₄oz) fresh borlotti beans
zest and juice of ¹/₂ lemon
salt
12 medium shallots, peeled and halved lengthways, leaving enough of the root to hold the shallots together
2 long thin aubergines, about 600g (1lb 5oz)
6 garlic cloves, sliced
6 small scallopini squash, quartered, about 300g (10¹/₂oz)

Preheat the oven to 180°C/350°F/Gas Mark 4. Halve and seed two of the peppers and chop the flesh coarsely. Slice two each of the chillies and tomatoes. Heat two tablespoons of olive oil in a saucepan over a high heat. Put in the peppers, red onions, sliced chillies and tomatoes. Fry over a high heat, stirring for 7–8 minutes until the vegetables are soft and the onion beginning to caramelise.

Add half of the basil and fry for a minute more, then add the stock or water. Bring to the boil, then lower the heat and simmer for 5 minutes. Remove the pan from the heat and leave it to cool for 30 minutes. Blend in a food processor, and pass the purée through a sieve, saving the liquid and discarding the vegetables.

Put the borlotti beans in a large saucepan of water, bring it to the boil, then lower the heat and simmer for about 10–20 minutes until tender. Drain the beans and toss with the lemon zest and juice, two tablespoons of olive oil and a little salt.

Put the remaining tomatoes on an oven tray with the shallots, drizzle with olive oil and sprinkle with salt. Roast in the oven for about 10–15 minutes until the shallots are soft and both vegetables are lightly coloured.

Chop the aubergines in quarters lengthways, and then in half across. Toss in olive oil in an oven dish and roast for about 10–12 minutes until tender and browned.

Cut the tops off the remaining peppers and scoop out the seeds. Chop the peppers diagonally into two or three large pieces. Chop the remaining chillies into thick diagonal slices. In a large wide pan, heat two tablespoons of olive oil. Add in the peppers, chillies, garlic and scallopini squash. Fry over a medium heat for 2–3 minutes, then add the remaining basil. Reduce the heat, cover the pan and stew for 30 minutes or so, until the vegetables are tender. Check occasionally to make sure the dish is moist, adding a little of the pepper broth if necessary.

Add the cooked tomatoes, shallots, borlotti beans and aubergines. Pour in the broth and heat the stew through for a few minutes. Season with salt, then serve.

Roasted Baby Aubergine with Lemon Basil, Chilli, Caperberries and Sheep's Cheese

These aubergines are lovely as part of an antipasti, but they also work very well as a starter served with some roast plum tomatoes and a little rocket. You can also make the dish as a warm salad using ordinary aubergines, sliced thickly into rounds and roasted.

Lemon basil has a lovely citric kick, but if you don't have any just use ordinary basil and a little lemon juice. Caperberries are the fruit of the plant of which capers are the flower buds. They have a similar but milder flavour, are larger and have pinkish flesh. You will find them, preserved in jars in some Mediterranean delis or food stores. The more widely available capers will also work well in this recipe.

Serves 4 as a starter

4–6 baby aubergines
olive oil
2 mild fresh chillies
2 small shallots, finely diced
30g (1¼oz) caperberries, thinly sliced
1 small bunch fresh lemon basil leaves, sliced
80g (2¾oz) hard sheep's cheese, such as Cratloe Hills, Manchego or Pecorino

Preheat the oven to 180°C/350°F/Gas Mark 4. Line the base of an oven dish with baking parchment. Halve the aubergines lengthways, brush the cut sides lightly with olive oil and place them, cut side down, in the dish. Brush the skin of the aubergine with olive oil too, and cover the dish loosely with parchment. Roast the aubergines in the oven for about 10–12 minutes until tender. The cut sides should be lightly browned.

While the aubergines are cooking, halve the chillies lengthways, remove the seeds and slice the flesh thinly. Put this in a small saucepan with the shallots and two tablespoons of olive oil. Fry gently for 1 minute over a low to medium heat, then stir in the caperberries and lemon basil, cook for a few seconds more, then remove from the heat.

Serve the aubergines warm, cut side up, with some of the dressing sprinkled over. Shave the cheese thinly and scatter the pieces over the aubergines.

Aubergine Parcels of Haloumi and Rocket with Roast Garlic and Shallot Raita

Preheat the oven to 150°C/300°F/Gas Mark 2. To make the raita, snip the ends off the garlic and shallots, toss them lightly in olive oil and roast in the oven for 15 minutes or so, until soft. Squeeze the flesh out of the skins and blend in a food processor. Add the yoghurt and pulse a few times to incorporate the garlic and shallot. Toast the mustard seeds in a heavy frying pan over a low heat for 5 minutes, then stir them into the yoghurt with the lime zest, chives and a pinch of salt.

Increase the oven temperature to 180°C/350°F/ Gas Mark 4. Cut a slice from two sides of each aubergine, then cut the remaining flesh into long slices about 0.5cm (¼in) thick. Brush these lightly with olive oil and roast them on a baking tray in the oven for about 8–10 minutes until fully cooked and lightly coloured. You will need 12 slices altogether, but prepare a couple of extra slices to allow for any parcels that break as you are making them.

Cut the haloumi into 12 slices. Heat a wide frying pan over a medium heat and brush the slices with olive oil. Fry the haloumi for about 5 minutes on each side until lightly coloured, transferring the cooked pieces to a plate. Squeeze the lime juice over the cooked haloumi. Chop the rocket coarsely.

Place the aubergines on a work surface with the best-looking sides down. Spread a thin layer of tomato pesto on each. Place a slice of haloumi across the centre of each aubergine slice, cover it with some rocket and fold over the top and bottom of the aubergine slice to form a tight parcel. Place the aubergine parcels, folded-side down, on an oven tray lined with baking parchment and bake for 5 minutes, just long enough to heat through. Serve with the raita.

Sundried tomato pesto

To make your own tomato pesto, soak 80g (2¾oz) sundried tomatoes in hot water for 20 minutes. Drain and blend the tomatoes in a food processor with 1 clove of garlic and 200ml (7fl oz) olive oil. A teaspoon of capers gives it a lovely edge too.

Serves 4

FOR THE ROAST GARLIC AND SHALLOT RAITA

4 garlic cloves, unpeeled
2 small shallots, unpeeled
olive oil
250ml (8fl oz) plain yoghurt
2 tsp black mustard seeds
zest of 1 lime
1 tbsp chopped fresh chives
salt

FOR THE AUBERGINE PARCELS

3 medium aubergines
olive oil
300g (10½oz) haloumi
juice of 1 lime
100g (3½oz) rocket
2 tbsp sundried tomato pesto (see below)

Rosa Bianca Aubergine with Chard and Pine Nut Filling and Roasted Pepper Sauce

The flesh of a Rosa Bianca is moist and juicy, so the filling simply adds texture and flavour without being a full-on stuffing.

Preheat the oven to 180°C/350°F/Gas Mark 4. Line the base of an oven dish with baking parchment. Halve the aubergines lengthways, brush the cut sides lightly with olive oil and place them cut-side down in the dish. Brush the skin of the aubergine with olive oil too, and cover the dish loosely with parchment. Roast the aubergines in the oven for 10–12 minutes until tender. The cut sides should be lightly browned.

Cut the stalk off the chard just below the bottom of the leaf. Slice the stalks about 1cm (½in) thick. Heat a tablespoon of olive oil in a medium pan and fry them for 5 minutes over a medium heat. Add in the wine and a little salt, bring to the boil, cover with parchment, lower the heat and simmer gently for 15–20 minutes until the stalks are tender. Set aside.

Cut the remaining stalk from the middle of the chard leaves and chop it finely. Heat a little olive oil in a medium pan and fry the stalk with the red onion and garlic over a medium heat for 5 minutes. At the same time, bring a saucepan of water to the boil, add the chard leaves and boil for about 3–4 minutes until tender. Cool them under cold running water, squeeze out the moisture and chop the chard finely before adding to the pan with the onion and garlic. Remove from the heat, leave to cool and then stir in the pine nuts and cheese. Season with salt and pepper.

Using a fork, carefully break up some of the flesh of the aubergines, leaving a good 1cm (½in) all around untouched. Gently press some chard filling into each aubergine for a loose filling. Put the aubergines, filled-side up, close together in an oven dish and return to the oven for about 5–7 minutes to warm through.

To make the pepper sauce, heat a little olive oil in a medium saucepan, chop the peppers and fry over a medium heat with the garlic for 2 minutes. Add the remaining wine and the water. Bring to the boil, lower the heat and simmer for 5 minutes. Put the contents of the pan in a food processor and blend to a smooth purée. Put the purée back in the pan, add the cream, return to the boil, then lower the heat and simmer for a minute. Season with salt and pepper.

To serve, pour a little sauce on each plate and place the aubergines on top. Serve a little of the braised chard stalks on the side.

Serves 4

2 large Rosa Bianca aubergines
olive oil
4 medium leaves of chard
100ml (3½fl oz) white wine
salt and pepper
1 medium red onion, finely chopped
2 garlic cloves, finely chopped
2 tbsp pine nuts, lightly toasted and chopped
40g (1½oz) hard cheese such as Desmond, Parmesan or Pecorino, finely grated

ROASTED PEPPER SAUCE

olive oil
2 red peppers, roasted, peeled and seeded
2 garlic cloves, finely chopped
100ml (3½fl oz) white wine
100ml (3½fl oz) water
150ml (5fl oz) double cream

Gooseberry Fool with Elderflower Syrup

Put the gooseberries in a large saucepan with the sugar and two tablespoons of the elderflower cordial. Bring this slowly to the boil, then lower the heat and simmer gently, stirring occasionally, for about 15–20 minutes until the gooseberries are very soft. Blend the mixture in a food processor, then pass the purée through a sieve and leave it to cool.

Serves 6–8

1kg (2¼lb) gooseberries
250g (9oz) caster sugar
200ml (7fl oz) elderflower cordial
400ml (14fl oz) whipping cream

Put the remaining cordial in a small saucepan, bring to the boil, then lower the heat and simmer for about 8–10 minutes until it has reduced to a syrup.

Whisk the cream until it forms soft peaks and fold in the cold gooseberry purée. Put the fool in a fridge to chill for an hour or more before serving. Serve it in individual dishes, and swirl some of the elderflower syrup over each one.

Gooseberry and Elderflower Rippled Parfait

Place the gooseberries in a large saucepan with 150g (5½oz) of the sugar. Heat gently, stirring until the sugar melts and begins to boil. Reduce the heat and simmer gently for about 5 minutes until the gooseberries just begin to collapse but are still green. Transfer the mixture to a food processor and blend to a smooth purée. Pass the purée through a sieve and leave to cool.

Serves 8

500g (18oz) gooseberries
250g (9oz) caster sugar
4 egg yolks
2 tbsp elderflower cordial
350ml (12fl oz) whipping cream

Place the egg yolks, cordial and the remaining sugar in a metal bowl over a pan of gently simmering water and whisk for about 7 minutes, until you get a thick and pale custard. Leave this to cool completely.

Whip the cream until it forms soft peaks, then fold this into the custard. Very gently, swirl the gooseberry purée through the custard to get a rippled effect.

Line a loaf tin with clingfilm and pour in the mixture. Freeze for at least 4 hours before serving. Serve with some amaretti or hazelnut biscuits.

Spice-marinated Figs with Honey, Thyme and Yoghurt Ice Cream and Sesame Brittle

This recipe calls for an ice cream machine. It is possible to make ice cream by freezing the custard in a bowl and stirring it occasionally to break up any ice particles that might be forming. However, there are so many ice cream machines available now, right down to some very inexpensive but effective models, and there is no comparison between the results achieved with and without one.

To make the sesame brittle, put the sugar and water in a small saucepan, bring to the boil, stirring until the sugar is dissolved, then lower the heat and simmer until caramel coloured. Pour onto a large sheet of baking parchment and sprinkle with the sesame seeds. Place another sheet of parchment on top and roll it to get an evenly thin finish. Leave the brittle until completely cold, then break it into pieces and store in a dry, airtight container.

To make the ice cream, put the milk and thyme in a saucepan and heat slowly until almost boiling. Remove from the heat and leave to infuse for 1 hour.

Whisk the egg yolks and sugar together until pale and thick. Reheat the milk to just below boiling and strain it onto the egg mixture, still whisking. Return this custard to a clean saucepan, bring to the boil, reduce the heat and simmer gently, stirring, until it has thickened a little. Add the honey, stir, then strain the custard through a sieve into a bowl. Leave to cool, then whisk in the cream and yoghurt. Freeze using an ice cream machine according to the manufacturer's instructions.

To prepare the figs, put the sugar, water and spices in a small saucepan and boil for 5 minutes. Remove from the heat and add the fruit juices and zest and the orange blossom water. Pour the marinade into a bowl and add the fig halves. Turn them until they are coated in the marinade and leave in a fridge for at least 1 hour, and up to 24 hours .

Heat a non-stick pan over a medium heat. Take the figs out of the marinade and put them cut-side down into the pan. Cook for 3–4 minutes. Strain the marinade into a bowl. Turn the figs over and add the marinade to the pan. Turn down the heat and cook gently for a further 5–8 minutes until the marinade has reduced to a slightly syrupy sauce. Serve immediately with the ice cream and sesame brittle.

Serves 4

FOR THE SESAME BRITTLE

150g (5¹/₂oz) caster sugar
1 tbsp water
2 tbsp sesame seeds, lightly toasted

FOR THE ICE CREAM

400ml (14fl oz) milk
1 tbsp fresh thyme leaves
6 egg yolks
75g (2¹/₂oz) caster sugar
50g (2oz) honey
100ml (3¹/₂fl oz) double cream
100ml (3¹/₂fl oz) yoghurt

FOR THE SPICE-MARINATED FIGS

150g (5¹/₂oz) caster sugar
150ml (5fl oz) water
3 star anise
1 cinnamon stick
juice of 1 lemon
zest and juice of 2 oranges
1 tbsp orange blossom water
8 fresh figs, halved

Growing in the dark

Beneath all the palaver, food is really just a fuel for our bodies. Or should I say, above all the palaver? No matter how much we amuse ourselves with it, or how much we elevate its role in our culture, the primary function of food is the purely practical one of nourishing our bodies. And yet, it is surely a testament to the human spirit that we have added so many layers of cultural and social importance to the preparation and consumption of this 'fuel'. We go to great lengths to make our food pleasurable, and to spread that pleasure in ways that range from intimate sharing to social ritual on a larger scale. As fundamental as food might be, to treat it simply as something to be shovelled into the body is to denigrate one of our most potently civilising graces.

The shapes, colours, textures and flavours of our food are now so highly varied that it is easy to forget where it all comes from. Sunlight, air and water create the basic chemistry behind everything we eat. It wouldn't be far wrong to say that we live on sunshine and water, which is a nice thought, conjuring images of a Garden of Eden full of fresh greenery and sweet fruit. Except, of course, the mythical garden had produce which needed only little management, allowing far too much time for things to go astray. If the inhabitants had stayed longer, if Adam's curiosity hadn't got the better of him, I'm sure they would have done a spot of gardening.

I started this book by looking at those vegetables that most obviously embody the essential life force of sunshine and water – the leafy greens that spring from the ground and grow towards the sun, a visible and potent sign of life. It is surprising, however, just how much we feed on plant life that grows in the dark. And so it is fitting to end the book with a look at that most unlikely source of nutrition and gastronomic delight: the foods we dig from the earth and those we cover to keep the sun away. These 'dark' foods might be considered our unexpected pleasures, ones we might have done without or never found. They are ancient somehow, perhaps in the way that many of them constitute, literally and symbolically, the very foundation of life, but are as modern, too, as anything we grow in the light. The plant roots and tubers that we produce for consumption now are very sophisticated, highly cultivated versions of their ancestors, about which people could once have had only an inkling of their potential. Their still primitive appearance masks generations of careful nurturing and development.

Curiosity and hunger have always been great motivators in the search for new foods, and they certainly would have played a big part in the development of unlikely plants or parts of plants into important elements of our diet. Hunger is a famously good sauce, and what else but a gnawing

THE CARROT'S QUALITIES ARE SIMPLE AND UP FRONT

tummy would make people go digging down into the earth to haul out tangled and muddy roots in the hope that they might be good to eat; or sifting through the rubble and decaying matter on the forest floor, not to mention poking around in the dank shadowy corners of caves and rocky outcrops? Well, yes, hunger of course, but as well as our naturally ingenious way of responding to necessity, there is also our instinct, still seen in every baby, to put something in our mouths in the optimistic hope that it tastes good. As well as sustenance, we are always on the lookout for new tastes and textures to excite our palates. So, even with hunger sated, we search around in unlikely places, looking for a taste buzz.

In some ways, there has been more ingenuity applied to the unlikely 'dark' foods than to the more obvious fresh greens. We have discovered and developed the roots and tubers that grow beneath leafy plants which themselves are not good to eat. Even when the leaf was good, we wondered if maybe the root might be too, or perhaps be even better? Carrots were for a long time eaten like parsley, prized for their delicate fronds, somewhere between herb and vegetable. Then we took a liking to the roots, manipulating them over time to a greater size and sweetness, even changing their colour. Parsley, in fact, went the other way, from a root valued for its flavour to a ubiquitous herb.

Then there are those plants, such as celery and seakale, that are good as greens but which we have discovered to be sweeter when kept pale, so we stick a bucket over their leafy heads to actually keep the sun away! We became so fascinated with the potentially offputting fungi that grow on or around trees that we cracked their secrets and learned to domesticate them. We train pigs and dogs to find peculiar-smelling truffles beneath the roots of trees, a food whose only connection with sunlight, air and water is that its parent life form has a benign relationship with the slow-growing tree it lives beneath.

Of course, the earth isn't really such an unlikely source of delicious sustenance. It is the repository of all that sunlight and water that feeds the plants above ground. Down below, plants store their energy, protect and concentrate it, and prepare for the time when they can use it to fuel new growth. Sometimes we wait for the fresh greenery; sometimes we greedily dig down and help ourselves to the energy source.

Because so much of what grows in the dark also keeps well, there is an inherent association between these foods and winter, and all that suggests: slow cooking, stews and braises, hearty warming food for cold nights. In winter, we need comfort food, dishes that make us feel safe and warm. Battening down the hatches and staying indoors, we use such foods not only to warm our bodies but to connect us to tradition and to our own histories, and to nurture a sense of belonging and security. This is the true 'soul food', food that nourishes us in ways that can't be measured by nutrition charts.

The holy trinity of roots: carrots, parsnips and turnips

These three vegetables are fixed together in my head, and I'm sure in the heads of many others too. In my childhood, they were served together as one dish more often than on their own. Mostly, they were chopped into rugged chunks and boiled, and sometimes the resulting collage was mashed with parsley and butter. Vegetable soup was the 'holy trinity' blended with a little potato and onion.

I say 'roots' now but then we simply called them 'vegetables'. The other vegetables, chiefly cabbage and potatoes, were clearly something else, not to be confused with the 'vegetables'. Cauliflower showed up occasionally on our table, and broccoli became a regular visitor shortly after it first arrived in the country. You know, I have often wondered about the phrase 'meat and two veg' as a description of traditional dinners. If potato were one of the two, what was the other? 'Meat and four, five or six veg' would have been a more accurate description of our meals.

Perhaps the absolute familiarity of the trinity is the cause of their being perceived as dull, ordinary and somehow from another time. They are certainly ancient and each of the three has a long history, and an exotic one too in contrast to their modern perception. I should exclude carrots from this image problem, however. While the parsnip and turnip have become marginalised and unglamorous, the carrot has held its own, and is still one of the most popular and commonly used vegetables. It's not surprising that the carrot is a real crowd pleaser and, maybe even more importantly, one that appeals to children. It's hard not to like a carrot, and hard to find someone who doesn't, other than the odd person who uses the aggressive defence of: 'Me? Vegetables? Nah, never touch them.'

The carrot's qualities are simple and upfront. It is brilliantly and cheerfully coloured, and handsomely elegant, whether long and thin or short and stout, or anything in between. While most roots have a degree of sweetness, often with an earthy undertone, the carrot's sugar kick is simple and clean, making it the most accessible vegetable, tastewise, for young palates.

A psychological brightness to match the carrot's colour lies in the fact that it is a summer vegetable as much as a winter one. The other roots are almost exclusively associated with the heavy cooking of winter and with the subsistence role of stored food. Carrots fit this image too, but they also have their day in the sun. Raw young carrots plucked straight from the earth are one of the delights of summer, adding a juicy sweetness to salads and lighting up plates of crudités at summer parties. Lightly cooked fresh carrots bring their crisp sweetness to warm salads as well as light dishes flavoured with fragrant spices, citrus and the lighter summer herbs of basil, marjoram, fennel, chervil and coriander.

Carrots have a long history and an ongoing place in most food cultures of the world. Right up there with tomatoes, these sweet charmers have been welcomed and ultimately treasured everywhere they showed up. It is said they came to Europe from the Middle East, particularly Afghanistan, where they were originally purple or very dark red. You can just imagine the fuss they would have caused, first as a rare and exotic treat, then as an incredibly useful addition to the diet as they became more readily available. Even now, right across the world, no matter how common they have become, carrots haven't lost their capacity to please. In an age when we have an insatiable appetite for novelty in everything, including our food, the purple carrot is enjoying something of a minor revival. However, it is ironic that it is being touted as rare and expensive while its bright orange descendant is so widespread and cheap.

In contrast to the carrot in its summer guise, nobody is ever going to offer you a fan of freshly cut turnip and batons of parsnips to dip into your guacamole. Well, I hope not anyway. That's not to denigrate the paler roots in any way. It's just not their time or place. While the carrot switches easily between the seasons, these other two are resolutely denizens of the colder months. You will sometimes come across them in summer (turnips more than parsnips) but they are not at their most sweetly dense and golden best. Sorry, I should clarify at this point that when I say turnip I am talking, in the Scottish sense, about the *swede* turnip only, or 'swedes', as they are often simply named. The other smaller white ones I neither grow, cook nor eat. I have enjoyed them on rare occasions in the hands of cooks who understand them, so I am prepared to admit this is a personal prejudice. Perhaps 'prejudice' is too strong; it's simply an absence of interest. Another day, perhaps.

Parsnips are similar to carrots in so many ways that it is worth looking at why one is so effortlessly popular while the other is variously seen as difficult, dull, challenging, boring and even downright unpleasant. The two roots are so closely related that they once shared the same name. While the carrot has made its way into every corner of the world, the parsnip has disappeared from the warmer parts of Europe where it was once a treat of Roman gardens and kitchens. Later, in medieval times, it was valued for its very useful combination of starchy texture and high sugar content.

But the parsnip has issues where the carrot is all sweetness and light. For one thing, it has a woody core and a tougher skin. I almost always cut the core from a parsnip unless I am cooking it soft to be puréed for soup. But perhaps the parsnip's best asset is also its most off-putting characteristic, namely its complex taste. It is as sweet as a carrot but the sugar is carried in a rich, earthy flavour that makes it the finest and most rewarding root to a lot of people, while to the rest of the population it is one best ignored.

As a child I was almost scared of the things, convinced that, as well as having a flavour akin to dirty lemonade, parsnips had spikes! My mind turned to this recently, over a bowl of smooth parsnip mash that I had cooked for a magazine spread. The angle of the feature was what we unfortunate vegetarians eat for Christmas dinner. I groan in affected weariness when the question pops up every year, without fail, then knuckle down to the job of spinning a different yarn to that of the previous year, though possibly similar to what I wrote the year before. Next year I think I'll have a go at reviving the nut roast.

The smoothness of the mash transported me back to the parsnips of my youth, the short bit of it before I refused to eat them because I'd become afraid of putting them in my mouth. The parsnips we ate were peeled and chopped into chunks or thick slices, each a full cross-section of the root. When parsnips get old, towards the end of winter, the cores become tougher and more fibrous. Sometimes too, they develop, short spiky shoots sprouting from the core into the flesh of the parsnip. I think it must have been a combination of these textures that spooked my young brain, which was always a little suspicious about food at that stage. It may only have been one unfortunate lunch or perhaps a sack of parsnips that lasted a week, but dinnertime at that age was no time for adventure, and I swore off the dangerous things for life.

Luckily, I got over it. A mere ten years of careful avoidance sorted that. Now, while I tend to take the carrot's easy charm for granted, I find the parsnip's complexity incredibly useful. There is even inspiration in its supposed difficulties. Carving out the core of a parsnip leaves a shape that suggests it would make good chips. So it does, and fritters too. The earthy flavour that becomes intensely but not cloyingly sweet when roasted makes parsnip a great ingredient for risottos, pancake fillings, ravioli, soups and that sublime mash. Parsnip works well with the hardier herbs such as rosemary and thyme, and with parsley and tarragon too, but it also shines with the more exotic flavours of spices such as coriander, cumin, fennel and cardamom.

There is an irony in that, surely. While the territory of the parsnip has retreated to the colder northern parts of Europe, at the same time it marries so beautifully in taste with the spices of the south and east that it is able to regain its former and rightful place among the pantheon of more exotic flavours. Think about roast parsnip in a couscous pilaf with fennel, coriander, lemon and chickpeas, and you will never consider it dull again.

If the parsnip is a vegetable with a small but quietly devoted following, the swede turnip is a class A, left-field cult at this stage in its history. Take a random poll in the room in which you are reading this: who likes turnip? There will be many dissenters, I'm sure, but if you don't have your own hand raised in favour, I might be up against it here. And yet, I don't think it's a hard case to make.

For a start, the turnip has no illusions about its place in the scheme of things. Strictly speaking, it's not even a root, but a swollen part of the stem that sits half in the ground and half out. It has never been glamorous, and isn't ever likely to be. Another vegetable would be mortified to be viewed the same way, but the turnip is used to shame. The carrot is outrageously popular and the parsnip at least has a noble history and a complex quality that gives it a good chance of a decent role in modern cooking, but the turnip is considered unfit for human consumption by more than half the people who even know what it is. And the other half are Scottish. Well, not quite. Although the turnip is most associated with Scotland, it has long been one of the most common and well-loved vegetables across Scandinavia and in Ireland. The name under which it operates in America is 'rutabaga', a derivative of its Swedish name, *rotabagge*, or 'red bag' (translated literally). Hence 'swede' too, I guess.

You will have heard the easy jibe often nervously thrown about by detractors of the turnip that it is food fit only for swine. Perhaps in a culture afflicted by the debilitating effects of snobbery and the paranoia of what is appropriate to eat, this would put you off a vegetable. Here, as in Scotland and Sweden, I don't think we mind too much eating what the pigs do if we recognise that it is good food in its own right. Only the socially insecure would worry about the association. Besides, pigs love food. I mean they genuinely love it, in the sense that they take real sensory pleasure from it as distinct from just filling their bellies. I'd trust a pig over a food snob any time. Nevertheless, it's unavoidably true that the turnip has become unfashionable and perhaps even the Irish and Scots are trying to dissociate themselves from a time when the pigs lived so close to us they were doing housework and learning basic sums.

A family I knew well when I was growing up had a novel use for turnips and went through quite an impressive quantity of them. Every month or so, a small van would pull up outside their house and a farmer would get out, lugging a sack of turnips up the garden path. He never stayed for tea, just dropped the sack against the side of the house and went on his way. He may have had a few more sacks to deliver, but would never have spoken of his routine. The family of the house knew the man well, otherwise the relationship could never have worked, but the transaction was always short and careful. Now, at the time, none of us had recipes for turnip soufflé or the least idea about how to reduce the roots to elegant nibbles. We just boiled them and ate them, as the saying goes. The family was small and had some quantity of turnips to get through in this simple way before the next lot arrived. And arrive it would, because the sack was eagerly awaited. Besides turnips, it contained the monthly supply of poitin – a type of homemade liquor – and a doorstep-delivered supply of good-quality and reputable poitin was not to be spurned simply due to an inability to get through a sack of turnips.

While you will sometimes find the swede turnip in summer along with its white cousin, it is as a stored winter food that it comes into its own. Then, it is a vegetable of rich, earthy sweetness with a dense yellow-orange flesh that has a wonderful ability to absorb flavour and fat. This makes it wonderful in mash and soups, as a roast vegetable and in long, slow braising. Turnips store well through the winter, though they may become fibrous and aquire an earthier taste as the 'hungry gap' of early spring approaches.

While it is rooted (no pun intended) in the culture and flavours of the cold north, its ability to soak up seasoning means it can be surprisingly good with richly spiced food. I'll come straight out and say it now: one of the best curries I ever had was made with turnip. It was a long time ago and there was the added incentive of outdoors-induced hunger and appetite lubricants.

To abridge the events of that evening somewhat, it involved spending a few hours in the bar of a remote island hostel. Meantime our self-appointed chef intended cooking dinner while not spending too much time in the kitchen. It was November and the local shop had two vegetables – cabbage and turnip. The cabbage was ragged and frost-burned, so we bought a turnip for the price of a packet of crisps. Mr Chef cut it into enormous wedges, fried some onions and spices, then added the turnip, coconut milk, yoghurt, cream and water and put the covered pot in a low oven while he rejoined the party. Several hours later, when the level of moaning from the famished throng actually penetrated his scheming brain, he volunteered to go upstairs and put on the rice. *Brown rice*, forty-five minutes' cooking time! That was the longest wait of my life for dinner, but also one of the most satisfying meals I've ever eaten. Yes, hunger is the king of sauces. In his own weird way, our chef knew what he was orchestrating, and he also knew that turnip doesn't cook quickly.

This is the essence of cooking turnip. It needs time and it's not much fun if undercooked. Even when roasting turnip, it is best to steam or parboil it for a few minutes first to make sure it achieves that perfect degree of soft moistness and intensity of flavour.

Two of the recipes in this section came from an evening in Paradiso when the chefs I was working with both claimed to have never eaten a turnip dish that pushed any pleasure buttons. I left work that night sporting a wide grin, while they looked damn impressed. We had made a filling for ravioli that paired turnip with the peppery, nutty flavour of some two-year-old Gabriel, the hard cheese made by my good friend Bill Hogan in West Cork, and doused the pasta parcels in a butter flavoured with sage, truffle and the sweetness of fried shallots. But the real challenge had been to make an elegant main course from a turnip. Staring at the large turnips on the bench, I began to see not their obvious roundness but their inner potential to be carved into a cube. That's a part of what I do for a living: stare at vegetables, wondering about their inner potential. Glamorous, eh?

From the cube, it was a small step to cutting thin square slices from it. Boiled and braised, these slices formed the basis of a galette, in which they were baked in alternate layers with a mixture of mushrooms and pecans. Of course, it looked like I had conjured up a couple of pretty fancy dishes just to prove a point, but I had been thinking about turnips for a week or more, being a little disgruntled that I hadn't put them on the menu yet that winter. I had learned something too – sometimes it takes a challenge to push a half-baked notion into something real and useful.

Turnip has one other glorious characteristic which should be a good enough reason to give it at least one chance in your kitchen. Almost alone among vegetables, and certainly far more than any other contender, the colour of turnip actually intensifies as it cooks. Check it out, then think about it. That is one cool root.

Beet, the pickled root

While the holy trinity of roots was an everyday staple of my childhood, there was another root we ate only occasionally. Salads didn't feature much on our table, but when they did they were usually accompanied by beetroot. They weren't really salads, more a plate of cold things. I don't think we even considered beetroot a vegetable, since it came in a jar of vinegar and sugar, pre-sliced into perfect circles. I've got some here now, as I write. I bought a jar this morning because beets were on my mind and I couldn't remember if I'd actually liked them as a child, nor how those pickled ones from the jars really tasted. I do remember the way they coloured everything they touched, especially the hard-boiled egg, an effect I found delightfully gross, as only a child can. They're good ... mmm ... I could eat them as a snack ... too sweet maybe, but with an acidic kick, though the beet itself is mild in comparison to how I have become used to it.

The process of jarring or pickling vegetables was invented to preserve surplus produce from the garden. It widened the range of foods available in winter and hence the nutrition obtainable from them, and also brought a ray of summer sunshine to the winter table. I have read references to the usefulness of pickled beetroot in winter salads of yesteryear, but we only ate salad in summer – at a time when fresh beets were, or should have been, in season. It's likely that while one summer's harvest was being picked for pickling, we were tucking into the previous year's supply.

My favourite way of preparing beetroot has more in common with the jarred version than I initially realised. It involves slicing partly cooked beets thinly and braising them slowly in olive oil, balsamic vinegar and sugar plus a hint of caraway seed. If you profess to hate caraway, cumin or fennel seeds are equally good. In fact beetroot likes the company of a lot of strong, distinctive flavours, from the sweet spices to the hot ones, bitter and pungent salad greens such as watercress and rocket, strong blue cheeses and soft, fresh, delicate ones, and the salty kick of olives and capers. Nuts are also good companions, especially hazelnuts, walnuts, pecans and pine nuts.

You will increasingly find beetroot of different shapes, sizes and even colours in the markets. These aren't really new, but their appearance surely signifies a growing interest in beets as well as our never-ending passion for variation. Two varieties which have the advantage – if you'd call it that – of not colouring everything they touch are the golden beets and the ones with concentric circles of pink and white. Both make handsome deep-fried crisps, as do all large beets in fact. The golden beets can be especially lovely in risotto and salads, but they can also lack that depth of character you might

want from a stand-alone beet dish. I use them occasionally, but I wouldn't go so far as to push a reluctant grower to provide them. With all beets, it is pretty much impossible to tell how they will taste before you cook them. If they are in good condition they will be firm; that goes for stored winter beets as much as for fresh summer ones – but that's about all you can tell. To obtain any more information you simply have to get to know your source, whether in the form of a grower, a retailer or just a seed packet.

Ultan grows two varieties. One is cylindrical, very deep purple in colour and possessing a rich, sweet flavour. I like these small-to-medium sized, though this is mostly for aesthetic reasons. The flavour is still excellent in slightly larger ones. They look elegant on a plate, whether whole or halved lengthways. The other, a round variety only slightly less intense in colour, I use more for dishes calling for mashed, chopped or puréed beets, such as in soups, curries, relishes and pickles.

The intriguing divergence of celeriac and its cousin celery

Celeriac and celery are essentially the same plant, manipulated in two different directions. The latter has long been cultivated for its stalks, which have been bred to be fat and juicy with a mild and crisply sweet flavour. Celeriac, on the other hand, is grown for the large swollen part at the base of its thin and bitter stalks. The edible part sits in the ground, half buried like a turnip. Both are descendants from wild celery, and both have been cultivated in their different ways since the seventeenth century. It is an intriguing divergence. The clear aim with celery was to increase the volume of the stalks but to somehow dilute the flavour of wild celery, which was considered overly bitter and 'green'. This blanching, which I'll be covering in more detail later, is traditionally done by keeping the sun off the green stalks as they grow, usually by 'earthing up' – literally scooping earth over the stalks as they try to reach the sunlight. Today, selective breeding has been used to produce varieties of celery that simply don't turn very green in the light.

At the same time that celery as we know it was being created, another pioneering bunch of people were focusing on the opposite end of the plant. Ignoring the bitter stalks, they worked on trying to get the tiny but edible root to create a swelling just at the surface of the ground. Don't ask: I've no idea how it was achieved – it's sheer alchemy to me, this turning of base plants into vegetable gold; but the genius of it is that all the flesh inside the swollen base is hidden from the light, a ball of delicate but intense flavour with no trace of the astringency of the leaves. In a way, celeriac is everything that blanched celery aspires to be, its taste comprising all the elements of celery, but milder and slightly nutty. I would go so far as to say that celeriac is somehow more sophisticated than its upfront cousin.

Up until not very long ago, celeriac tended to be smaller than the type we find in market stalls and supermarkets today, more gnarled and with a tangled knot of roots at the bottom – the removal of which caused the cook to have to hack away a lot of good flesh. Now, it is increasingly easy to find celeriac that is large, smooth, clean and practically spherical. This makes it much easier to work with, and less frustrating in terms of waste and trying to figure out how many you need to buy to get the quantity of usable flesh required. It may be that celeriac's ever-increasing profile is due to this new development towards user-friendliness. Anything that helps this classy root become more popular and easier to find is a good thing.

In the kitchen, celeriac makes great soup, especially if paired with hazelnuts, either cooked into the soup or as a garnish or salsa on top. It likes a kick of mustard too, and its earthy, seasonal quality makes it an evocative Christmas dinner ingredient. Over the years in the restaurant I have contorted slices of celeriac into a series of elaborate creations, and I have two favourites. One is the laborious but rewarding galette, which combines thin braised slices of celeriac with chestnuts, leeks and a hint of blue cheese. The other is the deep-fried fritter recipe I published in *The Café Paradiso Cookbook*, which I have revised for this book. It is simply the best way to eat celeriac.

Sunchoke, Jerusalem artichoke, topinambour... what's in a name?

It is a cruel irony that, while the sunflower is a plant that can't fail to bring a smile to the face, with seeds that are considered a fun and nutritious snack, its close relative the Jerusalem artichoke is generally regarded as a frumpy and troublesome root vegetable. But anyone who has seen a sunchoke growing knows what a noble plant it is, standing at least as tall as the loftiest sunflower, albeit with less impressive flowers. The edible tubers hanging on to the root system just below the surface can produce a heavy crop, so if you are growing them don't get carried away with planting. As a deterrent, it's also worth knowing that they can spread uncontrollably, taking over a garden in a few years of neglect!

SUNCHOKE

In the etymology of vegetables, which can be a minefield of bad translation, vanity and eccentricity, the tale of the sunchoke is one of the most convoluted. In France, it is called *topinambour* after the members of a Brazilian tribe who were being fêted as a novelty during their visit to the country in 1613, at the same time that the tuber was being introduced. This is despite the fact that the sunchoke had actually been brought to Europe from Canada, where it was popular with native tribes.

In Italy it was known as *girasole*, which at least makes some sense, given that it literally means 'sun flower'. It is generally accepted that 'Jerusalem' evolved from the sound of the Italian word rather than from any association with the Holy City. Well, if so, it seems a pretty flimsy reason to carry on calling it that forever.

For the long version of this story, check out Elizabeth Schneider's wonderful book *Vegetables from Amaranth to Zucchini*. She has a great appetite for, among other things, research in general and etymology in particular. What I really like about her investigations is the vexed tone she adopts when dealing with stupidly named new breeds of vegetables. It's a hobby horse of mine too, in case you hadn't noticed, especially when I feel I can't use a name because it's just too silly to write down.

At the same time, however, this is a subject I try not to get sucked into too often, so for my own purposes I simply adopt what I think is the most practical of a specific vegetable's names. Or perhaps the one I like best. It's hard to do trade in a vegetable that has a name you don't like or one that feels clumsy to say or read. And so, when I was told by my grower, Ultan, that 'sunchoke' was a legitimate alternative name for what we previously knew as Jerusalem artichoke, I could see new possibilities opening up for how to use the knobbly little tubers. It's true: a name can make that much difference. Write the old name on a menu and you might as well not bother cooking the stuff, just put them straight in the compost. 'Sunchoke' gives you the chance to at least get the dish to the table. Besides sounding better, at least the first half of the word conjures up the sunflower-like plant that the tubers come from. The other half, 'choke', still relates to the fact that someone a few hundred years ago thought the things tasted a bit like an artichoke, wrote it down, and the world blindly followed suit.

Besides its unwieldy former name, the sunchoke has a couple of other additional downsides attached to it. One is that it is just too damn knobbly and small to deal with, and way too fiddly to either peel or wash properly. Luckily, a few varieties are available now that are thin-skinned, relatively smooth and even quite large – the size of a small oblong potato. They do have to be peeled for soup or sauces, but if you are roasting them, they can be scrubbed easily and the thin skin is perfectly edible.

What isn't edible – or rather, digestible – in a sunchoke, however, is the carbohydrate or sugar it contains, called inulin. Because it is indigestible it causes wind. Nothing like as much as has sometimes been suggested, and certainly no more than the amount of flatulence caused by cabbage or undercooked beans, but because it is so easy to single out inulin as the culprit, the sunchoke will always be hounded by that legend.

Does it taste like artichoke? Well, it does a little but the subtle flavour that might be artichoke is a small part of the mix, which is dominated by that earthy sweetness that many roots and tubers have. Raw sunchoke, thinly sliced or grated, has a lovely crunch that can work very well in salads. Because there is no starch in sunchokes, they become meltingly soft when roasted or boiled. In fact, sunchokes can pass quickly from almost done to overcooked, so check occasionally with a fork when you are cooking them. The sunchokes should be soft inside but still firm enough to hold their shape.

Roasting is the simplest way to cook sunchokes, either as a side dish or to use in other ways, such as in risotto with leeks or with pungent greens like watercress or rocket. But, mostly, I use it in variations on a classic soup, or puréed and made into a velvety cream sauce for pancakes and timbales. Sunchokes also combine well with potato for a richly flavoursome mash, and if you get big ones they make great deep-fried crisps.

There is another vegetable trading under the name of artichoke – the Chinese artichoke. Don't ask where the name came from: it goes without saying that it isn't related to either of the other vegetables known as artichoke. This one is a very small tuber with a pearl-coloured skin over a ridged body, like a miniature, elongated Michelin man minus limbs. Whether you see it as beautiful or off-putting depends on whether it looks to you like a jewel or a just an oversized grub from the garden. It has a delicate flavour and can be eaten raw or lightly cooked. From a trial crop, I have eaten it both ways and it is hard to choose between them, though it does change when cooked. It was delicate, crisp and slightly acidic when raw. Later I cooked some Chinese broccoli for a warm salad and added the Chinese artichokes for the last minute of cooking. The texture became softer and the flavour sweeter. It is a potentially exciting addition to the palette of roots and tubers, though the most likely stumbling block is the trouble of harvesting the things. Crawling around on the ground to find the tubers, it would be very hard to see them as pearly jewels, and, besides, no grower will do that unless he loves the things himself. Time will tell.

One man's yam is another man's oca

Whatever doubts I have about the chances of Chinese artichokes ever becoming real and bountiful crops, oca, which we trialled at the same time, is the one I would do a little bullying for. Originally from South America, where it is still popular, oca is a tuber which clings to the roots of a very short, bushy plant. The plant itself is a handsome ground-covering one, with deep green shamrock-shaped leaves, pretty pink stems and occasional tiny yellow flowers. As attractive as the upper part is, the plant's real beauty lies under the ground. Stick a fork in and gently push it up by the base and you will be presented with a cluster of vividly coloured tubers. They may vary from pale golden to a cheerful pink, through to the most vibrant red. They are typically 4–6cm (1½–2½in) long, though they can grow much bigger, looking like stubby wrinkled fingers. The yield is good, or can be. (I suspect you should never make definitive statements like that around growers, lest you put a hex on their crops.) I have a preference for the darker ones, partly for aesthetic reasons, but also because I think they hold their flavour better when cooked. I have been known to make errors of taste based on aesthetics before, so until I do some blind tasting, don't quote me on that.

When Ultan first asked me if I would be interested in him growing oca, I muttered some mild encouragement, thinking he was talking about okra, the seedy green vegetable popularly known as 'ladies' fingers' and used in Indian and North African cooking, as well as in the gumbo stews of the southern parts of the US. I would have loved some locally grown okra but didn't think it was possible, and I wasn't going to get too excited just because Ultan had been poring over some glossy garden pornography again. When he dragged me into the propagating tunnel a few weeks later to proudly show me the progress of his 'okra', the penny dropped. I knew this vegetable from my time in New Zealand, which seems to be the only place outside of South America that has developed oca as a commercial crop. Confusingly, but somehow not surprisingly, in New Zealand it is called 'yam', even though they know it's not what the rest of the world understands by that word. So, in New Zealand everyone knows what you mean when you say 'yam', but in a muddy field in Ireland we were a little confused about what was in front of us. Not that we had any other yams to confuse the crop with; it was simply a matter of realising what we were dealing with and getting on the same wavelength as each other.

Given that only one person in the cook–grower relationship is doing any work during a trial crop period, which can take years, it is obviously important that a clear understanding and a sense of common mission exists. One careless sentence and the poor grower will be left trying to remember just why he is doing this and who exactly started that particular conversation. If that gives the impression that growers are sensitive, well ...

Luckily we were rowing the same boat in the same direction on oca, and once we decided to simply call it 'oca' and endure the endless explanations to punters, everything was fine and incredibly worthwhile. I had been harbouring two very strong memories of oca, to the extent that I would even say that I had a gnawing regret that I would never be able to work with them in Ireland. One memory was of a basic dish of yams roasted in honey and butter with a little citrus. The other was an Indonesian-style curry with peanuts and roasted yams; plus coconut too, I think. As yet, I simply hadn't had the opportunity to replicate it. Last year, because it was a small crop and I wanted the oca on the Paradiso menu, we came up with a warm salad, which meant we could keep it on the menu for a few weeks without actually being too carefree with the quantity of oca on each plate. I tried making the curry from memory once at home and it was good but not quite the dish I remembered. If the recipe is published here, it's surely because I cracked it with the increased yield this year. Or I might just have decided to try a different approach. Go check now! My God, but this is an exciting book! Don't get led astray, mind. Come straight back – I'm not finished here yet ...

It is said that oca shouldn't be harvested until the beautiful foliage has died away, or at least begun to fade. Before this, even though the tubers are fully grown, they are simply too unpleasantly acidic to be enjoyed. Even after this stage, oca often has a strongly acidic element, but it is balanced by a fruity sweetness. I say 'often' because the individual tubers can vary, being sometimes challengingly acidic and other times almost innocently sweet. This is the unique appeal of oca. I don't think there is another vegetable like it. Both the sweetest and most acidic of them are like fruit, plums perhaps, but with an earthiness that could only come from something that ripens underground. In the best examples, the flavour is balanced with a texture that is crisp as an apple when raw and meltingly soft when cooked.

When cooking oca, it is worth checking them often to make sure you take the cooked ones from the oven just as they are done. Overcooked oca is too soft; underdone, it has an unpleasant texture, like that of undercooked potato. And yet raw oca is delightful, so I suppose the rule is that if you are going to cook it, don't half-do it and don't overdo it.

Do growers dream of coconut-flavoured roots?

The mild flavour of both salsify and scorzonera has often been described as having hints of, among other things, artichoke. So they can both consider themselves lucky not to have been called 'carrot artichokes' or a variation on 'rootchokes'. Instead they both acquired quite beautiful names, evocative of something slightly exotic but revealing nothing of their subtle charm. Although they are related, it is not so close that they should have ended up being traded under the same name, as they often are. Scorzonera is sometimes called 'black salsify', and sometimes it is simply called 'salsify'! I have been using scorzonera for years and until recently had never cooked salsify. Yet I have always and only ever used the word 'salsify' to identify the vegetable I've been using. Why, when I know better? Well, despite the fact that I love the way scorzonera rolls off the tongue, I think I chose the slightly better-known name to cut down on the need for repeated explanations. Now that I have both vegetables from a local source, I have to make a decision. Own up and use both names in future, or ... you know, without another moment's thought, stick with 'salsify' for both.

The classic, or white, salsify is like a thin parsnip, often forked and sometimes even wrapped around itself, and it usually has a collection of hairy rootlets attached to its sides. Scorzonera, on the other hand, is a straight, cylindrical root with dark brown skin, though it has the same pearly-coloured flesh as salsify. While I have heard of the young shoots of the plants being eaten, I have never tried this. I have, however, snacked on the flower buds, which are delicious, having a subtle flavour reminiscent of artichokes. This is a surprising bonus from such earthy plants, and one that in no way inhibits the development of the roots for later harvesting.

Because of their long shape, and because it is preferable that they be fat as well, it is essential to grow them in stone-free soil, in so far as that is possible. But if you've successfully grown lovely, plump, long-legged salsify and scorzonera, it is then a tricky business getting them out of the ground without breaking the roots. Ultan uses an ancient tool called a parsnip fork, specially designed for a mission such as this. When the roots snap, the exposed flesh quickly discolours to a rusty hue, and they bleed a sticky milky white sap. It's like some alien life form being hauled out of its hidden habitat in a science fiction film, screaming incomprehensibly, 'The light, the light!'

The first time Ultan and I went to check out the crop he had planted months before, we witnessed this horror show. Then he took the bleeding – and I'd swear, struggling – root to a tap, rinsed it off and said: 'Here, taste that, it's just like coconut.' It wasn't his first time, then. I bit into it as he laughed at my timid face and the tiny nibble I had taken. I trust him absolutely as a grower but, well, he's not averse to the occasional prank. This time he was right – it was coconut. Just as the cheffy part of my brain was kicking in and beginning some improvisational work on raw scorzonera, the taste of coconut faded and the underlying, inevitable earthiness took over. The texture became dry and suddenly the experience was not unlike chomping on dried coconut that had been mixed with earth. No muddy flavours, thank God; more like the taste of a scorched football field on a warm summer's evening after you've being felled by a particularly hefty thump on the back. Long after I had spat out the tiny piece of root, I could still taste the earth it had grown in. It wasn't meant to be a prank, it's just that Ultan has extreme tastes and a fearless palate. He quite enjoyed his bite.

Because of its shape and relative smoothness, scorzonera can be a little easier than salsify to work with in the kitchen. The 'bleeding' is usually not an issue a few hours after the plant has been dug up, but both varieties still become sticky as you peel them and the flesh discolours quickly when cut and exposed to the air. For these reasons, you need to put the peeled roots into acidulated water as you go – that is, water with lemon juice added. Once peeled, they should be boiled for a few minutes, even if you intend to fry or braise them. This boiling stabilises the discolouring and the roots can then be cooked again or kept for hours before carrying on. If you are simply boiling the roots, there is no need to interrupt the cooking process; just simmer them until they are tender. But test them often because, as with most roots, the cooking time depends on a number of things, including the original texture of the root, how old it is and how long it's been out of the ground.

The flavour of both salsify and scorzonera is subtle but elegant, like a mild blend of sweet earthiness with hints of hazelnut and, yes, artichoke. It somehow adds up to more than the sum of its subtle parts. Well-cooked salsify makes a lovely soup, alone or with celeriac and potato, and it adds an elusive tone to mash or a cream sauce. Partly cooked or just lightly blanched, salsify can be roasted for risotto or pasta dishes, fried with other vegetables, especially mushrooms, or made into fritters, as in the celeriac recipe which I've included in this book. My favourite way to prepare salsify is to braise it in olive oil and white wine with a hint of sweet spice, such as star anise, nutmeg or fennel, to bring out the root's exotic character, which harks back to its Mediterranean origins.

SALSIFY

The lazy acre of spuds and other bad press for a miracle food

Flann O'Brien's brilliant early novel *An Béal Bocht*, published in 1941 and later translated as *The Poor Mouth*, is a surreal tale of the fantastical squalor and ferocious but strangely life-affirming desperation of Irish life in a semi-mythical time. Potatoes feature strongly, as do rain, funerals, debates on the Gaelic language and Gaelic-ness in general.

While the book is a satire on other sagas of unrelenting misery in Irish literature as well as on the humourless provincialism of Gaelic language revivalists, it also pokes fun at the fatalistic character of the Irish peasant. Life, in his view, is so hopelessly miserable it would be ridiculous to try to do anything about it. And as long as he has a few potatoes to keep body and soul together ...

This clichéd image of a lazy peasantry who would rather subsist on a basic diet of spuds than do any work isn't new. Potatoes had been carrying this association with indolence pretty much since their arrival in Europe from South America in the sixteenth century. Along with other misconceptions the tuber was burdened with, the idea took hold that farming potatoes required so little effort in proportion to the crop yield that farmers who went for it were bone idle by nature. Or it would make them so and thus encourage sin and sloth and ultimately bring down the whole of civilisation. Long before the famines of the nineteenth century, this perception of the Irish poor had taken hold in the minds of their supposed betters – an image perpetuated in another comic masterpiece, Spike Milligan's *Puckoon*, which has for a hero a man who wishes only to be allowed to lie about in ditches all day, avoiding work and his wife. Did potatoes make us lazy or were we by nature a bunch of layabouts just waiting for a crop to match our outlook? (Neither – it's a myth, of course, but bear with me ...)

O'Brien's final novel returned with typically fierce humour to the issue of the spud and how it affects our national identity and our over-reported heroic lethargy. *Slattery's Sago Saga* tells of an American who wishes to discourage the slovenly Irish from emigrating from their hovels in the Old Country to the great economic melting pot of the New World. To this end, the sago tree was to be introduced as a crop, thus providing the Irish with a food that was easy to produce and had even more starch than the flouriest of spuds. People would be so incapacitated by the increased starch levels that they wouldn't be able to think about leaving, never mind actually doing it. What exists of the book is hilarious but it was never finished. Perhaps Flann took to the sago?

On a more serious level, but in a similar tone, the potato is sometimes vilified as the cause of the Irish famines of the nineteenth century. For sure, the failure of potato crops left millions with little or no food. But what else could they have eaten in the circumstances? This vegetable sustained, virtually single-handedly, a huge population living on plots of land that couldn't otherwise support them except by potato growing and prayer. In reality, the potato was a miracle food whose attributes were abused for the usual reasons: greed, power and land ownership.

Less well known is the fact that, in other countries too, the potato played a vital role in people's general nutrition and hence was crucial to much of the social and economic change in Europe during the nineteenth century, especially the Industrial Revolution in England. After all, potatoes provide an almost 'complete' food that stores well and cooks easily and with little equipment. Hence they provided the perfect fuel for the new working classes of the chaotically growing industrial cities. In this environment, the baked potato would have revolutionised Western street food, providing easy meals for people with no cooking facilities and little money. You might expect that a simple plant tuber that facilitated such change would be lauded as a public hero, with a statue erected in every town square, yet ever since its arrival in Europe it was treated with suspicion and disdain, seen as potentially undermining society even as it was maintaining it.

More recently, despite a return to favour for much of the twentieth century when we simply ate the things without guilt or bad association, the poor spud has been getting a bad press once again. There has been a procession of diets scaring us off all carbohydrates, but especially potatoes and the tuber's great traditional rival, bread. Both have been wrongly portrayed as fattening and unhealthy. Although most of these diets have since been discredited, the stigma lingers to a degree. This business of avoiding carbs always seemed bizarre to me, given that every food culture in the world, now and historically, has had one or two carbohydrate staples as its nutritional cornerstone. Most of us typically live on carbohydrates supplemented with proteins and vegetables; we build our meals around carbohydrates, and have done ever since we stopped chasing our food across mountainsides.

Then there was a report – partly based on consumer surveys, partly on hearsay – that the potato was sliding down the league of our favourite staples. Why? Well, apparently, it is increasingly seen as a 'difficult' food: many of us no longer know how to cook it at home; we don't know how to build a meal around it; it doesn't go with pizza; and, anyway, it's dirty when you buy it and requires a certain amount of labour to prepare. Why bother when you can simply snip the corner off the pasta bag and pour the contents straight into a pan?

Possibly the most serious aspect of all this is the sense that the potato is becoming unfashionable again. In its simplest form, it is once again being seen, in some circles, as dull, low food, not fit company for the exotic ingredients we currently like to cook with. It is illuminating, if a little alarming, that in the drive to educate children to eat more vegetables, the potato isn't even classified as one, despite its high levels of potassium and vitamin C. Is this a careless oversight, or deliberate exclusion by official bodies staffed by people who themselves don't value the potato? Snobbish bias on the part of the aspiring middle classes?

As with every aspect of our lives influenced by fashion, it is an illusion that we are coming to this conclusion entirely by ourselves. Consumer choices are largely driven by the manufacturing and retail giants, who to a great extent decide not only what we eat but in what form we buy it. As our domestic appreciation of the potato goes down, our consumption of the vegetable in processed, value-added form just keeps on rising. Chip and crisp manufacturers continually widen their range to make sure every social strand has a potato snack to suit their sense of themselves. Tired of mass-produced cheese 'n' onion-flavoured crisps? Try kettle-fried mature Gorgonzola-flavoured, or perhaps Thai-style with sweet chilli and coconut. Underpinning this profiteering is the fact that potatoes at the farm gate are as cheap as the proverbial chips, and the power of the retail buyers is persistently driving the price down. What better thing to do with cheap food than process it, add perceived value by way of packaging and marketing, and sell it at a high price? The basic spud remains humble and low while its packaged offspring strive for upward mobility.

For all its sterling contribution to society, the potato tends to be seen as a side dish. When you bypass this mental hurdle, there are plenty of ways for potatoes to be the focus of a meal without incurring trauma. A gratin of layered slices, possibly with other vegetables like celeriac and leeks, and with or without cream and cheese, needs no accompaniment other than a salad, if you're so inclined. Potato cakes, pancakes and fritters need only a simple tomato sauce or aïoli. The first early potatoes of summer practically cry out to take centre stage, dressed only in butter and salt. Crushed potato, a cross between mash and fried potato, can be pressed into moulds and re-fried. This also makes a great base to construct elaborate dishes around, as in the gratin of potato, spinach and aubergine that we serve in Paradiso and which has been included on page 289. Potato is the heart and soul of Spanish tortilla, and the waxier varieties in particular make a surprisingly good ingredient in a tart with leeks or greens, and cheese. Potato gnocchi are surprisingly simple and enjoyable to make, as well as tasting great. In fact, the whole rolling process is something that kids like to get involved in, making preparing dinner as much fun as eating it.

Potato mash is probably my favourite comfort food, the one I turn to when I'm in recovery mode or just feeling like wrapping myself in a cocoon after the trials and tribulations of a busy day. It has also become something of a pick-me-up after a tough Saturday night in the restaurant kitchen – rich, buttery mash with braised puy lentils doused with chilli oil, washed down with icy beer. Mash is a great accompaniment to many dishes, but I don't think it should have to stay on the side. Lately, I've taken to thinking of mash as I do risotto. Like this basic rice dish, formerly a staple of Italian peasant cuisine, mash can be as rich or as frugal as you want, depending on how much butter, cheese, herbs or even vegetables you add to it. In fact, I like to eat mash in the same way I do risotto: served in a bowl with a wet stew or oily braise of vegetables. In the summer, this might be peperonata – the simple stew of sweet peppers in olive oil with garlic and basil – or courgettes and green beans with tomatoes, and, in the winter, cabbage with lentils. Not ten minutes before writing this, I had mash with Brussels sprouts in olive oil, tomatoes, ginger and thyme. Would I make that up? It was plate-lickingly good, and far from humble.

The whole issue of what variety of potato to use for which dish is one that is, if anything, becoming more complex. Once upon a time, and not so long ago, this was a simple enough job. The extremely floury types, such as Kerr's Pink, Records and Golden Wonder, maybe the old King Eddie too, were good for mashing, boiling and roasting. Roosters were the first new variety to arrive, filling the middle ground by making a good stand-in for floury spuds as well as being just about firm enough to hold their shape if necessary. For truly waxy potatoes, we have traditionally had to look to imports, but that is changing as tastes evolve and growers try to keep up. There is a greater demand for waxy potatoes and it would be a very healthy development if we could produce our own supply. Two of the most commonly available varieties right now are Charlotte and Nicola, and both have lovely dense flesh with a rich flavour that makes them really good roasted or steamed and served hot, dressed with butter or olive oil, as well as being perfect for warm or cold salads. This year we have been using 'Colleen' for mash, a relatively new variety developed for organic growing. (The ever-recurring issue of the peculiar naming of vegetables takes on a whole new dimension when it comes to potatoes. Where once they were called after the man – usually – who developed or popularised the particular variety, now they are mostly given girls' names. What's more, 'Colleen' is an anglicised spelling of the Irish word for 'girl'. Come on, lads, rein yourselves in!)

But all of this relates to Ireland. Reading American cookbooks, I come across references to potatoes I've never laid eyes on, let alone had the opportunity to cook. Similarly, most European countries have their own favourites. Even in England, I often don't recognise the varieties on sale. This is as it should be, with varieties being chosen to succeed in their particular environment as well as to satisfy the specific tastes of the population. But it makes it difficult to tell what kind of potato you're dealing with before you cook it – floury, waxy or somewhere in between. Buying directly from a grower or at a farmer's market, you can usually get the information directly from the source. And while supermarket packs sometimes give an indication of possible uses for the potatoes they contain, it is often too general.

The British Potato Council has a very useful starch-ometer kind of gadget on its website which gives a level of flouriness for the potato varieties it lists. It's a simple numerical scale. If you're unsure how the potatoes you've got are going to behave in the pan, check it out. Mind you, there's no guarantee they will be featured. Despite listing twenty or so types of potato, the website claims that a mind-boggling eighty varieties are grown in Britain alone. Rather better would be if potato packers adopted the flouriness scale and printed it on bags or sacks, or as a list at the point of sale.

Now, in case you think I'm an agent for the Potato Council, the website also has a promotion for a 'love your chips' campaign, which promotes chip eating in a nation already overdosing on the things. This even includes the question 'Do you know chips are made from potatoes?' I'm sure they wouldn't ask if they didn't feel the need to. The implications hardly bear thinking about.

However, there is one potato type that makes my heart sink – the 'baby roaster'. You hardly ever buy them for consumption at home, as the catering industry is almost entirely responsible for the invasion of restaurant kitchens and dining rooms by this lame excuse for a potato. The little knob-like things arrive in 10kg boxes, scrubbed clean and ready to pop in the oven, no prep, no cleaning. Some places don't even bother with the oven. They parboil them, then 'finish' them in a deep-frier. Finish indeed – your 'roast potatoes' are actually deep-fried! This might all be justifiable if we were talking about an irresistibly desirable vegetable here. But the baby roaster is not only insipid in flavour but is often too watery to be roasted in the first place. The typical life of these cutesy little things involves being grown, cleaned, packed, shipped, unpacked, roasted (or fried), carried to the table, cleared away and chucked in the pig-food bin. Their main purpose is to fulfil the kitchen's obligation to provide spuds, but they are little more than plate-fillers.

Some years ago, a farmers' representative was fuming about the increasing use of imported potatoes in Ireland, particularly by restaurants and hotels, demanding that a campaign be started to get the Irish catering industry to use homegrown spuds. Even if they were worth growing in the first place, we simply can't produce baby roasters here, as they are best suited to the sandy soil of Mediterranean countries. Government agencies are doing their bit, to some extent at least, by developing new varieties that might meet our need for a potato that looks well, holds its shape and can be produced in shapes and sizes that restaurants should find useful. In addition to the aforementioned 'Colleen', there are others such as 'Orla' and 'Setanta' that are showing promise. But it requires a commitment from restaurants too, to work with what is possible here rather than resorting to the easy option of using an imported variety because it is cheaper and less troublesome to prepare. That won't come easily from a sector that is so focused on reducing labour costs. However, what shouldn't be forgotten is that restaurants are, or can be, a frontline for movements in the food industry as well as shop windows for its produce. We respond to what is produced, of course, but we can influence it too.

Purple potatoes, ancient but newly exotic

New potato varieties are being developed all the time, in response to consumer demand and in an attempt to stay one step ahead of the old enemy, blight, which is still a threat to potato crops and the single biggest impediment to growers wanting to switch to organic cultivation methods.

While government agencies carry on the incredibly useful work of trialling new varieties of potatoes, individual growers run their own trials to find out what works best in their particular environment, as well as what works best for their own table or that of their customers. Unusual or little-known potatoes can seem exotic, whether they are new or ancient. One ancient variety is the Pink Fir Apple, producing long, knobbly spuds, and undergoing a spirited revival despite being slow-growing, prone to blight and offering a relatively small yield. The reason for its popularity is simple: it has a dense, creamy texture and a rich and nutty flavour that is unique among potatoes. The effect is almost fudgy, and if that sounds like something you'd want in a spud, you should definitely hunt these down. Simply steam them, coat them generously in butter, and season them with salt and pepper, then eat them slowly and sumptuously.

You may have noticed, in the previous paragraph, that I used the words 'exotic' and 'potato' in the same sentence. Well, I enjoyed the moment, whether you were paying attention or not. Even devoted potato lovers might mistrust the suggestion, however. Potatoes are staples, they fulfil a solid nutritional role, and we like them to be how we expect them to be. To a starch addict, there is little worse than a floury spud that mashes badly when it had promised to create meltingly fluffy pillows, or worse, a waxy one that turns into an unappetising lumpy gruel while boiling.

Nonetheless, if there are potatoes that might lay claim to the term 'exotic', they must surely include those with blue and purple flesh (though I'm inclined to drop the blue now; blue food doesn't do anything for me). These are truly ancient, in that there were wild versions growing in Peru over two thousand years ago. Of course the varieties we get now have been bred and re-bred, but their colour is not new. Neither is it a gimmick. In fact, the purple colour comes from the same beneficial antioxidant that makes vitamin-rich blueberries such a miracle food. The texture of most purple potatoes is medium floury, like the flesh of a Rooster, which makes them all-rounders. They are floury enough for chips, mashing or roasting, yet firm enough to boil, steam or use in gratins; and they are great in salads.

The first year Ultan trialled purple potatoes for Paradiso, the crop was small, so we decided to put a salad on the menu and do no more than test them for other uses. The crop came in high summer, so we teamed them up for the salad with broad beans, sheep's cheese and sunny herbs. When we tested the potatoes in other ways, they were decent mashed or roasted, but made amazing crisps. The flouriness, or starch level, was clearly just perfect for making crisps with a dry, crunchy texture that still managed to contain the full rich flavour of the potato. These crisps are increasingly showing up in packaged form in the fancy-nibbles sections of delis and supermarkets. I wouldn't usually say this, but … buy them, they are good. Better still, buy some purple potatoes and make your own. Anyway, we decided to serve the crisps with the salad too: purple potatoes presented two ways on your salad. How Irish is that?

You may read in some books that purple potatoes lose their colour when cooked, becoming anything from faded purple to a bluish grey. The potatoes of the first crop we worked with discoloured badly, to the extent that they looked downright unappetising. I was initially glum about the prospects of finding much use for them other than as crisps, which don't discolour. Then Victor the pastry chef, who had spent some time in a Michelin-aspiring kitchen, suggested we squeeze a little lemon juice over the potatoes after they had been steamed and cooled. Sounded unlikely to me at first, but it works: you can watch the chunks of cooked potato turning back to their original colour, and possibly even up a notch further. Very impressive, and it's good to know Michelin is useful for something besides tyres. Don't, however, go getting too trigger happy with the lemon juice, unless the potatoes are destined for a salad with a lemon dressing. The dressing on the salad we made pretty much chose itself, however, based on the fact the potatoes were already tossed in lemon juice.

The second year's crop, which was grown from seed potatoes saved from the first year, were a deeper shade of purple and never discoloured. I'm not even going to try to unravel that. Instead, my advice is to expect them to behave but keep a lemon handy.

Hidden plants bring sweet rewards

In a kitchen, 'blanching' usually means parboiling followed by plunging into cold water, and is often done to preserve colour in vegetables. Out in the garden, blanching is a method of protecting the stems of vegetables from sunlight so that instead of becoming tough, strong supporters of a mass of foliage, the leaves don't develop and the stems remain delicate and pale. It is the gardening equivalent of pampering your neo-gothic teenage children to see if they become even more sensitive by letting them spend all day in bed. (They certainly will.) Blanching can be done by covering the young stalks with sand or soil as they develop, by growing them indoors in a dark space, or by simply putting a bucket over the plant. Some bitter leafy greens, such as chicory, dandelion and endive, are blanched by tying them up closely so the inner leaves are hidden from the sun for a short time and they become pale and sweeter. (None of these methods is recommended for teenagers, however.)

The primary aim in blanching is to remove, or avoid the development of, the strong and often astringent flavours that green vegetables can have. Covered by a bucket or otherwise protected from the weather, the vegetable stalks carry on trying to grow towards the light but in a warmer environment and without the strain of having to support leaves. It is through blanching that celery became the domestic food we now eat in abundance, despite its ancestor having a bitter and almost overpowering flavour. There is a legend that the renowned Belgian Witlof variety of chicory was originally grown for its roots until some shoots accidentally developed in a dark shed and were found to be delicious. Other vegetables, such as asparagus and rhubarb, are blanched purely as a matter of taste and despite the fact that they are perfectly good to eat in their natural state. Even the leaves of swede turnips that have been left in the ground over winter to sprout shoots in spring can be made sweeter and more delicate by blanching. 'Forced' is sometimes used to describe blanched vegetables, usually when a vegetable has been grown earlier than its natural season or completely out of season. Mostly, though, the early arrival of vegetables is almost a side effect of blanching, caused by the cosy atmosphere of their bucket or dark room.

Under a bucket, a sheltered delicate jewel – seakale

Although seakale can be a delicious green, as has been discussed in 'It's a green thing', it is in its pale and delicate blanched state that it has earned a place in the aristocracy of vegetables. In its original wild state, growing in the shingle around the coasts of Europe, it was eaten as a nutritious green. Even then, the stalks would often be covered by shifting sand, leaving them pale and less bitter than the green leaves. It was cultivated in Italy during the Middle Ages and later had an extended heyday in England through the eighteenth and nineteenth centuries, when it was considered a real delicacy. Somehow, its popularity faded away and by the late twentieth century it had become something of an enigma, more known of than encountered. It's funny how it maintained its reputation as a delicacy even as its availability shrank almost to the point of it becoming gastronomic history, or even folklore. I had certainly heard about seakale long before I tasted it, and, knowing plenty of other food lovers for whom this is also true, I would say that this is fairly common.

There has been a renewed interest in seakale in recent years, particularly from high-end restaurants searching for unusual and rare ingredients. However, seakale remains difficult to get hold of unless you know someone who grows it, or can convince someone to grow it for you. I'm lucky in that regard because Ultan is usually one step ahead of my vegetable fantasies. One spring, as we walked past his array of kales and broccoli, he asked if I had ever tasted seakale. In a coincidence that I didn't really find surprising, I had tasted it for the first time just a week before. One of my chefs brought in two very precious stalks of blanched white seakale that he had managed to ... well ... let's say 'bring home' from a country house that grows a substantial amount of the stuff. Ultan himself had never tasted seakale, but was curious about it, and had just been offered some plants. If I hadn't just had my taste buds tingled, I would probably have dismissed it as one kale too many, but now I could see the potential. One part of my brain was thinking about how to turn seakale into an impressive dish (a little vain) and another was imagining how excited the customers would be to see it on the menu (a little naive).

BLANCHED SEAKALE

In practice, blanched seakale doesn't warrant, nor can it really tolerate, being overworked into complex recipes. The flavour is often described as having something of asparagus and artichoke about it, but that doesn't do any of them justice, as it is the unique individuality of all three plants that makes each of them a benchmark in the vegetable world. The cream-coloured stalks of seakale are delicate and subtle but in a divinely more-ish way. Their melting texture is slightly sweet with hints of earthy hazelnut. Unless you have access to a sufficient quantity whereby you might become bored of the simple approach of preparing seakale, there is no need to do any more with it than to boil or steam the stalks until tender and dress them with some butter and seasoning. The recipe given later is only a slight variation on this approach, a careful attempt to add flavour without drowning the essence of this precious vegetable.

Unlocking the powerful mystery of mushrooms

While the many-layered pleasures of seasonal wild mushrooms have been documented in 'Wild pickings', there are good-quality cultivated mushrooms to be had all year round. The rolling back of my uncomfortable relationship with mushrooms during the past year was largely due to my experiences of hunting for them in the fields and forests. Cultivated mushrooms had never been included in my little private phobia of fungi, which must have been more about where the mushrooms came from than how they tasted.

I may have inherited this fear from my father, who wouldn't touch the things, saying that they were dirty and nutritionally useless, not to mention being parasitic forms feeding off decaying life, so that eating mushrooms was a perversion of sorts. It's not that he wouldn't acknowledge the validity of their function in the cycle of life, simply that we had no business eating them.

It wouldn't have been an uncommon attitude to mushrooms in Ireland. Traditionally nervous of their dark side, we have for centuries ignored the wild mushrooms of the forest, and those who would touch any wild fungi at all mostly restricted themselves to the innocent field mushrooms that spring up in cow pastures. This lovable character is the ancestor of the ubiquitous white button mushroom of supermarket shelves. Perhaps it's no coincidence, then, that Ireland developed a strong industry producing the field mushroom's cultivated cousins, but has only touched on growing other varieties, especially the wood-borne ones such as shiitake and oyster mushrooms, which are so popular in other countries throughout the world.

Mushrooms may well be the strangest foods we eat. Because they have no roots and can spring up literally overnight, mushrooms were long thought to be individual life forms capable of spontaneous generation, simply inventing themselves out of nothing. It's no wonder that they were feared by many and revered by others as having all sorts of magical powers. It is well known that there are mushrooms that can make us ill or even kill us, and others that have strong hallucinatory effects. So it is not surprising that in many countries, especially China, mushrooms have long been used in a medicinal way too. Indeed, their medicinal properties are being investigated, and becoming increasingly accepted, by practitioners of conventional medicine.

Because of this combination of mystique and real power, there are endless stories and legends about mushrooms, of which my current favourite is that of the Berserkers, the ferocious stormtroopers of Viking armies. These guys often wore animal skins to strike fear into their enemies – or victims, more accurately – but their real secret was how they whipped themselves into a self-hypnotised frenzy of fearless, bestial savagery by howling, beating themselves and biting their shields. Oh yes, and chomping on special mushrooms. Their hallucinations of themselves as ferocious beasts usually carried over to the enemy, who somehow saw the same vision and turned to jelly soldiers.

Eventually humans figured out the mysteries of how mushrooms grow and what they are, even if some of their properties remain elusive. The mushrooms we see, pick and eat are the fruit of a life form, just as much as an apple is, though it is very difficult to see the parent because of how it is spread out underground or inside logs. This life form, mycelium, grows as a white strand of cells that can colonise a small space intensely or range across huge areas.

Of course, it's not accurate to classify mushrooms as parasites, and certainly not the ones we most like to eat. Of the three classifications of mushroom, one type is classically parasitic and feeds off its living host plant, usually a tree, eventually killing it. None of this variety is attractive to eat, which is something of a relief.

Then there is the extraordinary class of mushroom known as 'mycorrhizal' which forms a symbiotic relationship with trees. In this endearing marriage, the fungus breaks down organic matter in the soil for the tree to absorb and the tree responds by providing sugars to feed the mushrooms. Everyone is happy, and even more happily, some of the world's favourite wild mushrooms grow in this way, including chanterelles, ceps (or porcini), hedgehog mushrooms and truffles. Surely not a coincidence.

The third classification of mushrooms is called 'saprophytic', and these live on dead organic matter, such as fallen trees, straw and compost. This is not a parasitic relationship, quite the opposite in fact. Some, such as oyster and shiitake mushrooms, are 'primary' decomposers, actually breaking down the dead wood into compost, while others live on the compost, breaking it down still further. The all-conquering white button mushroom of the global supermarket is a compost dweller.

In a way, the huge success story behind the cultivation of this one variety, and the derision which the poor little thing often provokes, has tainted the perception of mushroom cultivation in general. However, when you consider how incomprehensible the mushroom once was – and to a great degree still is – the will to control and manipulate it, as well as the skill required, is really impressive.

If it is the nature of humans to try to tame and domesticate just about everything that appeals to them, the mushroom held out for a long time. The Chinese are said to have been cultivating shiitake mushrooms for almost a thousand years, but until the twentieth century this mostly involved enhancing the way the mushrooms grew in the wild – using cut logs instead of fallen trees. It was almost as much a question of herding as actual cultivation. Using the word 'herding' is more apt than you might think, given that some producers of shiitake consider them to be more like animals than plants. Now I know this might be weird territory for a vegetarian to be getting into but, remembering the classic guideline often quoted by vegetarians, about not eating anything with a face, have you ever seen a shiitake with one? If you answered yes, you should probably lay off the mushrooms for a bit. That aside, it is suggested that the shiitake has behavioural responses to things like music, erratic emotional environments and storms. All fungi like to produce their fruit after a shower of rain, but shiitake mushrooms love a wild storm. Even more bizarrely, they are said to be social, producing better when their host logs are stacked closely.

In Europe, although people had toyed with mushroom cultivation over the centuries, it wasn't until the 1700s that it was first developed as a commercial enterprise. In caves and old quarries outside Paris, it was discovered that the stable climate and predictable levels of humidity were conducive to consistent crops of mushrooms from a compost of horse manure and straw. The strain of fungus that produced so well in this environment was *Agaricus bisporus*, a close relation of the field mushroom.

You might say it's a pity that a better variety wasn't selected. Despite the phenomenal production and sales levels of the white button mushroom, it has become an icon of mass-produced bland food, and for good reason.

But, given my love of the field mushroom, I can't accept that the problem lies solely in the ancestry. The mushroom industry has managed to create one of the most insipid food products on the market out of something once held in awe for its powers, its mystery and its intense flavour. Picking the little things when they are so immature may be part of the problem but, in common with many large-scale operations across the food industry, it is more likely to be about the process of choosing and breeding strains of the variety that are more intent on achieving a large yield and quick growth. Those left to grow bigger, and especially the brown-capped varieties, including the Portobello, which is left to mature fully, have a much better flavour.

It could also be argued that every food that becomes widely and cheaply available loses some of its glister in the process, as our jaded palates tell us it is losing its power to please. It is a bad combination: the once exotic food becomes blander due to low production values even as its very ubiquity makes it less appealing to the consumer. It would be nice to think that the mushroom industry might save itself by switching to higher-quality strains with a focus on quality over quantity, and even to more interesting varieties.

None of this takes away from the fact that mastering the cultivation of mushrooms was quite a feat of understanding and technique. Even now, mushrooms involve the most convoluted growing process. Even more so for 'exotic' mushrooms – the shiitake, oyster, enoki and others. In theory, the process of producing a crop from the fruit of fungus is the same as for any other fruit or vegetable. You encourage the plant to grow and to attempt to reproduce itself, then you harvest the fruit or the flowers or the stems, leaves or whatever part you are interested in. With mushrooms, once you have overcome the first major hurdle, of getting the mycelium spawn to grow in the place where you want them to grow, you have only just begun, by comparison with propagating other plants. For one thing, the mycelium isn't in any great hurry to reproduce. It is more interested in growing itself than in producing fruit. It puts up fruit when it wants to move somewhere else, and that can mean waiting until it has effectively used up the space it's in and all the available food. The mycelium, meantime, is very happy living and growing in the log, until it gets to the time when it feels a need to find a new home. Then you get a few shiitake for supper.

In the modern industry, white mushrooms and their brown cousins are grown mostly in the compost of animals, or manure. For the primary decomposers like oyster and shiitake mushrooms, the medium most used is the sawdust by-product of the hardwood timber industry. This is mixed with grain bran, for nutrients, in bags or wrapping of some kind, and sterilised by cooking. To replicate the need of the mycelium to put up fruit, the spawn has to be introduced and then encouraged to grow until it has literally turned the mixture into a solid white structure of fungus. Getting it to do this involves detailed adjustment of the climate conditions of light, shade and darkness, as well as temperature and humidity. Having grown to the point where it clearly can't get any more food, nor continue to grow even if it had any, it might put out fruit in an attempt to move on. If conditions are right, of course, conditions which are different, and therefore have to be carefully recreated, to those required for the growing period. It clearly isn't a business for unskilled optimists.

At the same time, there are still producers of shiitake mushrooms who use a variation on the earliest cultivation method: inoculating logs and storing them outdoors to let them get on with it, with a little support and encouragement – the 'herding' method mentioned earlier. They claim to produce superior mushrooms but in much lower yields than indoor production, and command a heftier price too.

Despite the technical challenges, the production of specialist types, especially shiitake and oyster mushrooms, is already on the same scale as that of the Agaricus varieties, and growing. Worldwide, that is. Ireland remains a producer of white Agaricus mushrooms, but almost exclusively an importer of the others.

However, the real challenge to mushroom growers lies in to what extent they can succeed in cultivating the mycorrhizal fungi – those that live symbiotically with living trees. Given that these include the iconic truffles, ceps and chanterelles, coupled with our appetite for taming the wild, it would seem foolish to bet against it. Already, there are truffle nurseries producing trees, usually oak, beech or fir, which have been inoculated as saplings with the mycorrhiza of truffles. So if you'd like to have your own truffle crop, you can buy a few inoculated trees, plant them out and wait a few years, maybe even as many as ten, to see if any truffles show up. For a smaller, if less exciting gamble, you can get kits to grow various mushrooms at home, including inoculated shiitake logs.

For some reason, the needs of ceps and chanterelles haven't quite been figured out yet. The 'yet' is almost inevitable, as is the likelihood of truffle farming becoming more predictable and successful. As much as I admire man's tenacity in this, I can't help feeling that it might be better if some things were left to nature, with their mysterious allure intact.

In the kitchen, cultivated mushrooms are generally prepared in much the same ways as those from the wild. Some are best fried quickly, others stewed in their juices; some like butter, and wine, others cream and herbs.

I think it's fair to say that all mushrooms like garlic and salt. Three cultivated varieties have become constants in my kitchen, and this has as much to do with access to reliable supplies of good-quality mushrooms as it does to any personal favouritism.

Portobellos are the large brown-capped descendants of the common white field mushroom. Some of these monsters can weigh over 100g (3½oz) each; indeed, you can feel their density when compared to a field mushroom of the same circumference. The promise of this weighty texture is delivered in a rich, earthy flavour, especially when roasted. They are excellent simply roasted or grilled, but even better if the cap is filled or topped with complementary flavours. I like Portobellos with strong cheeses, especially blue or smoked varieties, as well as with oily nuts such as walnuts, pecans or pinenuts. Sage, parsley and thyme are also good with these mushrooms, as is the smoky flavour of Spanish paprika.

Oyster mushrooms come in a range of variations, but most are soft and delicate with a mild flavour. An exception is the king oyster, which is firm and dry, with something of the texture of a small cep. It is satisfyingly chewy when cooked but with the subtle flavour of all oyster mushrooms. King oysters are best sliced and fried briefly in plenty of butter over a high heat, followed by a short time stewing at a lower temperature. Being quite firm, they don't absorb flavours the way the open-gilled Portobello does, but they pair well with sage and garlic, cream and mustard, and a generous splash of alcohol such as white wine, cider or brandy.

Despite their place in the global market, I still think of shiitake mushrooms as resolutely Asian and so tend to use them in Eastern types of dishes such as broths and stir-fries flavoured with coconut, chillies, ginger and coriander, or in miso-based soups. Shiitakes have a chewy texture which lends itself to roasting too.

The imperfect harmony of cooks and growers

In this final chapter, as in the first three, I have been looking at a range of different vegetables – some that are old favourites and others that are new to me, and possibly to you too. It has been informative for me too. As much as this has been an exercise in putting down what I know about certain vegetables, it has also been an exploration of what there is to learn in the daily, weekly and seasonal business of working with them. I am aware that the sum total here is only a fraction of what there is to know and of the potential of the vegetables themselves, both in the field and in the kitchen. Even with the ones that seem to have always been in my repertoire, there is still so much to discover. With others, such as oca and seakale, to pick just two from this chapter, I have only just begun to scratch their surface, so to speak, in terms of appreciating their qualities and working out how to show them off to best advantage in my cooking.

This is the endlessly fascinating thing about using fresh vegetables, most of which have been produced virtually on my own doorstep. Every crop of every season will be different and will bring frustrations as well as increased knowledge and understanding. Because growers nurture the plants from seedlings, inevitably they are more in touch with all this than cooks, though in an ideal world it would be more equal. In this respect, I envy growers their affinity with the produce, but never the work involved. Each to their own, I suppose. Indeed, most growers wouldn't fancy the long hours in the heat of a kitchen either. I often think of something said by Myrtle Allen of Ballymaloe House, a woman who is both a cook and a gardener, about the uneasy relationship between the two, to the effect that cooks expect everything too soon and all at once, and gardeners resent the cooks sneaking into the vegetable beds and making off with everything just for one meal. It is difficult for the needs of the two to be always in accord. However, we can't work in isolation, and it is through the ongoing collaboration of growers and cooks that we will continue to learn and our food culture will continue to evolve and thrive.

Celeriac Fritters with Caper and Rosemary Aïoli

These make a lovely finger food, snack or very casual starter. If you want to serve them as a formal starter, place a little pile of them on a plate with a ramekin of the aïoli to dip into and a garnish of rocket or watercress salad. My favourite is rocket salad with fresh pear and a simple citrus and olive oil dressing.

To make your own rosemary oil, put two sprigs of fresh rosemary in a pan with enough olive oil to cover them. Heat the oil very gently for a few minutes, but don't let it get so hot the rosemary begins to fry. Remove from the heat and leave for 30 minutes. Strain the oil into a large jug and dilute it with more olive oil to taste. It should have a strong hint of rosemary but not be overpowering.

For the aïoli, squeeze the roasted garlic flesh out of its skin, then put it in a food processor with the egg, egg yolk and mustard and blend for 1 minute. With the motor still running, add the oil in a slow, steady stream until you get a thick dipping consistency. Add the capers, season with salt and pepper and blend for a few seconds only.

Peel the celeriac by slicing the skin off with a knife. Chop the flesh into pieces just over 5mm (¼in) thick, small enough to be eaten in two bites. Cook these in boiling water for 5–8 minutes, until just tender. Cool under cold running water.

Whisk the eggs and milk together. Mix the breadcrumbs and cheese together. Coat the celeriac pieces first in flour, then in the egg mix, and finally in the breadcrumbs. Heat some vegetable oil in a deep-fryer or large saucepan to about 170°C/325°F. If using a saucepan, put a few breadcrumbs in the oil to test the temperature. If the bread floats and becomes golden after about 15 seconds, turn the heat down to hold the temperature. Deep-fry the fritters in batches until crisp and lightly browned. Keep them warm in the oven while you cook the rest. Serve with the aïoli as a dip.

Serves 6–8 as a starter

FOR THE CAPER AND ROSEMARY AÏOLI

4 garlic cloves, roasted (see page 144)
1 egg
1 egg yolk
1 tsp Dijon or other hot mustard
200ml (7fl oz) rosemary-infused olive oil (see method)
2 tsp small capers
salt and pepper

FOR THE FRITTERS

1 medium celeriac, approx 600g (1lb 5oz)
2 eggs
100ml (3½fl oz) milk
200g (7oz) fresh breadcrumbs
50g (2oz) Desmond, Parmesan or other hard cheese, very finely grated
100g (3½oz) plain flour
vegetable oil, for deep-frying

Cabbage Timbale of Celeriac and Chestnuts with Porcini and Oyster Mushroom Sauce

You will need four metal rings or pastry rings of 7–8cm (2³/₄–3¹/₄in) diameter to make individual timbales. You can also make this like a large cake in a single loaf tin or a flan ring with a removeable base and slice it into individual portions.

    I usually serve this with fresh mushrooms, either oysters alone or mixed with wild mushrooms when we can get them.

Preheat the oven to 200°C/400°F/Gas Mark 6. Discard the outer leaves of the cabbage, or save them for another dish. Cut the stalk from as many of the paler leaves as you need to line your four metal rings or larger tin. Cook the leaves in boiling water for about 3–4 minutes until tender, then refresh in a bowl of cold water. Drain the leaves in a colander, then pat them dry with kitchen paper.

    Peel the celeriac and slice the flesh into pieces ¹/₂cm (¹/₄in) thick. Boil these for 2 minutes, then drain them and transfer to a baking sheet. Brush the slices with olive oil and roast them in the oven for 5 minutes.

    Lower the oven temperature to 180°C/350°F/Gas Mark 4. Melt the butter in a wide pan and cook the chopped leeks over a high heat with the garlic and thyme for about 7–8 minutes, stirring. If there is a lot of liquid in the pan when the leeks are tender, pour it off before continuing. Add the mustard and cream and continue cooking over a high heat for 3–4 minutes more. Remove from the heat and leave to cool completely, then stir in the eggs and chestnuts. Season with salt and pepper.

    Place the four metal rings on a baking tray then line each with cabbage leaves so there is a single layer all round and enough overlapping to cover the top. Line the cabbage base with a layer of celeriac, then press in a layer of the chestnut mix. Repeat this, then finish with a layer of celeriac. Fold over the overhanging cabbage leaves and press gently. Brush the tops with olive oil and cook for 15–20 minutes in the oven until the timbales are firm, occasionally moistening them with a splash of stock or water.

    To make the sauce, soak the porcini in the hot water for 20–30 minutes. Heat the butter in a wide pan and fry the shallots, garlic, thyme and oyster mushrooms over a medium heat for 5 minutes or so until the mushrooms are almost tender.

Serves 4

FOR THE TIMBALES

1 Savoy cabbage
1 large celeriac, approx 800–900g (1³/₄–2lb)
olive oil
1 tbsp butter
300g (10¹/₂oz) leeks, washed and diced
2 garlic cloves, finely chopped
1 tsp fresh thyme leaves
1 tsp Dijon or other hot mustard
100ml (3¹/₂fl oz) double cream
2 eggs, beaten
300g (10¹/₂oz) cooked chestnuts, coarsely chopped
salt and pepper

FOR THE SAUCE

25g (1oz) dried porcini mushrooms
200ml (7fl oz) hot water
1 tbsp butter
2–4 small shallots, finely chopped
2 garlic cloves, finely chopped
leaves from 1 sprig fresh thyme
200g (7oz) fresh oyster mushrooms, sliced
100ml (3¹/₂fl oz) double cream

Add in the porcini and their liquid. Bring to the boil, then lower the heat and simmer for 5 minutes. Add the cream and continue simmering for a few minutes more, until the sauce has thickened a little. Season with salt and pepper.

To serve, turn each timbale onto a plate, bottom-up, and spoon some mushroom sauce over the top.

Beetroot and Pomegranate Tabbouleh with Orange-marinated Feta

You will need to put two medium beets through a juicer to get the 225ml (7¹/₂fl oz) of beetroot juice needed to give this salad its vivid colour. Alternatively, boil two extra beets, blend with a bit of water and pass the purée through a fine sieve.

Put the feta in a bowl. Stir together the orange zest and juice and olive oil and pour it over the feta. Turn the cheese to coat it in the marinade then leave for 2 hours or more.

Warm the beetroot juice and pour it over the bulgur in a large bowl. Stir once, and leave it to stand for 20 minutes.

Chop the cooked beetroot into small dice. Remove the seeds from the pomegranate, discarding the skin and pith.

Add the beetroot, pomegranate and the rest of the ingredients to the bulgur with three or four tablespoons of the feta marinade. Serve in a large serving dish with the feta around the edge of the salad.

Serves 4

225ml (7¹/₂fl oz) beetroot juice
150g (5¹/₂oz) bulgur wheat
200g (7oz) beetroots, cooked and peeled
1 pomegranate
50g (2oz) fresh flat leaf parsley, coarsely chopped
25g (1oz) fresh mint leaves, coarsely chopped
1 tbsp cumin seeds, lightly toasted
3 tbsp lemon juice

FOR THE ORANGE-MARINATED FETA

200g (7oz) feta, cut into 2cm (³/₄in) dice
zest of 2 oranges
juice of ¹/₂ orange
100ml (3¹/₂fl oz) olive oil

Braised Carrots with Spices and Cider

Preheat the oven to 180°C/350°F/Gas Mark 4. Melt the butter in a flame-proof oven dish and fry the carrots, garlic, ginger, coriander and cumin over a medium heat for 2 minutes. Add the nutmeg, orange zest and cider, season with salt and pepper, and bring to the boil. Remove from the heat, cover the dish loosely with baking parchment and put it in the oven for about 30 minutes. The carrots should be very tender and the liquid almost all gone. Add some more cider or water and cook a little longer if the carrots are not yet tender.

Serves 4 as a side dish

1 tbsp butter
400g (14oz) carrots, sliced diagonally
1cm (1/2in) thick
2 garlic cloves, sliced
1 tsp grated fresh root ginger
1 tsp coriander seeds, cracked
1 tsp cumin seeds
1/2 tsp freshly grated nutmeg
zest of 1 orange
150ml (5fl oz) dry cider
salt and pepper

Braised Scorzonera with Star Anise

Scorzonera roots can be sticky and dirty, so peel them over newspaper or a wide tray. Cut into pieces about 6-10cm (1½-4in) long and drop into a saucepan of water to which you have added the juice of one lemon. Bring to the boil, simmer for 5 minutes, then drain.

Heat the olive oil in a pan and add the scorzonera, whole garlic cloves and the star anise. Cook over a medium heat for 5–7 minutes, until the scorzonera is coloured a little, then add the wine, stock and some salt. Cover with baking parchment and simmer slowly over a low heat until the scorzonera is tender. This could take 40–50 minutes. You may need to add a little more stock or water occasionally if the pan is becoming too dry.

Serves 4 as a side dish

4–6 whole scorzonera, washed and peeled
juice of 1 lemon
50ml (2fl oz) olive oil
2–3 garlic cloves
2 star anise
50ml (2fl oz) white wine
100ml (3½fl oz) vegetable stock or water
salt

Sunchoke Cream Soup with Sheep's Cheese Risotto Balls and Truffle Oil

The risotto balls in this soup are based on the classic Italian dish of 'arancini', where the balls are the size of oranges. These balls are much smaller so you need only a very small amount of risotto. It is really too small a quantity of risotto to make, so I recommend you either make risotto for lunch while you prepare dinner or that you make more of the balls than you need for this dish and have them in tomato sauce the following day. They keep very well in a fridge (before frying) for up to two days.

I use a combination of two cheeses – Knockalara, a soft, fresh and mild cheese; and the more strongly flavoured Cratloe Hills, which is a 6–9 month old hard cheese with a texture like Manchego or Pecorino.

Serves 4

FOR THE RISOTTO BALLS

1 tbsp soft sheep's cheese
1 tsp hard sheep's cheese, grated
4 tbsp cooked risotto
vegetable oil, for deep frying

FOR THE SOUP

oil or butter, for frying
2 medium onions, finely chopped
2 garlic cloves, finely chopped
700g (1lb 8oz) sunchokes, peeled and chopped
75ml (2½fl oz) white wine
700ml (22fl oz) vegetable stock or water
4 tbsp double cream
1 tsp white truffle oil
1 tsp finely chopped fresh chives

To make the risotto balls, combine the cheeses. Take a scant tablespoon of risotto, form it into a ball in your hand, then make an indentation in the ball. Take a small piece of the cheese mixture and press it into the risotto, then reform the risotto into a ball around the cheese. Press well to ensure the rice is firmly stuck together. Leave the balls in the fridge for at least 20 minutes before frying.

Heat a little oil or butter in a large saucepan, add the onions and cook gently for 7–10 minutes until they become translucent. Add the garlic, sunchokes and wine, bring to the boil, then lower the heat, cover with a piece of baking parchment and simmer for 8–10 minutes. Add the stock or water, bring it back to the boil, then lower the heat, put the lid on and simmer for 15–20 minutes until the sunchokes are soft.

Blend the soup to a fine purée, then pass this through a sieve and return it to a saucepan. Add the cream and reheat gently. Do not allow the soup to boil. Just before you serve, stir in the truffle oil. However, if you are making enough for leftovers, only add the truffle oil to that which you are about to serve.

While you are reheating the soup, heat some vegetable oil to 170°C/325°F in a large saucepan or electric deep-fryer. If using a saucepan, drop a small piece of risotto mixture into the oil to test. If it floats quickly and fries gently, the oil is ready. Turn the heat down to hold the temperature. Drop in the chilled risotto balls and fry them for 2–3 minutes until lightly coloured.

Divide the soup between four serving bowls and place a deep-fried risotto ball in each one. Sprinkle some chives over the top to serve.

Warm Salad of Roasted Oca and Pak Choi with Peanut, Lime and Coriander Dressing

Preheat the oven to 180°C/350°F/Gas Mark 4. Place the halved oca on an oven tray and roast them in the oven for 15–20 minutes until the oca are soft inside. Test each one with a skewer or by squeezing with your fingers, and remove them as they're cooked.

Make a dressing by whisking together the ginger, lime juice and sugar.

Heat a wide pan on the stove and put in the pak choi, spring onions, chilli, soy sauce and 2 tablespoons of water. Simmer this over a high heat for 2 minutes, stirring until the pak choi has softened.

Place a mound of the pak choi on each of four plates, and top with the roasted oca. Scatter on some roasted peanuts and fresh coriander, then spoon some of the dressing over each salad.

Serves 4

16–20 medium oca, washed and halved

4–6 heads baby pak choi, leaves separated

4 spring onions, diagonally sliced

1 fresh red chilli, halved, seeded and thinly sliced

1 tbsp soy sauce

2 tbsp peanuts, roasted, peeled and coarsely chopped

1 handful fresh coriander leaves, chopped

FOR THE DRESSING

1 tbsp grated fresh root ginger

100ml (3½fl oz) lime juice

2 dsp caster sugar

New Potato and Summer Vegetable Soup with Salsa Verde and Mascarpone

This is a very fresh soup for which the vegetables are lightly cooked. By using waxy new potatoes that won't break down to give a heavy, starchy texture to the soup, you will get a light but satisfying summer dish.

To make the salsa verde, pulse the first seven ingredients in a food processor. Add the olive oil and blend briefly to get a thick pesto-like consistency.

In a large saucepan, heat the olive oil and gently fry the spring onions, garlic and new potatoes for 5 minutes over a low to medium heat. Add the stock, bring it to the boil and simmer for 5 minutes. Add the green beans, courgettes and tomatoes, and simmer for 5–10 minutes more, until the potatoes are tender. Add the broad beans or peas for the last minute of cooking. Season with salt and pepper.

Ladle the soup into deep bowls and stir a tablespoon of salsa verde into each. Put a teaspoon of mascarpone into the middle of each portion and serve.

Serves 4

FOR THE SALSA VERDE

25g (1oz) fresh basil
50g (2oz) fresh parsley
25g (1oz) fresh mint
2 garlic cloves
4 spring onions, chopped
1 mild fresh green chilli, halved, seeded and chopped
1 tsp capers
200ml (7fl oz) olive oil

FOR THE SOUP

2 tbsp olive oil
4 spring onions, thinly sliced
4 garlic cloves, chopped
500g (18oz) new potatoes, washed and diced
750ml (1¼ pints) vegetable stock
100g (3½oz) green beans, chopped
100g (3½oz) courgettes, diced
4 tomatoes, peeled, seeded and diced
50g (2oz) fresh small broad beans or peas
2 tbsp mascarpone cheese
salt and pepper

Seakale with Lemon Thyme Butter and Pine Nuts

Bring some water to the boil in a large saucepan (just boil enough water to cover the seakale when it is added). Add the lemon juice. Trim any leaves from the top of the seakale stalks and discard. Put the stalks in the boiled water, bring back to the boil, then lower the heat and simmer gently, uncovered, for 7–10 minutes until the seakale is tender. Drain off the remaining water, and remove the pan from the heat. Add the butter, lemon thyme, and a little salt and pepper. Shake the pan a few times so that the butter melts and coats the seakale. Transfer the seakale to a serving plate and pour all of the herbed butter over it. Sprinkle the pine nuts over and serve.

Serves 4

juice of ½ lemon
400g (14oz) whole blanched seakale stalks
2 tbsp butter
leaves from 1–2 sprigs lemon thyme
salt and pepper
1 tbsp pine nuts, lightly toasted and cracked

Salsify, Carrot and Mushroom Stew with Cider-tarragon Cream and Smoked Cheese Polenta

This recipe came about from a challenge at Paradiso to make a main course from root vegetables. Of course, the addition of mushrooms adds to its appeal, and everyone loves a cream sauce. At the time, we had a source of hedgehog mushrooms, which were fantastic in this dish because of their firm texture and intense flavour. King oysters are good too, if you can get them, as are shiitake. In fact any mushroom that doesn't leak too much brown liquid when cooked will do, even the very large white button types that haven't quite opened out.

It may seem unusual to serve a stew with a cream sauce. However, the stew is quite dry and intense, so the cream adds a contrast in both flavour and texture, as well as offering moisture for the polenta to absorb.

You can serve the stew without the cream sauce by simply adding more of each of the liquids in the stew itself – olive oil, cider and tomato passata.

I use smoked Gubbeen cheese to give the polenta a mildly smoky flavour. If using another smoked cheese, you may need to reduce the quantity. To add some greenery to the plate, we sometimes rest each piece of polenta on a little mound of spinach flavoured with nutmeg.

Serves 4

FOR THE SMOKED CHEESE POLENTA

1 litre (1³/4 pints) vegetable stock

200g (7oz) coarse maize

1 tsp salt

1 tsp smoked paprika

100g (3¹/2oz) smoked Gubbeen cheese, grated

olive oil

FOR THE STEW

300g (10¹/2oz) salsify

juice of 1 lemon

300g (10¹/2oz) carrots

50ml (2fl oz) olive oil

4 garlic cloves, thinly sliced

leaves from 1 sprig fresh thyme

150ml (5fl oz) dry cider

2 tbsp butter

100g (3¹/2oz) shallots, thinly sliced

150g (5¹/2oz) mushrooms, whole or in large pieces

1 tbsp tomato passata

1 tbsp chopped fresh parsley

salt and pepper

FOR THE CIDER-TARRAGON CREAM

150ml (5fl oz) cider

300ml (10fl oz) double cream

2 tbsp fresh tarragon leaves, coarsely chopped

To make the polenta, bring the stock to the boil in a large saucepan, then whisk in the maize and salt. Whisk until it comes back to the boil, then reduce the heat to very low and simmer the polenta, stirring occasionally for about 20 minutes until the grains are very soft. Stir in the paprika and smoked cheese. Line a shallow baking tray, about 20x30cm (8x12in), with baking parchment and tip the polenta in (the polenta should be about 1–1.5 cm (¹/2in) thick). Leave it to cool, then cut it into any shape you like. I like triangles.

Preheat the oven to 180°C/350°F/Gas Mark 4.

To make the stew, peel the salsify and cut into diagonal pieces about 4cm (1¹/2in) long. Keeping the peeled salsify in water to which you have added the lemon juice will stop it from discolouring. Peel or wash the carrots and cut them into similar slices. Heat the olive oil in a flame-proof oven dish and add the vegetables, garlic and thyme. Fry them over a medium heat for 5 minutes. Add the cider and bring it to the boil. Cover the dish with baking parchment, then braise in the oven for 20–30 minutes until the vegetables are tender.

Raise the oven temperature to 200°C/400°F/Gas Mark 6. In a large shallow pan, heat the butter over a medium heat, add the shallots and mushrooms and fry for 5–7 minutes until almost tender. Add the braised salsify and carrot, passata, parsley and some salt and pepper. Stew the vegetables for a few minutes to mingle the flavours and to reduce the liquids until almost gone.

To make the cider-tarragon cream, put the cider in a small pan, bring it to the boil, then lower the heat and simmer for about 5–7 minutes until it is reduced by half. Then, add the cream and reduce again to get a slightly thickened pouring consistency. Stir in the tarragon and a little seasoning.

At the same time, brush the polenta pieces lightly with olive oil and bake them in the oven for 7–10 minutes, until crisp and golden.

To serve, pile some stew in the centre of each plate, pour some sauce around and place three or more pieces of polenta in the sauce.

Oca with Spinach, Coconut and Cashews

This is based on the massaman curry recipes of southern Thailand. The sweet spices work really well with the fruity acidity of the oca. Serve with rice or lentil dhal.

Blend the onion, chillies, lemongrass, ginger, garlic, spices and fresh coriander in a food processor to a fine paste. Heat the vegetable oil in a large saucepan and fry the paste for 5 minutes over a medium heat, stirring often. Chop the oca into bite-size pieces if they are large, or leave small ones whole. Add them to the pan and continue frying for 10 minutes more. Pour in the coconut milk, and enough stock or water to just cover the oca. Bring it to the boil, then lower the heat and simmer, uncovered, for 15–20 minutes until the oca are tender.

Meanwhile, cook the spinach in boiling water for 3–4 minutes then drain and squeeze out the moisture. Chop the spinach coarsely. Add the cooked spinach and the roasted cashews to the curry, and season it with salt.

Serves 4

1 medium onion, chopped
1 or 2 fresh green chillies, halved, seeded and chopped
2 sticks lemongrass, chopped
1 tbsp grated fresh root ginger
2 garlic cloves
1 tbsp coriander seeds
seeds from 6 cardamom pods
½ tbsp cumin seeds
4 cloves
½ tsp ground nutmeg
½ tsp ground cinnamon
1 handful fresh coriander leaves
2 tbsp vegetable oil
500g (18oz) oca, washed
400ml (14fl oz) coconut milk
vegetable stock or water
400g (14oz) spinach
80g (2¾oz) whole cashews, roasted
salt

Swede Turnip and Leek Curry

Preheat the oven to 150°C/300°F/Gas Mark 2. Peel the turnip by slicing the skin off with a sharp knife. Chop the flesh into large chunks at least two bites each. Bring a medium saucepan of water to the boil and cook the turnip chunks for 7–8 minutes, then drain.

In a large flame-proof oven dish, heat the butter and fry the leeks, chilli, ginger and spices over a medium heat for 5 minutes. Add the turnip chunks, cream, a generous seasoning of salt and the vegetable stock or water. Bring this to the boil, stir in the yoghurt and transfer the dish to the oven. Bake the curry slowly for about 60–90 minutes until the vegetables are very tender and beginning to soften.

Serve with rice and beer.

Serves 4–6

1 large swede turnip
2 tbsp butter
2 large leeks, sliced 2cm (3/4in) thick
6–8 bird's eye chillies, ground
1 tbsp grated ginger
1 tbsp coriander seeds, ground
1 tbsp cumin seeds, ground
1 tbsp fennel seeds, ground
1 tsp turmeric
250ml (8fl oz) double cream
salt
200ml (7fl oz) vegetable stock or water
500ml (18fl oz) plain yoghurt

Shiitake Mushrooms with Aubergine, Mustard Leaves, Coconut and Rice Noodles

I like this best with tagliatelle-shaped rice noodles but the thinner linguine style is good too.

Slice the aubergine into strips about 4cm (1¹/₂in) long and 1cm (¹/₂in) thick. Heat the vegetable oil in a wide pan or wok and fry the aubergine and mushrooms together over a high heat for 5 minutes. Add the spring onions, tomatoes, chillies, garlic, ginger and coriander and cook for 2 minutes more. Add the coconut milk, mustard leaves and basil, bring it to the boil, then lower the heat and simmer for 2–3 minutes.

At the same time, bring a large saucepan of water to the boil and cook the rice noodles according to the packet instructions. This usually involves soaking and/or simmering for 2–5 minutes, depending on the type of noodle. Drain the cooked noodles well and divide between four bowls. Use a spoon to put some vegetables on each portion, pouring in the coconut broth too. Squeeze some lime juice on top and serve.

Serves 4

1 long Japanese-style aubergine
2 tbsp vegetable oil
200g (7oz) shiitake mushrooms, halved
6 spring onions, diagonally sliced
4 tomatoes, halved and thinly sliced
4 dried bird's eye chillies, chopped
4 garlic cloves, sliced
3cm (1¹/₄in) piece fresh ginger, sliced
1 tbsp coriander seeds, ground
1 x 400ml (14fl oz) tin coconut milk
50g (2oz) mustard leaves, coarsely chopped
small bunch fresh Thai basil leaves, coarsely chopped
150g (5¹/₂oz) rice noodles
1 lime, halved

Thyme and Wild Garlic Mash with Sprouting Broccoli, Sweet and Hot Peppers and Puy Lentils

This is one of an endless number of possible variations on mash as the focus of a simple dinner. The basic model is mash accompanied by some greens flavoured with tomato, often garlic and chillies too and richly moistened with olive oil. Kale and cabbage are good, as are beans and courgettes in summer. A simple version of peperonata, the sweet pepper stew, is good too, or a moist ratatouille. You could also flavour the mash with cheese or different herbs, but don't go so far that it is no longer mash but a complicated potato-based dish. This is comfort food we're doing here, not a dinner party.

Serves 4

1.2kg (2³/₄lb) floury potatoes
150ml (5fl oz) milk
100g (3¹/₂oz) butter
leaves from 2 sprigs fresh thyme
4 spring onions, finely chopped
salt and pepper
4 tbsp olive oil
2 small red onions, halved and thinly sliced
500g (18oz) sprouting broccoli stalks, about 6–7cm (2¹/₂–2³/₄in) long
4 garlic cloves, sliced
1–2 fresh chillies, halved, seeded, and thinly sliced
4 ripe fresh or whole tinned tomatoes, halved and sliced
4 tbsp cooked Puy lentils
100ml (3¹/₂fl oz) vegetable stock or water

Peel and steam the potatoes until soft. Heat the milk in a large saucepan until warm but not hot, then add the butter allowing it to melt before adding the potatoes. Turn off the heat and mash the potatoes with a potato masher. Stir in the thyme and spring onions, and some salt and pepper.

While the potatoes are steaming, heat 2 tablespoons of the olive oil in a wide pan or wok, and fry the onion, broccoli, garlic and chillies over a high heat for 3–4 minutes, stirring constantly until the onion begins to brown. Add the tomatoes and continue frying for 2 minutes more. Add the lentils and a little stock or water to prevent the vegetables sticking. Cover the pan and reduce the heat to let the vegetables simmer for a few minutes. When the broccoli is tender, add the remaining 2 tablespoons of olive oil and a little salt. Depending on how moist you want the dish, you may want to add a little more stock too.

Serve a generous mound of mash on four warmed plates. Spoon on some vegetables and pour some of the pan juices over each portion.

Gratin of Crushed Potato, Spinach, Spiced Aubergine and Fresh Goat's Cheese with Thyme and Caper Cream

Serve this with a braised vegetable, such as fennel or scorzonera and some simple fresh greens.

Preheat the oven to 180°C/350°F/Gas Mark 4. Chop the aubergine into medium dice, toss in olive oil and roast in the oven for about 10–12 minutes until cooked through. Leave the oven on to cook the gratin.

Meanwhile, heat a little olive oil in a large saucepan, cook the onion for 2–3 minutes, then add the garlic, chillies, spices and thyme. Continue cooking over a medium heat for about 7–8 minutes until the onion is soft. Add the tomatoes, wine and purée to the saucepan and cook until reduced to a thick sauce, about half an hour. Add the roasted aubergine.

Peel and steam the potatoes, then chop them coarsely. Heat 2 tablespoons of olive oil in a wide, heavy frying pan, then toss in the potato chunks. Keeping the temperature high, brown the potatoes, all the while turning them and breaking them down into smaller chunks with the side of a slice, until you have a dish somewhere between very well-fried potato and chunky mash. Add the chives and season with salt and pepper.

Cover an oven tray with baking parchment and place four 7–8cm (2¾–3¼in) diameter metal or pastry rings on it. Line the rings with parchment, cutting the paper to rise 1cm (½in) above the ring. Press in a layer of potato to come about halfway up a metal ring, then a smaller layer of spinach, followed by one of spiced aubergine to bring the gratin up to the top of the paper. Place a slice of fresh goat's cheese on top. Repeat with the remaining three rings, then bake them in the oven for 15 minutes.

To make the thyme and caper cream, bring the stock and wine to the boil in a small saucepan then lower the heat and simmer for about 5–6 minutes to reduce by half. Add the cream and reduce again to get a slightly thickened pouring consistency. Stir in the capers and thyme and a little seasoning.

Place each gratin on a serving plate, remove the metal ring and paper and serve with the thyme and caper cream.

Serves 4

FOR THE GRATIN

500g (18oz) aubergine
olive oil
1 medium onion, finely chopped
6 garlic cloves, crushed
2 dried bird's eye chillies, ground
2 tsp cumin seeds, ground
2 tsp coriander seeds, ground
leaves from 2 sprigs fresh thyme
4 ripe tomatoes, chopped or 1 x 400g (14oz) tin chopped tomatoes, juice discarded
100ml (3½fl oz) red wine
2 tsp tomato purée
600g (1lb 5oz) potatoes, medium floury, such as Roosters
1 tbsp chopped fresh chives
salt and pepper
300g (10½oz) spinach, cooked, cooled and chopped
200g (7oz) fresh goat's cheese log, sliced into 4 rounds

FOR THE THYME AND CAPER CREAM

100ml (3½fl oz) vegetable stock
100ml (3½fl oz) wine
300ml (10fl oz) double cream
2 tsp tiny capers or chopped capers
1 tsp fresh thyme leaves

Parsnip, Fennel and Quinoa Pilaf with Pickled Lemon, Mint and Coriander, and a Harissa-yoghurt Sauce

The fruity acidity of pickled lemon brings a lovely counterbalance to the sweetness of the vegetables. If you don't have, or can't get, pickled lemon, use the zest of one lemon and the juice of a half instead. The harissa-yoghurt sauce adds a nicely disguised kick of heat to the dish.

Preheat the oven to 180°C/350°F/Gas Mark 4. Quarter the parsnips and remove the cores. Chop the flesh into wedges about 3cm (1¼in) long. Toss these in a little olive oil in an oven dish and roast them for about 20–30 minutes, turning occasionally, until tender and beginning to caramelise.

    Heat 2 tablespoons of olive oil in a large saucepan and fry the onion, fennel and garlic over a medium heat for 10 minutes, until beginning to colour. Add the cumin and coriander seeds, turmeric and quinoa and continue to fry for a further 5 minutes. Add the stock, bring it to the boil, cover the pan, then reduce the heat and simmer for 15–20 minutes until the quinoa is tender. Stir in the parsnips, pickled lemon, mint, fresh coriander and season with salt.

    While the pilaf is cooking, stir the harissa paste and yoghurt together, to be served alongside the pilaf.

Serves 4

600g (1lb 5oz) parsnips

olive oil

1 medium red onion, halved and thinly sliced

1 fennel bulb, quartered, core removed, and thinly sliced

2 garlic cloves, sliced

2 tsp cumin seeds

1 tsp coriander seeds, cracked

1 tsp turmeric

100g (3½oz) quinoa

300ml (10fl oz) vegetable stock

4 slices pickled lemon, chopped

1 tbsp chopped fresh mint leaves

2 tbsp chopped fresh coriander

salt

FOR THE HARISSA-YOGHURT SAUCE

1–2 tsp prepared harissa paste

200ml (7fl oz) plain yoghurt

Caramelised Beetroot with Caraway and Walnuts

Preheat the oven to 170°C/325°F/Gas Mark 3. Cook the beetroots in boiling water for about 20–30 minutes until just tender. Cool the beets under cold running water, and rub their skins off with your fingers. Slice the beets thinly and toss them in a large oven dish with the caraway seeds, olive oil, balsamic vinegar and sugar. Add enough water or vegetable stock to bring the liquid level to about 1cm (¹/₂in) in the dish. Cover it loosely with baking parchment and place the dish in the oven for 40–60 minutes. The liquid should be evaporated and the beets beginning to caramelise. Toss the walnuts through the beetroots before serving.

Serves 4–6

800g (1³/₄lb) medium beetroots

2 tsp caraway seeds

2 tbsp olive oil

2 tbsp balsamic vinegar

2 tbsp caster sugar

50g (2oz) walnuts, thinly sliced

Galette of Braised Turnip, Portobello Mushroom and Pecans with a Red Wine Sauce

At Paradiso we serve these galettes with braised scorzonera and some simple Brussels sprouts flavoured with a little orange.

Preheat the oven to 170°C/325°F/Gas Mark 3. Peel and trim the turnips so that you can cut thin slices about 7–8cm (2¾–3¼in) square and about 0.5cm (¼in) thick. A mandoline is very useful for doing this but a good sharp knife is fine too. Cut four slices per portion, sixteen in all. Bring a large saucepan of water to the boil, add the turnip slices, return to the boil and cook for 7 minutes. Drain the slices, then transfer them to one or two oven dishes. Heat the butter, white wine and stock together in a saucepan until the butter melts, then pour this over the turnip slices. Season with a little salt, cover loosely with foil and place the dishes in the oven. If after 30 minutes they are not yet tender, continue cooking, ensuring that they don't dry out, until they are fully cooked but not too soft to handle. The liquid should be almost gone .

Serves 4

FOR THE GALETTES

2 large turnips
4 tbsp butter
100ml (3½fl oz) white wine
100ml (3½fl oz) vegetable stock or water
salt and pepper
4 large Portobello mushrooms
melted butter or olive oil
100g (3½oz) pecans
100g (3½oz) cream cheese

FOR THE RED WINE SAUCE

400ml (14fl oz) red wine
200ml (7fl oz) tomato passata or puréed tinned tomato
1 small red onion, finely chopped
2 garlic cloves, chopped
½ stick celery, chopped
1 sprig fresh thyme
2 whole cloves
4 tbsp cold unsalted butter, diced

Turn the oven temperature up to 190°C/375°F/Gas Mark 5. Place the mushrooms on an oven tray, brush them with butter or olive oil, season with salt and roast them for about 10–12 minutes until they are tender. Chop the mushrooms coarsely and put them in a food processor with the pecans. Pulse carefully to get a coarse purée. Mash or fold in the cream cheese by hand.

Reduce the oven temperature to 180°C/350°F/Gas Mark 4. To make the sauce, place the wine, tomato, onion, garlic, celery, thyme and cloves in a saucepan and bring to the boil. Reduce the heat and simmer for 15 minutes, then blend and pass the purée through a sieve. Return the sauce to a pan, bring back to the boil, reduce the heat and simmer again until reduced by half. Season lightly with salt and pepper.

Place four slices of turnip on an oven tray lined with baking parchment and cover with some of the mushroom-pecan mixture. Place another turnip slice on top, and repeat until each galette has four turnip layers and three of mushroom. Press gently on each galette, brush the tops with a little melted butter and place in the oven to heat through for 7–10 minutes.

Just before you serve the galettes, heat the reduced red wine sauce and whisk in the butter over a high heat. The sauce will thicken and become a little glossy. Place a galette on each plate, pour the sauce around them and garnish with thyme.

Turnip and Gabriel Cheese Mezzaluna with Sage Butter, Pecans and Shallots

These quantities will make about 20 'mezzaluna' – which translates literally as 'half moons' in Italian. We serve three as a starter, but five is a generous meal with a simple salad on the side. For instructions on making fresh pasta, see page 216.

Preheat the oven to 130°C/250°F/Gas Mark ¼. Put the sugar, maple syrup and water in a small saucepan and heat gently until the sugar has melted. Stir in the pecans, then lay them on an oven tray lined with baking parchment. Place in the oven for 20 minutes. Remove the tray from the oven and leave the pecans to cool and become crisp, then slice them thinly.

To make the filling, peel the turnip with a sharp knife, cut it into small dice and steam for about 10–12 minutes until tender. Leave to cool. Blend the turnip to a smooth purée in a food processor, or mash well by hand. Place the purée in a pan with the cream and cook it over a low heat, stirring often for 5–7 minutes until the purée has thickened to a very stiff consistency. Season with salt and pepper and cool it again. Stir in the cheese.

Cut 20 circles with a diameter of 8cm (3¹/₄in) from the pasta sheet. Place a teaspoon of the turnip filling in the centre of each one and brush the edges with water or beaten egg. Fold each pasta circle in half, pressing firmly to seal the edges, taking care to ensure that there are no air pockets in the parcels.

Leave the butter at room temperature for 15–20 minutes to soften, then stir in the sage leaves. Heat a tablespoon of olive oil in a frying pan and fry the shallots over a high heat for about 5–7 minutes until they become crisp and lightly coloured. Leave them in a warm place.

To cook the mezzaluna, bring some water to the boil in a large saucepan and drop in some of the parcels. Don't overcrowd the pot. Put the sage butter in a wide shallow bowl and place this on top of the pot so the butter becomes very soft but doesn't completely melt. Simmer the parcels for 3–5 minutes until the pasta is done – checking occasionally is the only way to know. Carefully take the cooked parcels from the water and put them in the bowl with the butter. Keep these warm while you cook a second batch.

To serve, place the mezzaluna on warm plates with a generous amount of the melted sage butter. Place a spoonful of shallots in the centre and scatter some glazed pecans over the top.

Serves 6 as a starter, 4 as a main meal

FOR THE PECANS

30g (1¹/₄oz) caster sugar
1 tsp maple syrup
1 tbsp water
50g (2oz) pecans

FOR THE MEZZALUNA

250g (9oz) turnip
1 tbsp double cream
salt and pepper
60g (2¹/₄oz) Gabriel cheese (or mature cheddar or Parmesan), finely grated
1 fresh pasta sheet, approx 16x100cm (6¹/₄x40in); or 2 16x50cm (6¹/₄x20in) sheets
water or beaten egg
150g (5¹/₂oz) butter
2 tbsp chopped fresh sage leaves
1tbsp olive oil
250g (9oz) shallots, halved and thinly sliced

Grilled Portobello Mushrooms with Potato Pancakes and Tarragon Cream

Think of this as a rich brunch, needing only a simple salad garnish or some eggs if you are really hungry and in need of comfort food.

This recipe makes eight potato pancakes which can also be a base for a complex dinner. In Paradiso we sometimes serve them with some roasted artichokes stuffed with olives and cheese. They also make a great snack, as well as a decent foil for a dryish stew.

I like to fry the pancakes in metal rings (about 7–8cm (2³/₄–3¹/₄in) in diameter) to give them a perfectly circular shape, but it isn't really necessary. The pancakes will hold together well without any support.

Serves 4

2 tbsp butter
2 garlic cloves, crushed
4 large Portobello mushrooms
2 tbsp soured cream
2 tsp chopped fresh tarragon
1 tomato, peeled, seeded and finely diced

FOR THE POTATO PANCAKES

4 medium potatoes, thickly grated
4 small shallots, finely sliced
leaves from 1 sprig fresh thyme
2 rounded tbsp plain flour
2 eggs, beaten
olive oil

Preheat the oven to 200°C/400°F/Gas Mark 6 and leave the butter at room temperature for 20–30 minutes.

To make the potato pancakes, combine all the ingredients except the olive oil in a large bowl and mix well. Heat a heavy or non-stick frying pan over a medium heat and brush it lightly with olive oil. Place the rings in the pan (or not, as you prefer) and drop a tablespoon of the potato mixture into each, pressing it in to get a flat surface. Fry the pancakes for 5 minutes, then flip them over, press them down. and fry for a further 5 minutes until golden on both sides.

Stir the garlic into the butter. Spread the butter on the mushrooms and roast them in the oven for about 10–12 minutes until tender.

Mix the soured cream, tarragon and tomato together. Spoon a little mixture onto each roasted mushroom. Place the mushrooms on four of the pancakes and top with the other four pancakes, pressing down gently. Serve immediately.

Root Vegetable Crisps

Root vegetable crisps are a fashionable snack. You can make them yourself from just about any root vegetable or tuber, using one of these two basic methods. I always use the frying method but the oven variation works too though the crisps can tend to be hard rather than crisp, and drier too. Not necessarily a bad thing, just slightly different.

- sea salt
- black pepper
- ground chilli
- a mix of ground spices such as cumin, coriander and chilli
- lime or lemon zest, very finely grated
- orange zest with ground fennel seeds
- good quality dried herbs such as oregano, dill or chives

Because they shrink when cooking, it is best to use large vegetables, though this isn't an issue when it comes to turnips! Carrots, turnips and parsnips all behave much the same. Beetroots tend to have more sugar and therefore burn more easily, so I drop the temperature by a few degrees for them. Sunchokes are a revelation when deep-fried, becoming wonderfully crisp with an intensified flavour, as are purple potatoes.

The vegetables need to be cut thinly and evenly. You can do this with a sharp knife and a steady hand, or a strong wide peeler. However, there is no getting away from the fact that it is best to use a mandoline, a gadget with a very sharp blade and numerous settings to dictate the thickness of the cut. Please bear in mind, not just the first time but every time you use a mandoline, that it can be a very dangerous thing if used carelessly. Buy one with a guard and never slice without it on.

The ingredients are simple – root vegetables and cooking oil. If you are using the oven method, you might want to use olive oil. Otherwise I suggest a stable vegetable oil such as rapeseed, groundnut or sunflower.

Method 1

Heat some oil in a deep-fryer or large saucepan to 170°C/325°F. If you are cooking the crisps in a saucepan of oil, either use a thermometer or test with a slice of vegetable. If the oil hisses and bubbles gently when you drop the slice in, it is hot enough.

Slice the vegetables thinly. The second thinnest setting on a mandoline is usually good. If you are unsure, again, test a slice.

Drop in some vegetables, being careful not to overcrowd the pan, and fry them until they are lightly coloured. Stir occasionally to ensure even cooking.

Remove the cooked vegetables from the oil and put them to drain on a tray lined with absorbent paper. They will still be slightly soft but will crisp up as they cool. While they are still warm, sprinkle the crisps with sea salt and anything else you fancy. Leave them in a warm place to cool down and become crisp.

Method 2

Preheat the oven to 200°C/400°F/Gas Mark 6. Slice the vegetables thinly, as above. Put them in a bowl and toss them in a little oil, just enough to lightly coat the

continued overleaf

vegetables. Lay the vegetable slices in a single layer on an oven tray and bake them for 20–30 minutes until they are lightly coloured. Remove the crisps to a tray of absorbent paper and sprinkle with sea salt and any other flavourings you want to use. Again, they will crisp up as they cool down.

Parsnip Chips

Because of the sugar content in parsnips, these chips will burn easily on the outside if the oil is too hot.

Serves 4–6

4–6 large parsnips

vegetable oil, for deep-frying

salt and pepper

Peel and quarter the parsnips. Cut out the woody core, then chop the parsnips into chips about 1cm ($^1/_2$in) thick. Try to keep the chips of relatively even thickness otherwise thin ends will burn while the rest cooks through.

Boil the chips in water for 5 minutes, drain and dry on kitchen paper. Heat some vegetable oil to 170°C/325°F in a deep-fryer or large saucepan. If using a saucepan, test the oil by dropping in a small piece of parsnip. If it floats and sizzles gently, turn the heat down to hold the temperature. Drop in the parsnips and fry them for about 7–8 minutes until they are crisp and lightly coloured. Remove the cooked chips and drain them on kitchen paper. Season with salt and pepper.

Roast Parsnip Mash

Preheat the oven to 190°C/375°F/Gas Mark 5. Toss the parsnips in olive oil then roast in an oven dish covered loosely with baking parchment for about 12–15 minutes until tender and golden. Remove them from the oven and purée in a food processor.

Peel the potatoes and steam them until tender. In a separate saucepan, heat the milk and butter until the butter begins to melt, then add the potatoes and mash them. Stir in the parsnips and chives and season with salt and pepper.

Serves 4

400g (14oz) parsnips, peeled and diced

olive oil

600g (1lb 5oz) floury potatoes

150ml (5fl oz) milk

4 tbsp butter

1 tbsp chopped fresh chives

salt and pepper

Roast Sunchoke Risotto with Lemon-thyme Oil

Preheat the oven to 180°C/350°F/Gas Mark 4. To make the lemon-thyme oil, combine the olive oil, lemon zest and juice and thyme in a jug or jar. Shake well or blend and set aside.

If you wish to decorate the finished dish with sunchoke crisps, take out the four largest sunchokes and make crisps with them according to one of the methods on pages 296–298.

Take 500g (18oz) of the sunchokes and slice them. Heat a little olive oil in a large saucepan, add in two of the onions and cook gently for 7–10 minutes until they become translucent. Add 2 cloves of the garlic and the 500g (18oz) of sliced sunchokes. Cover with a piece of baking parchment and stew for 5 minutes. Add the stock, bring it to the boil, then lower the heat, cover with the pan lid and simmer for 20 minutes or so until the sunchokes are soft. Remove the pan from the heat and blend the mixture to a fine purée, then pass this through a sieve to get a thinnish broth. You will need about 1.2 litres (2 pints), so add more stock or water now if necessary. Put this broth back in the pan and keep it warm.

Chop the remaining sunchokes into pieces about 2cm (³⁄₄in) long. Toss them lightly in olive oil on an oven tray and roast them for about 10–12 minutes until just tender and lightly coloured.

Heat two tablespoons of olive oil in a large saucepan and gently fry the remaining onion and garlic for 5 minutes. Add the rice and toast it over a medium heat for 10 minutes, stirring often. Add the white wine, bring to the boil, then lower the heat and simmer, stirring until it has been absorbed. Now add in a ladle or two of the hot sunchoke broth. Let this simmer until it is absorbed, stirring often, then add more broth. Continue in this way until the rice is just tender and almost dry. It will take about 20 minutes. Now add the roasted sunchokes, chives, butter and half of the cheese. Season well.

Serve immediately on warm plates, with the sunchoke crisps on top. You may need to blend or shake the lemon-thyme oil again. Pour a little around each risotto. Offer the remaining cheese on the side.

Serves 4

FOR THE LEMON-THYME OIL
200ml (7fl oz) olive oil
zest and juice of 1 lemon
leaves from 2 sprigs fresh thyme

FOR THE RISOTTO
1kg (2¹⁄₄lb) sunchokes, washed and peeled
olive oil
3 medium onions, chopped
4 garlic cloves, chopped
850ml (1¹⁄₂ pints) vegetable stock
320g (11¹⁄₄oz) carnaroli or arborio rice
120ml (4fl oz) white wine
2 tbsp finely chopped fresh chives
60g (2¹⁄₄oz) butter
60g (2¹⁄₄oz) hard cheese, such as Desmond, Parmesan, or a mature goat's or sheep's cheese
salt and pepper

Oyster Mushrooms in Sherry Vinegar on a Leek and Sheep's Cheese Frittata

Try to get king oysters for this dish, for their firmer texture. If using a softer mushroom, shorten the cooking time. Serve this with some crusty bread or a potato dish.

My favourite Irish hard sheep's cheese is Cratloe Hills. A mature Manchego or Pecorino would also be delicious.

In a heavy frying pan, heat a little olive oil and fry the leek and garlic over a medium heat for about 8–10 minutes until tender. Beat the eggs in a bowl, season with salt and pepper and stir in the cheese. Heat the grill to a medium-low temperature. When the leeks are done, stir the egg mixture into the pan, lifting the edges of the forming frittata to allow the uncooked egg to flow underneath. When the frittata is almost set, place the pan under the grill to finish cooking.

Meanwhile, heat 2 tablespoons of butter in another pan and fry the mushrooms and shallots over a medium heat for 2 minutes, then turn the heat down a little and let the mushrooms stew in their juices for 5 minutes more. When the mushrooms are tender, stir in the sherry vinegar, parsley and remaining tablespoon of butter. Season well with salt and pepper.

Slice the frittata and divide between four plates. Spoon some mushrooms and their juices over each portion.

Serves 4

FOR THE FRITTATA

olive oil

1 medium leek, washed and thinly sliced

2 garlic cloves, sliced

6 eggs

salt and pepper

30g (1¼oz) hard sheep's cheese shavings

FOR THE MUSHROOMS

3 tbsp butter

300g (10½oz) oyster mushrooms, thickly sliced

2 small shallots, thinly sliced

2 tbsp sherry vinegar

1 tbsp chopped fresh parsley

Index

Acknowledgements

The production of this book has been much more of a collaboration than it might appear from the credit on the cover. First of all, big thanks to Sara Wilbourne for kick-starting me once again. Thanks to Jenny Heller for her creative input and vision and to Lizzy Gray for her firm but gentle support throughout. Thanks to Jon Hill and Emma Ewbank for their wonderful design skills. Cristian Barnett's exquisite photography and Linda Tubby's interpretive food styling were both a revelation to me. Kate Parker's eagle-eyed editing has made something like sense of my often chaotic ramblings.

The book is also a collaboration with the people who produce the food featured here, particularly Ultan Walsh. It has been one of the most rewarding aspects of writing this to fully realise how closely we work together and how his knowledge, energy and humour drive my approach to food. Many others in the food culture in and around Cork have contributed information, knowledge, philosophy and opinion and, Cork being Cork, I know they won't mind remaining nameless.

Finally, I am indebted to everyone in Café Paradiso, especially the kitchen staff for holding the show together so well while I was both mentally distracted and often physically awol. Take the rest of the day off.

About the author

Denis Cotter is the owner and chef of the celebrated Café Paradiso in Cork, Ireland, where his unique take on vegetarian cooking is heavily influenced by local vegetable and cheese producers. He is the author of two previous books, *The Café Paradiso Cookbook*, published in 1999, and *Paradiso Seasons*, 2003. The latter won 'Best Vegetarian Cookbook in the World' at The Gourmand World Cookbook Awards.

Find out more about Denis and Café Paradiso at:
www.cafeparadiso.ie

For information on Ultan Walsh, go to:
www.gortnanain.com